Impacts *of the* COVID-19 Pandemic *on* Chinese *and* Chinese American Women

Impacts *of the* COVID-19 Pandemic *on* Chinese *and* Chinese American Women

Racisms, Feminisms, and Foodways

ZIYING YOU

INDIANA UNIVERSITY PRESS

This book is a publication of

Indiana University Press
Office of Scholarly Publishing
Herman B Wells Library 350
1320 East 10th Street
Bloomington, Indiana 47405 USA

iupress.org

© 2025 by Ziying You

All rights reserved
No part of this book may be reproduced or utilized in any form or by any means, electronic or mechanical, including photocopying and recording, or by any information storage and retrieval system, without permission in writing from the publisher.

First Printing 2025

Cataloging information is available from the Library of Congress.

ISBN 978-0-253-07333-4 (hdbk.)
ISBN 978-0-253-07334-1 (pbk.)
ISBN 978-0-253-07335-8 (web PDF)
ISBN 978-0-253-07336-5 (ebook)

CONTENTS

Acknowledgments   *vii*

List of Abbreviations   *xi*

1. Global Asian Folklore Studies, Feminisms, and Anti-Asian Racisms   1

2. Building New Homes: Chinese Immigrant Mothers, Communities of Support, and Political Activisms during the Pandemic   36

3. To Return or to Stay: Chinese Women International Students and Their Transnational Experiences during the Pandemic   67

4. Coming Out of "the Fog": Chinese Adoptees, Antiracist Solidarities, and Remaking Chinese/Asian American Identities   104

5. "Going Home": Chinese Lay Buddhist Women, Diverse Agencies, and Hybrid Communities   145

6. Fluid Foodways, Racisms, and Everyday Lives   175

7. Conclusion   209

Appendix: List of Contributors   *219*

Bibliography   *223*

Index   *243*

ACKNOWLEDGMENTS

BECAUSE OF THE CHANGING GEOPOLITICS and unpredictable sensitivities that could impact the well-being of many people, I have chosen not to disclose the names of many individuals who have provided me with invaluable help, support, and insights. I am sincerely thankful to one and all.

First and foremost, I give heartfelt thanks to all the people who shared their stories, voices, and life experiences with me. Without their generosity of time and spirit and their trust and support, there would be no research project and no book. Sincerely, this book is for them. I truly regret that I could not fit all of their stories and voices onto these pages.

This project started with my collaboration with a group of amazing scholars in China after the outbreak of the coronavirus in late 2019. I admired their courage as they conducted important research to record the unforgettable stories of the many Chinese people who experienced and survived the pandemic from 2020 to 2023. I hope that one day their research and achievements will be shared with the world.

After the pandemic spread globally, I started to interview Chinese and Chinese Americans about their experiences of and reflections on the pandemic. Initially, I encountered difficulties in recruiting study contributors, but I was fortunate to receive valuable assistance from Andy Dai, the president of Huagen Chinese School, who kindly helped me recruit about twenty participants, and I also employed snowball sampling techniques to further expand the pool of contributors. From the fall of 2020 to the summer of 2021,

Zoe Seymore worked as my research assistant at the College of Wooster (CoW), and she recruited twenty-six Chinese adoptees in the United States for interviews. It was my first time conducting research with Chinese adoptees. Their stories and voices changed my research agenda, and as a result, I reframed my research questions and overarching themes.

After the Atlanta spa shootings in March 2021 and in response to the increasing incidents of violence and racisms targeting the Asian, Asian American, and Pacific Islander (AAAPI) communities, Désirée Weber and I supported our student leaders Coco Liu, Zoe Seymore, and Alicia Krielaart to organize the March for Asian Lives at CoW. I am sincerely grateful to all the faculty, staff, students, community members, and allies who participated in our planning meeting, the march, and subsequent events. As requested by some AAAPI students, I designed and taught Anti-Asian Racism at CoW in the spring of 2022. This class provided a safe space for students and other members of the community to express their thoughts, feelings, and reflections on anti-Asian racism while also providing a path forward for civic engagement, advocacy, and community activism. I also worked with my students to organize an AAAPI lecture series. I would like to thank all the invited speakers and everyone who participated in the lectures and supported our social justice endeavors.

At CoW, I would like to express my deep gratitude to many colleagues for their unstinting support. I am deeply grateful to research assistants Zoe Seymore, Siyan Ji, Zhen Guo, Adam Hinden, Minh Nguyen, and Lijiayi Wang for their important help and assistance. Many other friends and colleagues in academia also assisted me in numerous ways.

I owe tremendous thanks to Meng Ren for connecting me with Professor Ying Lu at New York University. Ying is a beloved leader and activist mother in AAAPI communities, and her full stories are presented in chapter 2. I am deeply grateful to Ying for her significant leadership, guidance, mentoring, and support. Ying connected me with a group of amazing activist mothers, and many important AAAPI civil rights groups and organizations. I feel fortunate to have witnessed the important historical moments of passing the AAPI curriculum bills in New Jersey and would like to thank everyone who has been involved in advocating for AAPI curricula in many states across the country. Thank you all for making history and making us visible!

On June 23, 2022, I cofounded the Writing 15 Minutes Every Day WeChat group and happily worked with several Chinese professor mothers and colleagues in the US and China. Together, we set up our daily goals and complete our daily writing tasks. We call each other sisters even though most of us have never met face-to-face. We have supported each other going through the pandemic and other crises in our lives. Every sister in the group shines brightly, and every one is a warrior. I feel very blessed to have worked with them, and I still write every day!

During the writing of this book, I also participated in different writing groups at CoW. I am deeply grateful to colleagues who participated in the writing groups and brainstormed with me about my book structures and chapter outlines. They encouraged me to focus on the most important things in my writing and helped me balance work and life. I am thankful to them for cheering me on and supporting me as I wrote this book.

Parts of this research project were presented at various conferences and invited lectures, including the American Folklore Society annual meetings; the Association for Asian Studies annual meetings; the conference of the International Society for the Study of Chinese Overseas; Hawai'i International Conference on Chinese Studies; the Women's, Gender, and Sexuality Studies South Conference; and others. I am deeply grateful to my collaborators and the organizers, chairs, panelists, and audiences who participated in these events and shared their insightful questions, comments, and feedback with me.

Many friends and family members sustained me with their support and kindness in every way, and I owe them my heartfelt gratitude. I truly regret that I cannot thank everyone here. Although I did not mention you specifically here, you are on my mind and heart. This book is for you all.

The professionals who staff the Indiana University Press are like a gift from heaven. Beginning with Allison Blair Chaplin and Sophia Hebert, acquisitions editors, and Nancy Lightfoot, project editor and manager, and ending with Samantha Heffner, marketing and publicity manager. Their courtesy, expertise, and guidance as well as their willingness to have dialogues with me over the many decisions involved in producing a book made the work an integrative, cooperative, and rewarding process. I am very grateful to Allison Gudenau, project manager, and her team for copyediting my manuscript. I also want to thank René Rodgers, my developmental editor, who provided lots of great advice and suggestions. I am also grateful to my anonymous reviewers for engaging, insightful, and invaluable comments, recommendations, and feedback at crucial stages of this book's production.

I started my new job as Associate Professor in the Department of Comparative Literature and Intercultural Studies at University of Georgia (UGA) on August 1, 2024, and I am also affiliated with Center for Asian Studies and the Institute for Women's & Gender Studies. My colleagues at UGA passionately welcomed me and provided invaluable support in completing this book through its publication. I am deeply grateful to them for their role in my success.

Acknowledgments   ix

None of the aforementioned people or institutions are responsible for the interpretations or any shortcomings in the book.

Parts of my discussion in the introduction about Global Asian Folklore Studies and anti-Asian racisms are published under the title "Defining Global Asian Folklore Studies" in the *Journal of Folklore Research* 61 (3) in 2024.

ABBREVIATIONS

AAPI	Asian American(s) and Pacific Islander(s)
AAAPI	Asian(s), Asian American(s), and Pacific Islander(s)
AAJIL	Asian American Justice + Innovation Lab
AANHPI	Asian Americans, Native Hawaiʻians, and Pacific Islanders
ABC	American-born Chinese
AFS	American Folklore Society
AWUC	Asian Women United of California
AYA	Asian Youth Act
AYR	AAPI Youth Rising
BIPOC	Black, Indigenous, and people of color
BLM	Black Lives Matter
CAAC	Civil Aviation Administration of China
CCA	Chinese and Chinese American
CDC	Centers for Disease Control and Prevention
CEA	China Eastern Airlines
CoW	College of Wooster
CSCIO	China's State Council Information Office
CSSA	Chinese Students and Scholars Association

DEI	diversity, equity, and inclusion
EQ	emotional quotient
FBI	Federal Bureau of Investigation
GAFS	Global Asian Folklore Studies
GSE	Garden State Equality
HCS	Huagen Chinese School
ICH	Intangible Cultural Heritage
IIE	Institute of International Education
JAF	*Journal of American Folklore*
LGBTQ	lesbian, gay, bisexual, transgender, queer or questioning
LGBTQIA+	lesbian, gay, bisexual, transgender, queer or questioning, intersex, asexual, and allies
MIT	Massachusetts Institute of Technology
MUVNJ	Make Us Visible New Jersey
NGO	nongovernmental organization
OCCS	Ohio Contemporary Chinese School
OCF	Ohio Chinese Festival
OPG	OCCS Parents Group
PCE Club	Parents and Children Education Club
PCEI	Parents and Children Education Identifications
PCR	polymerase chain reaction
PPE	personal protection equipment
SAH	Stop AAPI Hate
TBC	Tibetan Buddhist Center
TEAACH	Teaching Equitable Asian American Community History
UN	United Nations
WHO	World Health Organization
WASU	Wooster Adoptee Student Union

Impacts *of the* COVID-19 Pandemic *on* Chinese *and* Chinese American Women

1

GLOBAL ASIAN FOLKLORE STUDIES, FEMINISMS, AND ANTI-ASIAN RACISMS

ON MAY 5, 2023, Dr. Tedros Adhanom Ghebreyesus, the director general of the World Health Organization (WHO), declared "with great hope" an end to COVID-19 as a public health emergency, emphasizing that this did not mean COVID-19 was no longer a global threat (UN News 2023). Tedros stressed that the virus was still killing people and mutating, and there remained risks of variants emerging that could cause new surges in cases and deaths. The decision to terminate the state of emergency was not taken lightly; it was a result of meticulous analysis of data conducted by the Emergency Committee led by the WHO. For more than twelve months, the pandemic had been on a declining trend; highly effective vaccines had led to immunity increasing, death rates decreasing, and the pressure on once overwhelmed health systems easing. Tedros said, "This trend has allowed most countries to return to life as we knew it before COVID-19" (ibid.). However, he expressed the view that the pandemic's impacts had laid bare political divisions both within nations and between them. Trust among people, governments, and institutions was eroded, fueled by a deluge of misinformation and disinformation. Tedros also acknowledged the extensive damage inflicted by the virus on the global community, including severe economic disruptions that wiped trillions from gross domestic products, disrupted travel and trade, forced business closures, and pushed millions into poverty.

According to the WHO's Coronavirus Dashboard, which has collated key statistics since early in the pandemic, globally, as of 6:07 p.m. CEST (Central European Summer Time), May 31, 2023, there were 767,364,883 confirmed cases of COVID-19, including 6,938,353 deaths, reported. As of May 30, 2023, a total of 13,375,580,553 vaccine doses had been administered (WHO 2023). As the continuing and complicated impacts of COVID-19 become more evident, it seems time to take perspective, even as the pandemic continues to leave indelible marks on our world. Enduring scars serve as a constant reminder that new viral threats will inevitably emerge, carrying their own devastating consequences. We need to acknowledge the numerous mistakes that were made during the pandemic and the ways in which our existing tools and technologies were not best used to combat the virus. To prevent a recurrence of such mistakes, we must make a solemn commitment to ourselves, as well as to future generations, that we shall never repeat those mistakes. Notable among these errors were instances of lack of coordination, inclusion, equity, and solidarity. Our collective experiences should catalyze positive changes and foster a heightened determination to make a diverse, equitable, and inclusive society for all.

This book adopts inclusive frameworks that integrate decolonizing, antiracist, and feminist perspectives to deconstruct the structures of power, exploitation, and misrepresentation inherent in the White Western colonial matrix. The focus of this study is on the diverse lived experiences, struggles, actions, and achievements of various marginalized Chinese and Chinese American (CCA) women, including Chinese immigrant mothers, international students, transracial adoptees, and Chinese lay Buddhist women. This book examines how these women responded to anti-Asian racisms and the multiple crises of the pandemic and how they define, articulate, and exert their strengths, agencies, and strategies to enable their marginalized communities to not only survive but also achieve success and well-being.

The new coronavirus broke out in Wuhan, China, in late 2019. On January 23, 2020, the Chinese central government imposed a lockdown in Wuhan and other cities in Hubei Province. On March 11, 2020, Dr. Tedros Adhanom Ghebreyesus declared COVID-19 a global pandemic. On March 14, 2020, President Donald Trump declared a "national emergency" to free up federal resources to combat the coronavirus in the US; new travel restrictions into the US went into effect on the same day. Schools and other public places were closed, and I had to keep my five-year-old son, Lucas, and my two-year-old daughter, April, at home. It was one of the most challenging times in my life.

Reading the news about the rapidly evolving pandemic and learning about how the early lockdowns affected people's lives worldwide, I felt very depressed and anxious—it was like witnessing a fast train coming off its rails, and I could do nothing to stop it. At the same time, I felt like I was juggling three full-time jobs simultaneously: college professor, full-time mother to

Fig. 1.1. *SPLIT*, 2022, drawn by my son, Lucas.

two young children at home, and full-time schoolteacher for my son's online classes. Balancing these responsibilities was demanding and challenging—not only was I living through the pandemic myself, but I was also supporting my students and children through the crisis. The surge in anti-Asian hate crimes and racisms during this time was heartbreaking and added to the stress, and it revealed the barriers caused by systemic racisms in our united fight against COVID-19. Like everyone else, I struggled to adapt to the rapidly changing pandemic and its impacts on our lives. However, I found hope in the support of those around me—my students, colleagues, friends, and family. We did the best we could to help each other and create communities of support in times of crisis.

As a Chinese immigrant woman in the US, I constantly felt torn between different worlds, and the distressing news from those worlds weighed heavily on my soul (see fig. 1.1). This experience was not unique to me; I heard similar stories from many CCA women as we faced multiple marginalizations and oppressions during the pandemic. Through this book, I aim to present the diverse lived experiences of Chinese immigrant mothers, international students, transracial adoptees, and lay Buddhist women in the US during the COVID-19 pandemic while examining how these experiences intersect with social structures and notions of race, ethnicity, gender, power, and health. Ultimately, I hope that no one will have to endure such divisiveness, trauma, or loss in the future.

What Has the Pandemic Taught Us about Racisms?

In this study, I draw on virtual ethnography, interviews, class surveys, social media analysis, and personal narratives of Chinese immigrant mothers, international students, transracial adoptees, and lay Buddhist women who were born in China and lived in the US (permanently or temporarily) during the COVID-19 pandemic to examine social and cultural impacts of the global pandemic on them. Particularly, I examine how they experienced and responded to surging anti-Asian racisms and how multiple crises associated with the global pandemic changed their daily lives, (dis)identifications, and foodways. I also explore how individuals relating to one or more identifications form a community in which folklore often helps them bond, communicate, and express shared cultural values.

Why did I choose the four particular groups I did for my study? The ways in which these specific groups experienced and coped with COVID-19 make them strategically significant for examining marginalized agencies from decolonial, antiracist, and feminist approaches. The pandemic experiences of these groups render hypervisible the intersecting power structures of race, ethnicity, and gender that have always been operative but became nearly unavoidable to confront during the COVID-19 pandemic. For many contributors, COVID-19 became a galvanizing moment of identity crises, (dis)identifications, and agency building. For many Chinese immigrant mothers whom I studied, the pandemic brought a sense of crisis awareness of themselves as non-White subjects living within White neoliberal feminist paradigms of motherhood. Most painful was the way COVID-19 racialized them and their children as the "yellow peril" or diseased other. They coped by building diverse communities of support based on the identities for which they were being discriminated against. For international students, the surging anti-Asian racisms, travel bans, geopolitical tensions, and many other factors pushed them to identify more strongly as racialized subjects in America, thus aligning them more closely with US-born Chinese Americans and their historical lineage tied to the Chinese Exclusion Acts of the nineteenth and twentieth centuries. Their lived experiences illustrate how COVID-19 produced transnational racialized identifications among Chinese students that transcend national borders and citizenship lines. Similarly, transracial adoptees, who came to disidentify from Whiteness, came out of the fog to identify as Chinese/Asian Americans during the COVID-19 pandemic, engaging in anti-racist activisms, reclaiming cultural connections to Chineseness/Asianness, and creating spaces of belonging for themselves. These stories offer counter-narratives to the dominant portrayal of COVID-19 as a period of debilitating mental health for youths and for Asian Americans especially. The adoptees' practices of self-care and cultural resilience make this demographic especially important to consider when examining diverse forms of creative agencies from marginalized groups vis-à-vis health and mental health. As for lay Buddhist women, I did my fieldwork with them in rural northern China in 2019 and then studied this group in the US after the COVID-19 outbreak. The lay Buddhist Chinese diasporic women are often absent in religious studies in general and Buddhist studies in particular. I use a feminist decolonizing approach to interpret Chinese lay Buddhist women's diverse agencies and highlight their subjectivities and their own constructions and perceptions of agencies. Decolonization returns to CCA women the power to decide how they want to live.

Because the terms *race* and *racisms* are so loaded, I will begin with some definitions. According to Michael Omi and Howard Winant (2015, 205), race "is a concept that signifies and symbolizes social conflicts and interests by referring to different types of human bodies." Race is a social construct that differs by time and place and draws on arbitrary criteria for categorizing people. It "has been a master category, a kind of template for patterns of inequality, marginalization, and difference throughout U.S. history. . . . No other social conflict—not class, not sex/gender, not colonialism or imperialism—can ever be understood independently of it" (9). Racism "creates or reproduces structures of domination based on racial significations and identities" (237). Stuart Hall (1980) argues that we cannot understand racism as a general thing; there are multiple racisms that are always situated in particular social, economic, political, cultural, and historical contexts. These multiple racisms are all related but distinctive in their origins and contours. The racisms triggered by the coronavirus echo the long-standing specters of "yellow perils" and discrimination faced by Chinese and Asians in different parts of the world throughout the history of the Chinese and Asian diasporas (Billé and Urbansky 2018; Hsu 2016; Richard M. Lee 2003; E. Lee 2015, 2019; Lee and Yung 2010; McClain 1994; Ngai 2021). Mae Ngai (2021) argues that the Chinese Question—the idea that the Chinese pose a racial threat to democracy and Euro-American civilizations—has been circulated again and again in different places and at different times. Although the Chinese Question originated in the late nineteenth-century politics of racism, colonialism, and capitalism, it has gained greater attention in our own time due to the intense competition between China and the West. During the pandemic, US president Donald Trump repeatedly referred to the coronavirus as the "Chinese virus" or "Kung flu" to deflect attention from his mishandling of the pandemic. These repeated invocations of the Chinese Question through racist language and xenophobic accusations had a disastrous impact on people of Chinese and Asian ancestry across America. This book presents the stories of CCA women who fought against both the coronavirus and anti-Asian racisms as well as the dynamic processes of their (dis)identifications through community building, political activism, sharing their narrative voices, participating in religious activities, and returning to traditional foodways during the pandemic. The ultimate goal of this study is to contribute to public health and social justice efforts and to develop better strategies to respond to racism and crises in our global world.

America has predominantly operated as a colonial empire, and after the decline of the Civil Rights Movement, its governance shifted to a racial dictatorship that utilized force, violence, and hegemony—a concept defined as governing through institutional coercion and propaganda (Omi and Winant 2015). This approach involved disseminating messages and perspectives through various institutions like education, healthcare, science, the economy, business, religion, media, entertainment, the judiciary, the police, and the military. These institutions promoted an ideal of a free and humane society while masking the reality of oppression faced by marginalized groups. The US empire has relied on federal and state-enforced terrorism and violence to maintain "order" and "stability" while upholding the pillars of White supremacist ideology and systemic racism. Many racisms are deeply ingrained in American society, shaping institutional policies as well as individual and group thoughts, speech, and behavior (Prahlad 2021).

Although race, racialization, and racism have been important barriers in everyday lives, existing scholarship in folklore studies has rarely centered explicitly on these key themes (Prahlad 2018, 2021). Anand Prahlad (2018) articulated three significant weaknesses in mainstream American studies of folklore and folklife. First, there was a lack of self-awareness among folklorists, particularly White folklorists, regarding their own positionality in race, class, gender, and ability. Prahlad argued that failing to recognize their positionality along these dimensions undermines the integrity of folklorists' research, especially when studying cultures outside their own. He criticized both White and Black folklorists for often overlooking the influence of their racial identities on their work, leading to a narrow understanding of "what folklore is and who the folk are" and to the neglect of the lived experiences of people outside conventional groups (2018, 730–31). The second weakness Prahlad identified was the failure to contextualize folklore within broader racial, political, and social dynamics. Prahlad pointed out that folklore studies had historically been constrained by outdated conventions that ignored significant cultural and political developments among African Americans and other racial groups. This resulted in folklore studies that were disconnected from the realities of racial politics and social change, often resorting to stereotypical and exoticized portrayals of racial groups. The third weakness was the insulatory nature of folklore studies and the failure to expand folkloristic discourses to engage with Black philosophical scholarly traditions and race theory. Prahlad argued for the expansion of folkloristic discourses to include insights from Black studies, critical race theory, Latino studies, Native American studies, Asian American studies, African studies, and other disciplines that address racial issues more comprehensively.

At the 2020 American Folklore Society Francis Lee Utley Memorial Panel, "Race and Racism in the Practice and Study of Folklore," Prahlad (2021) pointed out that the core practices of American folklore studies—such as a strong attachment to nostalgia, perceiving folk groups as small, adopting a materialist approach, emphasizing genres, having an isolationist standpoint, rejecting external theoretical frameworks, and focusing solely on aesthetically pleasing things—collectively hinder any significant disciplinary transformation that could compel folklorists to address race and other social categories as essential intellectual endeavors. Consequently, folklore studies have struggled to effectively tackle the most pertinent and socially relevant issues of any given era throughout its existence. John Roberts (2021, 267) stated, "The influence of systemic racism as a historical phenomenon has and continues to be insidious and often invisible in exerting its influence on how we perform institutional roles, implement institutional policies, and even manage social relationships in our contemporary lives." When turning this panel into a *Journal of American Folklore* (*JAF*) special issue, Lisa Gilman (2021, 250) commented: "It is this blindness, this invisibility, that can be the most insidious: unless we recognize our own positionality, our own complicity, our own accountability, we (as individuals, a field, a society) will never change." She further stated that folklorists often prided themselves for their work "at the margins" and tended to "value the expressivity and artistry of 'everyday people,' often with an emphasis on those who experience oppression, violence, or marginalization within the contexts in which they live and express themselves" (250). Paradoxically, she stated that this dedication to social justice often produced "the fantasy" that folklorists weren't racists or, at least, weren't contributing to racisms and other forms of oppression. She reminded us that the field of American folklore studies was not only "out of and in the service of white dominance" but also "our organizations and the work we do continues to feed social stratification and power differentials" (250). Echoing their statements, Juwen Zhang (2023c, 209) expressed his hope that "many folklorists in and outside AFS will join together to engage in dialogues crossing existing boundaries and to make folklore studies truly 'at the very center of humanistic study.'"

I hope that this book will not only advance the dialogues and discussions about how best to enhance the lives, representations, and vitalities of CCA women in American society but will also create awareness about the adverse impacts that the global pandemic and racisms have on CCA women going forward. It is also my hope that the research questions posed by this book will translate into actionable, effective, and sustainable solutions that will strengthen personal, community, institutional, governmental, national, and global interventions to cope with the lasting impacts of the pandemic and racisms. As Dr. Martin Luther King Jr. (1965) said, "The arc of the moral universe is long but it bends toward justice." It is my dream that the study stemming from the questions that have been posed will not only illuminate the opportunities for listening, learning, strategizing, and implementing but also actively foster our collective pursuits of social justice and gender equality.

PERSONAL NARRATIVES AND VIRTUAL ETHNOGRAPHY

To understand CCA women's experiences of and responses to the pandemic and racisms, my collaborators, research assistants, and I conducted qualitative, structured, narrative interviews with eighty-six contributors from February 2020 to June 2022. Their personal narratives reveal how challenging the life situations of CCA women in the US were during the pandemic as they fought both the coronavirus and surging anti-Asian racisms. The contributors were recruited through online groups, online postings, local Chinese school networks, and referrals from participants (snowball sampling). Their ages ranged from eighteen to sixty-five years. Their educational backgrounds ranged from completing high school to holding doctoral degrees. All the interviews were conducted virtually, and each interview lasted between one and four hours.

In addition, I used virtual ethnography from 2020 to 2023 to participate in many online activities with local communities that I study. Virtual ethnography is conducted on the internet and adapts the traditional, in-person ethnographical method to the study of online virtual worlds and online communities (Boellstorff et al. 2012; Hine 2000). Moreover, virtual ethnographic fieldwork and interviews were used together with global media reports and social media postings due to the global impacts of the pandemic. To protect confidentiality, most study participants have been given pseudonyms, though some contributors agreed to use their real names.

In addition, I distributed class surveys in two courses at the College of Wooster (CoW) in 2021–22: Food and Religion in China and Anti-Asian Racism. The latter was requested in March 2021 by my Asian and Asian American students in the March for Asian Lives student movement after the Atlanta spa shootings in which a White gunman killed eight people, six of whom were Asian women. When teaching, I asked my students to reflect on their personal experiences of and reflections on various forms of anti-Asian racism and changing foodways during the pandemic. The data collected from both courses are integrated into my content analysis anonymously. Moreover, I collected and processed data from popular social media platforms, such as WeChat and Facebook, and conducted a comparative analysis to identify the main challenges, coping strategies, and community building activites of CCA women during the pandemic.

I hope this book offers complex and nuanced portraits of CCA women in the US. They come from diverse cultural and socioeconomic backgrounds and are not confined to middle-class or upper-middle-class segments of society. Some contributors are the children of entrepreneurs and engineers, doctors and drivers, teachers and officials, and workers and peasants in mainland China. This book explores the diverse lived experiences of CCA women with different class backgrounds and their unique paths across national borders.

Here I draw on personal narratives as a key method to study the lived experiences, struggles, and achievements of CCA women in coping with racisms and the multiple crises of the pandemic. Personal narratives and storytelling provide a powerful and transformative means of understanding and expressing experiences, identifications, and social dynamics for individuals from marginalized communities (Tate 1983). Individuals can share their lived experiences, challenge dominant narratives, and resist oppressive systems, and therefore these narratives serve as a platform for marginalized voices, allowing women, gender nonconforming individuals, and minorities to reclaim agencies and assert their diverse realities. For example, during the women's movement of the 1970s, the act of sharing personal narratives became a form of activism that contributed to raising consciousness. By recounting their own experiences of violence and sexism, women realized that these issues were not isolated incidents but were systemic problems embedded within society (Kalčik 1975). This realization prompted efforts to address these issues in social and political spheres.

Personal narratives were defined as folklore and established as a legitimate folklore genre when Sandra Dolby Stahl (1977, 1989) drew on theories of folkloristic performance, deconstructive criticism, and reader-response theory to present a meticulously developed methodology for studying personal narratives, the stories that people tell based on their own experiences. As Stahl notes, personal narratives are closely related to other established genres of folklore, such as memorates, local character anecdotes, or family stories. Although the contents of personal narratives may not be traditional, Stahl (1989, 13) states that "the values or attitudes reflected in the stories are culturally shared and thus traditional." Personal narratives reveal rich detail about the values, beliefs, attitudes, and emotions of the narrators and of their audiences. They can also illuminate the social and cultural contexts in which they are produced and performed.

By centering on personal narratives, this study recognizes the complexity and intersectionality of race, ethnicity, class, gender, and sexuality and highlights the nuanced ways in which power, privilege, and oppression operate in people's lives. Moreover, personal narratives foster empathy and connection, enabling individuals to empathize with others' experiences and challenge their own preconceived notions. Through the exploration of personal narratives, this study engages in a process of knowledge production that acknowledges the significance of individual stories as sources of insight, critique, and social change (Collins 2009).

Theoretically, this book integrates decolonizing, feminist, and antiracist approaches and centers on personal narratives that have contributed to the construction and transformation of society and self during the pandemic. Folklorists have played important roles in the "vernacular turn" in contemporary academic fields and public discourses (R. Bauman 2008; Goldstein 2015; Primiano 1995) and the growing interest in Indigenous knowledge production and vernacular responses to diseases and disasters (Briggs 2021; Briggs and Mantini-Briggs 2003, 2016; Goldstein and Shuman 2012; Horigan 2018; Lindahl 2012; Lindahl et al. 2022; Wilson 2013). They have also contributed to our understanding of the intersections of folklore, health, and trauma as well as the grassroots agency in public health (Blank and Kitta 2015; Bridges, Brillhard, and Goldstein 2023; Kitta 2019; You and Zhang 2022; Zhang and You 2022). Diseases are often intertwined with social and cultural issues, and folklorists have formed new ways of engaging with public health professionals and local communities. In *Theorizing Folklore from the Margins*, Solimar Otero and Mintzi Auanda Martínez-Rivera (2021, 9) urge folklorists to work with communities on the ground to "challenge and expand our understanding of vernacular expressive cultural practices, as well as the theoretical approaches used by folklorists." I am answering these calls by creating spaces for further dialogues and collaborations between folklorists and Asian, Asian American, and Pacific Islander (AAAPI) communities, whether they focus on how we faced the pandemic together or ways to collaborate to create a more diverse, equal, and inclusive "post-pandemic society" (Foster 2020).

ACTION-BASED AND FUTURE-ORIENTED GLOBAL ASIAN FOLKLORE STUDIES

This research seeks to combine the study of global Asias with the field of Critical Folklore Studies to create a subfield, Global Asian Folklore Studies (GAFS), in which we explore the role of folklore in creating global Asias by making and remaking their fluid boundaries. GAFS embraces a range of research collaboration methods with AAAPI communities and integrates interdisciplinary, intersectional, decolonizing, and feminist approaches to look at the racialized and gendered experiences of AAAPI individuals and communities on the ground. GAFS recognizes the importance of migration, allows for the examination of both new and old forms of displacement, and aims to advance our understanding of how technology is creating new forms of connectivity and bridging distances and divisions. As a dynamic field, GAFS redefines the scope of folklore studies on global Asias, providing spaces for sustainable intellectual exchanges that transcend disciplinary, institutional, and field boundaries.

As an action-based and future-oriented field of study, GAFS uses diverse methods to address the root causes of anti-Asian racisms, marginalization, and exclusion and aims to understand and transform the ways knowledge, values, and beliefs are produced. By critically examining the discursive positionings of social institutions and using oppositional narratives and action-research methods, GAFS seeks to approach the existing social systems as the subjects of theoretic critique and social transformation.

Like Critical Folklore Studies, GAFS goes beyond simply criticizing established hierarchies of truth and power, and its objectives extend beyond mere policy changes. GAFS can involve projects that aim to create "oppositional knowledge structures" and to integrate this knowledge with tangible political actions while continually fostering opportunities for in-depth ethnographic engagement (McDonald 2020, 405). This form of activist scholarship strives for policy changes by observing, discovering, analyzing, and presenting narratives, ways of life, and experiences that challenge the mainstream. It advocates for the acknowledgment of peripheral, marginalized, and excluded groups that are typically overlooked in conventional discourses. Thus, GAFS is entangled in the politics of recognition and representation, actively intervening in the construction of worldviews and reshaping normative knowledge through storytelling and other forms of expressive cultural practices (Delgado 1989).

Despite the significance of GAFS, Juwen Zhang (2023c) noticed the invisibility and absence of Asian American folklorists in American folklore studies. By "Asian American folklorist," he means "any folklorist, with or without Asian ancestral legacies, who holds Asian American folklore as their primary research area and, for most of them, as their personal identity" (208). He further pointed out that in recent discussions on advancing folklore studies—including the *JAF* special issue "Critical Folkloristics Today" (Mills and Westerman 2020), the Francis Lee Utley Memorial Panel "Race and Racism in the Practice and Study of Folklore" in *JAF* (N'Diaye 2021; Prahlad 2021; John Roberts 2021), and four essay collections published by Indiana University Press: *Advancing Folkloristics* (Fivecoate, Downs, and McGriff 2021), *Theorizing Folklore from the Margins: Critical and Ethical Approaches* (Otero and Martínez-Rivera 2021), *What Folklorists Do: Professional Possibilities in Folklore Studies* (Lloyd 2021), and *Culture Work: Folklore for the Public Good* (Frandy and Cederström 2022)—none of the over one hundred contributions addresses the issues of Asian American folklore or groups, and there are no contributors who (self-)identify as Asian American folklorists. I aim to fill in the gaps by envisioning GAFS as an intellectual hub, facilitating interdisciplinary dialogues, and providing tools for comprehending and navigating the complexities of cultural tensions and conflicts.

In *Implied Nowhere: Absence in Folklore Studies*, Shelley Ingram, Willow Mullins, and Todd Richardson (2019, 7) aim to explore "new paradigms in folklore studies" by uncovering and integrating what has been "absent" in folklore studies because there are "things that have been implied to be nothing and things that are nowhere implied," which hold significant influence over both ideology and actuality in the field. Viewing folklore studies through the lens of absence allows me to identify several areas that are currently lacking attention and consideration. First, global Asian folklore—including Asian, Asian Diaspora, and Asian American folklore—remains understudied in folklore studies (Zhang 2015a, 2015b, 2023b, 2023c). Second, the study of AAAPI women has been further marginalized in the field. Third, AAAPIs have often been portrayed as victims of systemic racism, and AAAPI women, despite their recent actions to combat social injustice, have been implied as passive victims of both racism and sexism. By making the invisible visible, this book centers on the stories, voices, and actions of CCA women in their responses to anti-Asian racisms and the multiple crises of the pandemic, highlighting the diverse agencies and strategies they used to advocate for social justice and change—not only for their communities but for all marginalized and oppressed communities.

The Integration of the Study of Global Asias with Critical Folklore Studies into GAFS

GAFS integrates the study of global Asias and Critical Folklore Studies. Scholars often examine global Asias as transnational, inter/intra-Asian, multidisciplinary frameworks through critical perspectives such as (im)mobilities, (in)visibilities, globalization, neoliberalism, capitalism, communication, and representation (Azuma 2021; T. Chen 2018, 2021; Chen and Chua 2007; Chen and Hayot 2015; Leong 2021; Ryang 2021; Yano 2021). This study builds on but also complicates such investigations. I propose that global Asian folklore mobilizes communities, discourses, practices, and power relationships in the ongoing process of building social justice. This process is also intertwined with national, gendered, racial, and ethnic dynamics on the ground. Here global Asias serve as a conceptual "infrastructure that makes critical conversation across the silos of knowledge production that structure academia—discipline, field, area, period, methodology—possible without interpellating interlocutors and practitioners into singular, synonymous, or even especially allied subject positions" (T. Chen 2021, 1001). Christine R. Yano (2021, 851) defines global Asias as "transnational, transhistorical, and transgeographic flows, whether of peoples, ideas, practices, goods, diseases, and environmental concerns of Asia and its related communities (both inside and outside Asia) across time and space." The study of global Asias aims to revolutionize academic approaches to the study of Asia and its diverse diasporas "by making figure-ground reversal and the grounded relation between objects/contexts of study fundamental aspects of its conceptualization of Global Asias as an architecture that can be collectively built to generate conversation and debate across siloed sites of academic knowledge" (T. Chen 2021, 1001).

By linking the fields of Asian studies, Asian American studies, and Asian diaspora studies, the study of global Asias has focused on "how institutional fields of academic knowledge production operate historically and contextually to influence the scholarly understanding of the politics, cultures, societies, aesthetic practices, and peoples of Asia" (T. Chen 2021, 1001). By unsettling Asian studies' assumptions through critical race and ethnic studies methods, vocabularies, and priorities—while simultaneously leveraging Asian studies' focus on questions of place, regional awareness, and linguistic expertise—the study of global Asias has been advanced to challenge the

US-centrism of concepts governing the Asian diaspora perpetuated by Asian American studies.

GAFS engages with the study of global Asias through the lenses of Critical Folklore Studies (Buccitelli 2020; González-Martin 2020; McDonald 2020; Mills 2020; Mills and Westerman 2020; Otero and Martínez-Rivera 2021). David A. McDonald (2020, 404) frames Critical Folklore Studies as "a problem-centered and participatory mode of inquiry that foregrounds the affective, communicative, and performative capacities of human behavior to mobilize oppositional and emancipatory knowledge in the pursuit of social justice." He argues that activist-oriented Critical Folklore Studies advance the principles of applied and public folklore in new approaches that address social justice and aim to alleviate systemic forms of violence causing precarity and marginalization. These new approaches challenge the assumptions about precarity and propose emancipatory alternatives to support activist ideals. McDonald thinks that adopting these new approaches is crucial for revitalizing folklore studies, making positive impacts within the communities in which we work, and expanding the potential of folklore for public goods. Indeed, in times of global pandemic, conflict and violence, widespread inequality, environmental crises, and forced (im)mobilities, we—as critical scholars—need to utilize our expertise to address structural inequalities based on diverse lived experiences on the ground and collaborate with local communities, stakeholders, and policymakers to build social justice. When defining new Critical Folklore Studies, Margaret A. Mills emphasizes that it is an ongoing and dynamic process with local variations, as the targets and tactics of disempowerment and marginalization are constantly evolving in the fluid realms of politics. She also points out that it is "a work in progress" that requires continuous "assessment of impact against current needs and capacities" (Mills 2020, 384).

GAFS is nothing new in itself; however, it has never been framed as a collective framework but, rather, has been practiced by various scholars, professionals, and writers who have incorporated diverse perspectives and theoretic sources to respond to the needs and concerns of Asian and Asian American communities on the ground (Ayeshah and Garlough 2015; Bender 2017; Khan 2015, 2018; Kim and Livengood 2015; Ku, Manalansan, and Mannur 2013; Leary 1999; J. Lee and Nadeau 2010, 2014; Magat 2015, 2019; Marshall 2021; Zhang 2015a, 2015b, 2023a, 2023b, 2023c). For instance, the *Asian Ethnology* special issue "Intangible Cultural Heritage (ICH) in Asia: Traditions in Transition" suggests the possibility of a wider "pan-Asian" heritage paradigm distinguished by an emphasis on intergenerational transmission of expressive culture and an explicit acknowledgment of the dynamic nature of ICH. The authors further propose that this paradigm opens opportunities to examine continuity and innovation in cultural transmission and reproduction, vibrant and dynamic hybrid forms of creative cultural expressions, and the recognition of the complexities of political, religious, and historical fields that cultural practitioners have to negotiate for their traditions to continue to resonate with local communities, government patrons, and international sponsors (You and Hardwick 2020). Another *JAF* special issue, "New Perspectives on the Studies of Asian American Folklores," advocates for the studies of Asian American folklores in both academic and public folklore sectors (Zhang 2015a). This issue's contributors emphasize the importance of recognizing and embracing diversity among the category "Asian Americans," which is an integral segment of the traditionally defined "American folk groups" (Ayeshah and Garlough 2015; Khan 2015; Magat 2015; Zhang 2015b). They advocate for the studies of Asian American folklores as legitimate fields of American folklore scholarship, developing diverse methodologies to achieve their goals. When defining Asian American folklore studies, Fariha Khan (2018) focuses on the diverse peoples of Asia as they navigate their lives in the US, acknowledging and responding to the history of racisms and stereotypes of the Asian "model minority" and "forever foreigner." According to her, these studies specifically challenge Eurocentric ethnic folklore theories and methods by highlighting the unique ways in which diverse groups within Asian American communities create and sustain folkloric identities and by raising the questions of whether there are emerging pan–Asian American or transnational identities evident in various traditions. Building on these important scholarships, GAFS fosters diverse perspectives to counter AAAPI homogeneity and embrace various approaches for collaborative research with diverse AAAPI communities that aim to advance the studies of such communities by any folklorist, regardless of their race or ethnic background. These joint efforts help ground ethnography and analysis in ethical methods that effectively address the complicated and nuanced realities of being/becoming an AAAPI person.

Echoing Prahlad's (2021) recommendations for significant changes in folklore studies, GAFS moves away from genre-centered perspectives to broader social and political dynamics to understand and navigate the complexities of cultural tensions and conflicts. Folklore here is viewed as "the essential, invisible stuff that holds everything else together, as the ideological, cellular, and neurological, and as a part of human DNA rather than as the actual collectibles" (Prahlad 2021, 264). This move involves questioning our fundamental notions such as "what it means to be human" (264). In particular, GAFS focuses on the diverse narratives, traditions, and cultural expressions of AAAPI communities and creates spaces to facilitate meaningful dialogues, cultural exchanges, and mutual understanding among people from diverse backgrounds. GAFS can play a pivotal role in these paradigm shifts, acting as an intellectual hub that connects AAAPI communities and cultures and enabling folklore studies to emerge as one of the most pertinent and esteemed disciplines in the twenty-first century.

GAFS is more than an academic research subject, analytical or conceptual category, or matter of transnational or cross-border framing (Azuma 2021). GAFS is where different institutionalized fields of academic studies, public folklore, and social justice work can intersect or interact and where scholars, students, activists, artists, and community members can work together toward common goals. They can work together to go beyond area-based institutional traps and show what forward-looking and future-oriented scholarship and actions could do.

Armed with a critical awareness of transnational realities and the global inequality of power, GAFS can engage in inclusive and productive conversations and collaborations with African American studies; Latinx or Latino/a/e studies; Indigenous studies; women's, gender, and sexuality studies; and disability studies. The epistemologies of diverse communities explored in this book demonstrate how GAFS has the capacity and responsibility to integrate theory and practice in meaningful ways that make important impacts. Such attempts would also contribute to the strengthening of racial, ethnic, and cultural coalitions across diverse communities and foster a deeper mutual understanding between various racial, ethnic, and cultural groups, within academia and beyond.

GAFS draws on the approach of intersectionality to look at the problems of discrimination, inequality, and oppression faced by AAAPIs before, during, and after the pandemic. Intersectionality provides multiple analytical lenses to interrogate race, class, gender, ethnicity, and other dimensions of difference that shape our lives today and to contest existing ways of understanding the structures of inequality (Crenshaw 1991; Thornton Dill and Zambrana 2009). Moreover, it calls for modes of community engagement, coalition building, political actions, and ways of understanding antiracism, equality, rights, liberation, and empowerment informed by multiplicity.

Similar to Critical Latinx Folklore Studies (González-Martin 2020), GAFS embraces interdisciplinary and intersectional approaches, and the goal is to look at the racialized and gendered experiences of AAAPI individuals and communities as well as the problems of discrimination, inequality, and oppression faced by them in their everyday lives. The significance of migration is also recognized in GAFS, which allows us to examine ongoing forms of exodus and resettlement as well as both new and old forms of displacement while also acknowledging that displacement could occur even when people stay in place. GAFS aims to advance our understanding of the emerging forms of connectivity by technology and the growing prominence of the digital in bridging distances and divisions. As a dynamic and interdisciplinary field, GAFS reconceptualizes the parameters of academic research on Asia and its diverse diasporas and establishes the basis for sustaining intellectual exchanges that transcend disciplinary, institutional, and field boundaries. Furthermore, exploring global Asian feminist and decolonizing approaches is crucial in defining GAFS.

GLOBAL ASIAN FEMINISMS

Here I intend to integrate AAAPI feminisms, Women of Color feminisms, and transnational feminisms into global Asian feminisms, which expand our understanding of diverse feminist agencies and political activisms. By recognizing diverse experiences, struggles, actions, and contributions of AAAPI women from diverse backgrounds, these integrations challenge the limitations of mainstream White Western feminist discourses and theories. The integration of AAAPI feminisms sheds light on the unique intersectional experiences of AAAPI women, addressing issues of racisms, immigration, and (dis)identifications and seeking to dismantle systemic racisms and invisibility that AAAPI women often face in both mainstream feminist discourses and society at large. Simultaneously, the inclusion of Women of Color feminisms into global Asian feminisms recognizes the diversity within Asian and non-Asian communities. Women of Color feminisms emphasize the experiences and struggles of women from various racial and ethnic backgrounds, including but not limited to those of Asian descent. This integration fosters solidarities and challenges the tendency to homogenize AAAPI experiences, recognizing that different racial and ethnic backgrounds intersect with gender in complex ways. Furthermore, transnational feminisms contribute to the development of global Asian feminisms by acknowledging the transnational flows of people, ideas, and activisms. They emphasize the interconnectedness of women's experiences across national boundaries, challenging nationalist frameworks and promoting transnational solidarities. Overall, the integrations of AAAPI feminisms, Women of Color feminisms, and transnational feminisms into global Asian feminisms are crucial for fostering a more inclusive understanding of the diverse lived experiences, struggles, actions, and contributions of AAAPI women. By recognizing the complexities of identifications, power, and global dynamics, these integrations pave the way for more intersectional and transformative feminist political activisms and movements. In short, the ultimate goal is to build a more diverse global Asian feminist praxis that commits unequivocally to the fight against all kinds of discrimination faced by AAAPI and Black, Indigenous, and People of Color (BIPOC) women. When presenting discourses and practices of integrated global Asian feminisms and cross-boundary feminist solidarities, I consider similarities and differences among feminist actions in and across Asia and North America.

AAAPI feminist voices challenge White feminist hegemony and heteropatriarchal nationalism. Early pioneering publications focused on AAAPI women's histories, experiences, and perspectives provide important foundations for making racialized gender oppressions and struggles visible and articulating potential solutions to fix the problems and raise more feminist and antiracist consciousness (AWUC 1989; Hune and Nomura 2003; Kim, Villanueva, and AWUC 1997; Lim and Tsutakawa 1989; Moraga and Anzaldúa 1981; Shah 1997; Võ and Sciachitano 2004). In their important edited volume, *Asian American Feminisms and Women of Color Politics*, Lynn Fujiwara and Shireen Roshanravan (2018) examine how race, gender, sexuality, class, and citizenship have shaped Asian American communities and politics. The book's contributors reflect on what theoretical interventions, resistant strategies, and epistemic shifts shape the field of Asian American feminisms; how the key concepts, theories, practices, and strategies interact with the coalitional politics of Women of Color and US Third World feminisms; and what tensions or disconnections push against and reconstruct the potentials of the politics of Asian American feminisms.

As a demographic category, the identity "women of color" is often used to refer to those legally classified in America as "non-White" and "female," and it is used "in its cross-racial feminist coalitional meaning and historical emergence at the intersection of the 1960s US civil rights, antiwar, gay and women's liberation movements" (Fujiwara and Roshanravan 2018, 8). Therefore, this term is intentionally used in relation to and with distinctions from "transnational" or "global" feminisms. To address what Kimberlé Crenshaw (1991) came to theorize as the "intersectionality" of oppressions and illustrate how marginalized peoples become invisible on multiple fronts of struggles, Fujiwara and Roshanravan (2018) use the capitalized term *Women of Color* to "invoke cross-racial feminist coalitions and the cultural, scholarly, and activist work they generated" (2018, 9).

Transnational feminisms are understood as disruptions of traditional constructions of nation-states and connections across different communities grounded in solidarities with BIPOC in the US. The rapid increase in economic globalization and the swift global flows of peoples, cultures, and information have intensified the significance of developing transnational understandings of contemporary issues. Transnational feminisms have provided distinct perspectives on women's lives and deepened our understanding of the gendered aspects of global processes. In *Transnational Feminism in the United States*, Leela Fernandes (2013) examines how transnational feminist perspectives shape how we create and disseminate knowledge about the world within the US and how national narratives and public discourses affect transnational feminist paradigms. Adelyn Lim (2015) argues that transnational feminism is not premised on a collective identity, and instead, it should be understood as a collective frame of action. She demonstrates that acknowledging the differences of diverse women activists who advocate for different agendas leads to a more comprehensive understanding of the connections and commonalities in the relations among those involved. In *Making Transnational Feminism*, Millie Thayer (2010) draws on ethnography to look at transnational feminist alliances and view them from the local perspective of two women's movements in Northeast Brazil. She discovers rural women and feminists in nongovernmental organizations appropriating and translating global gender discourses, negotiating with each other over political resources, and devising strategies to defend their autonomy from distant donors. In doing so, she argues that the Brazilian organizations contribute to the creation of a transnational feminist political space—a "counterpublic," where movements debate strategies, articulate new identities, and strive to develop alternative social practices. Feminist alliances in this space are marked by a delicate balance between solidarity and self-interest, between collaboration and contention.

By integrating AAAPI feminisms, Women of Color feminisms, and transnational feminisms into global Asian feminisms, I focus on cross-cultural, cross-boundary mediations and negotiations, and engage in critical reflections on global Asian feminist solidarities to strengthen broader coalitions formed in the ongoing fight for social justice and gender equality. In theory, the integration of AAAPI feminisms, Women of Color feminisms, and transnational feminisms opens the door for interdisciplinary, cross-spatial, cross-temporal, and comparative work that contributes creative perspectives to GAFS.

In *Feminism without Borders: Decolonizing Theory, Practicing Solidarity*, Chandra Talpade Mohanty (2003) calls on feminists to adopt a decolonizing approach, which is also antiracist and anticapitalist. Mohanty (2003, 3) articulates a positive feminist vision of a "world that is pro-sex and [pro]-women, a world where women and men are free to live creative lives, in security and with bodily health and integrity, where they are free to choose whom they love, and whom they set up house with, and whether they want to have or not have children . . . a vision in which economic stability, ecological sustainability, racial equality, and the redistribution of wealth form the material basis of people's well-being." To achieve this vision, "everyday feminist, anti-racist, anticapitalist practices are as important as larger, organized political movements" (4).

GENDERED EXPERIENCES OF THE COVID-19 PANDEMIC AND FEMINIST AGENCIES

In this section, I examine the significance and implications of adopting gender-focused perspectives in addressing the multifaceted crises of the COVID-19 pandemic. Gender is a complex process of social construction of identities that we perform (Butler 1999) along a spectrum, with male and female representing just two (binary) identities (Goertz and Mazur 2008). Moreover, gender is highlighted as a critical "analytic category" (Waylen 1997, 206), offering valuable insights into policy, institutions, education, health, politics, and economy as well as family and community dynamics and the interactions among them. Jean Grugel and colleagues (2022) show that gender is a pivotal determinant in creating unequal health outcomes and how gender intersected with race, ethnicity, age, migrant status, sexuality, geography, and particularly poverty to exacerbate risks for numerous women's groups during the pandemic.

The COVID-19 pandemic shed light on the preexisting gender inequalities present in different aspects of life and exacerbated gender gaps significantly. The pandemic has been reported by several organizations as the largest setback to gender equality in history. According to the Global Gender Gap Report published on July 13, 2022, it is projected to take 132 years to close the gender gap globally (WEF 2022). The specific challenges faced by women vary across countries due to cultural, religious, and socio-political factors. In general, the implementation of social distancing and "stay at home" orders inadvertently heightened risks and burdens faced by women and girls, with scarce policies to alleviate these negative impacts. Moreover, the economic repercussions of the pandemic plunged numerous families into severe financial distress, posing both immediate and prolonged threats to women and girls. During such turbulent times, the risks of sexual abuse, adolescent pregnancy, child or early marriage, and human trafficking escalated, significantly undermining the sexual and bodily rights of women and girls, with far-reaching and enduring ramifications. Furthermore, women were disproportionately affected by job losses during crises and tend to face more challenges than men in regaining employment once the crisis subsided (Grugel et al. 2022). Despite our adjustment to the "new normal" during the pandemic, women continued to endure sufferings and hardships (George and Kuruvilla 2021). The gender-focused analyses conducted in this book have played a crucial role in unveiling the alarming, threatening, and painful experiences faced by women during the pandemic.

My goal here is to illustrate the imperatives to formulate public policies and legislation that not only support and empower women and girls but also cater to their unique needs, situated as part of broader patriarchal structures and systems that often exploit, marginalize, and harm women and girls. Meanwhile, I understand the importance of acknowledging that gender extends beyond simplistic and conventional definitions of "women." My commitment to understanding and addressing the lived experiences and challenges faced by CCA women, constrained by my expertise, space, and research challenges, leads me to focus on how the pandemic affected them and how they coped with its multiple crises. I approach this focus with the understanding that it is part of more extensive and inclusive strategies on gender for building a diverse and equitable future society for all.

When exploring the unequal impacts of the pandemic, my research focuses on the experiences, narratives, reflections, actions, and contributions of CCA women who have been highly vulnerable and marginalized on multiple levels since the COVID-19 outbreaks. How have anti-Asian racisms and multiple crises of the pandemic affected CCA women? How have these women coped with the multiple harms of racisms and the pandemic? How have they defined, articulated, and exerted their creative agencies and resilience in mobilizing together to fight for individual, family, and community well-being as well as social justice? Exploring these questions within specific contexts, I present the diversified, complicated, and nuanced struggles, actions, negotiations, and achievements of Chinese immigrant mothers, women international students, transracial adoptees, and lay Buddhist women in the US during the pandemic.

Agency as a key concept in social thought has challenged feminist theorists to understand its limits when individuals interact with oppressive social structures. In the late 1990s, feminist theories of agency shifted from emphases on resistance, empowerment, and negotiation within oppressive social structures to frames that discern secularist biases and expand the definition to include self-authorship and the creative and generative aspects of agency (McNay 2000; Mahmood 2005). Lois McNay (2000) articulated a generative agency attuned to strategies that individuals use in their struggles to appropriate and change cultural meanings and resources. She later argued that an emphasis on self-authorship better captures how individuals respond in ways that impede, strengthen, or inspire social changes (McNay 2003).

In this book, I intend to dismantle White Western definitions of feminist agency that emphasize free will, individualism, personal freedom, and preferences for rational thought and propose to return the power to CCA women to articulate and remake their innovative agencies within particular social, cultural, and political contexts. My research illustrates different forms of feminist agencies exerted by CCA women in global contexts in times of crisis and thus contributes to our broader understanding of the diverse ways that CCA women interact with their traditions, build communities, craft solidarities, and engage in social justice.

This study, approached through gendered and racialized lenses, aims to make a valuable contribution to feminist scholarship on lived experiences of women during the COVID-19 pandemic (Adeola 2021; Banerjea, Boyce, and Dasgupta 2022; Dugarova 2020; George and Kuruvilla 2021; Grugel et al. 2022; Higginbotham and Dahlberg 2021; Krasny 2023; Sobti and Sobti 2023). By shedding light on the challenging realities CCA women face in the US, this book highlights their ongoing struggles for equal rights in every aspect of life. It seeks to draw the attention of governments, institutions, policymakers, and scholars to the remarkable efficiency with which women serve their families, communities, and society as well as to their emergence as leaders in navigating the challenges posed by the pandemic. The unprecedented circumstances of COVID-19 underscored the vital role women play in sustaining diverse, equal, inclusive, and resilient communities. Ultimately, this book reinforces the effects of women's empowerment even in the face of one of the largest health crises witnessed by human beings.

In the following sections, I first introduce anti-Asian racisms in the US before and during the pandemic and historicize the lived experiences of CCA people in the contexts of racial discourses and larger political and social forces. Then, I present the key themes of homemaking, belonging, and communities of support throughout the book.

Anti-Asian Racisms in the US before and during the Pandemic

There are various forms of anti-Asian racisms across time and space, and Jennifer Ho (2024) has labeled them collectively "global anti-Asian racism"; they have endured for centuries, particularly in the guise of "yellow perils," which view Asians as threats to national security and democracy. They have been prevalent in Europe and the Americas against Asian immigrants and refugees but are also found in Africa, Australia, and in Asian nations as well.

Anti-Asian sentiments have invariably emerged in places where Asian immigrants and refugees have settled.

There has been a long history of Asian immigration to the US, and hostile attitudes toward these migrants have been part of that history. By the late sixteenth century, driven by capital logic and ambition, empire-colonizers built global networks and technologies to connect all parts of the world to the West in the name of commerce and Christianity. Asians sailed around trade routes worldwide and first visited North America briefly in 1587 (Hsu 2016). British colonists took over Indigenous territories in Hawai'i and other nearby regions, driving out Indigenous cultures and replacing them with commercialized practices for personal profits. These commercialized practices required laborers—often called "coolies"—who predominantly consisted of Asians and Asian Americans, including Chinese, Japanese, Koreans, Filipinos, and Indians. They worked inhumane hours on plantations in arduous conditions and for very low pay, and they were seen as "savages" in the eyes of White people. These Asian immigrants struggled to claim acceptance and equality in the US.

In the 1850s, the California gold rush sparked Asian immigration to the US, especially Chinese immigrants who were seeking a source of income for their families; they also found other jobs, including constructing the western half of the Transcontinental Railroad (1863–69). Amid this wave of immigration, San Francisco became a harbor for anti-Asian sentiments and actions. The president at that time, Ulysses S. Grant, was in support of legal restrictions on Chinese immigration, and the number of women entering the country fell dramatically as a result. Segregated schools later followed as well, separating the Chinese from the rest of the population (Hsu 2016).

From 1852, Chinese immigrants were discriminated against and attacked by White Americans, primarily for their eating habits (e.g., they were described as rat-eaters or lizard-eaters), and were stigmatized as posing an economic threat, being unable to comprehend the principle of democracy, and bringing filth and disease with them (Chang 2003; Roberts 2002). Prejudice against the Chinese was given legal backing with the passage of explicitly anti-Chinese legislation—for instance, on May 2, 1882, the first Chinese Exclusion Act was passed, followed by further discriminatory legislation in 1904, severely restricting Chinese immigration to the US (Tung 1974).

While Asians experienced some forms of racisms and discrimination, each Asian community went through different experiences, varying according to region, political orientation, class, gender, and livelihood. Exclusion stemmed from widely held beliefs in the inferiority and unassimilability of Asians as a biologically distinct race. Social Darwinism and eugenics contributed to the justification of discrimination against Asians and the corresponding policies such as immigration controls, bans on naturalized citizenship, and limits on economic options and political participation (Hsu 2016).

Anti-Asian racisms reached a new high with the 1942 incarceration of Japanese and Japanese Americans in concentration camps. The Japanese military force attacked the US naval base at Pearl Harbor in Hawai'i on the morning of December 7, 1941, leading to America's entry into World War II. Doubting Japanese Americans' loyalty, Franklin Delano Roosevelt signed Executive Order 9066, which forced all Americans of Japanese descent into internment camps. Over 110,000 Japanese Americans were incarcerated, and 79,000 among them were American citizens. Many were given only a few days' notice, and most of them ultimately had to leave their homes, properties, livelihoods, and life savings behind. In internment camps, many families were separated and lived difficult lives in remote areas. The physical and economic erasure through internment camps left a painful mark on the history and psyche of Japanese and Japanese Americans as well as Asian Americans (Yano 2020).

Despite the challenges of facing anti-Asian hate and racisms and the resulting struggles to claim acceptance and equality in the US, Asian peoples continued to immigrate to the country and managed to make a life for themselves and their children. The Chinese played a major role in pushing the law that certified if you were born in the US, then you were a US citizen (E. Lee 2015). During World War II, the recognition that the US and China were allies brought about a substantial, if not a complete, revision of American attitudes toward China and the Chinese people. All Chinese exclusion laws were repealed in the US in December 1943 (Tung 1974). After World War II, the worldwide struggle against communism compelled the US to cultivate friendships with Asian nations and peoples, including the many emergent postcolonial states, such as India, Korea, Vietnam, Malaysia, Cambodia, Indonesia, and Burma. Soon the 1952 McCarran-Walter Act abolished altogether the racial bars on citizenship and granted immigration quotas to all nations (Hsu 2016).

During the Cold War, the multifaceted competition between the US and the Soviet Union pitted capitalism against socialism and made America open its door widely to attract highly educated, professional workers, particularly those in nuclear arms, space exploration, and other important technology fields required for research and development. After the passage of the Immigration and Nationality Act of 1965, the US welcomed large numbers of highly educated and professional workers, such as scientists, engineers, medical personnel, and similar. This act had a huge effect on the increase in Asian immigration, causing many different Asian groups to be spread out all over the US.

The term "Asian American" was coined by activist-scholars Yuji Ichioka and Emma Gee in conjunction with establishing the Asian American Political Alliance in 1968 and the founding of Asian American studies at UCLA in 1969 (Yano 2020). From its beginnings, this term was not intended as a demographic group but "as a new self-defining political alliance between Asian ethnicities in the United States," and it "arose out of the oppositional political struggle of the 1960s" (127).

Since the 1960s, Asian immigrants and Asian Americans have been labeled "model minority" subjects: "educated, employable, hard-working, and politically compliant" (Hsu 2016, 99–100). The concept of the model minority became a stereotype during the 1960s when the Civil Rights Movement continued the fight for equality for all Americans. It is used to pit Asian Americans against other communities of color, particularly Black Americans. White-dominated news publications ran articles extolling the ways Asian Americans capitalized on the American dream with their emphasis on education and a strong work ethic. By doing this, it delegitimized centuries of systemic racisms and racist policies that shaped the experiences of all communities of color. It has also created a hierarchy within ethnic minority groups and created unrealistic expectations of minorities. The White-invented label "model minority" has not protected Asians and Asian Americans from systemic racisms and discrimination. Rather, it has exaggerated the polarization, interrelated racializations, and relational positioning among communities of color (Yano 2020).

Yano (2020, 129) argues that "stereotypes perform their own kind of violence, whether physical, psychological, or emotional." These stereotypes both disable and enable identity politics within one's racialized self and make one invisible in the assimilation framework. In particular, the "model minority" stereotype has created a lot of pressure for AAAPI individuals to conform to the White-dominated culture, and some passively accept that they must hide or abandon their home culture, values, and identities to prevent discrimination. This has led many AAAPIs to feel stressed, embattled, isolated, and inadequate, leading to many mental health issues. To dismantle these harmful stereotypes, AAAPI communities have rallied against the systemic racism that splits and hurts us all.

Systemic racism is defined by Rosalind S. Chou and Joe Feagin in *Myth of the Model Minority: Asian Americans Facing Racism* (2016) as follows: "Our concept of *systemic racism* thus encompasses a broad range of racialized realities in this society: the all-encompassing white racial frame, extensive discriminatory habits and exploitative actions, and numerous racist institutions. This white-generated and white-maintained system entails much more than racial bigotry, for it has been from the beginning a material, structural, and ideological reality" (5). Chou and Feagin draw on forty-three in-depth interviews conducted from 2005 to 2007 to present experiences of racism among Asian Americans from various nations and social classes and assess the effects of racial stereotyping and discrimination in a variety of settings. According to them, anti-Asian racism and discrimination occur in everyday life in public places in such forms as being called slurs, being attacked in the streets and shops, being failed by the legal system, being the recipients of hate from their own neighbors, and being ignored through inadvertent silent acceptance from the Asian American community. Everyday racism also occurs in educational settings—from elementary schools to colleges—and in workplaces: bullying in schools with lack of action from administration, social divisions during projects, issues in romantic relationships, lack of representation in schools and colleges, discrimination at work due to accents or stereotypes, and an inability to stand up for oneself. Accordingly, everyday resistance to racism comes in many different forms, including strategies such as direct confrontation, rejection of the White racial frame, construction of a counterframe, correction of miseducation, reexamination of stereotypes, shifts in peer groups, production of tangible political change, community action, and creation of self-definition and self-valuation. In conclusion, Chou and Feagin advocate for significant political and social change, noting, "In such situations the racial framing and hierarchy can be restructured again, perhaps even replaced, if substantial numbers of Americans of diverse backgrounds can be brought to a full consciousness of how racial oppression operates in society—and if they *organize* collectively and effectively to bring about that significant societal restructuring" (232).

The collective actions and social changes visualized by Chou and Feagin came into reality during the COVID-19 pandemic when anti-Asian racisms reached a peak globally. In the US, Donald Trump tweeted the phrase "Chinese virus" on Twitter on March 16, 2020, although the WHO urged people to avoid terms like the "Wuhan virus" or "Chinese virus," fearing it could spike a backlash against Chinese and Asian people. Trump's single tweet fueled exactly the kind of backlash the WHO had feared, and it was followed by an avalanche of tweets using the hashtag #chinesevirus, among other anti-Asian hashtags and phrases (Hswen et al. 2021). Trump's repeated use of the phrase "Chinese virus" exacerbated the long-existing anti-Asian racisms in the US and perpetuated systemic racisms against communities of color. Globally, the pandemic exaggerated racisms and xenophobia against marginalized groups in different countries. Discrimination targeted groups who were thought to have caused and spread COVID-19, including the residents of Wuhan and African communities in China; ultra-Orthodox Jewish communities in the US, UK, and Israel; and Black/Asian/mixed ethnic communities in the US and UK (Zhou and Gilman 2021). From 2020 to 2022, the proliferation of various rumors, conspiracy theories, and fake news significantly contributed to the rise of anti-Asian racisms and racist divisions within families, societies, groups, and communities (Bodner et al. 2021; Zhang 2023b). Some conspiracy theories circulated online that blamed China for deliberately creating or releasing the virus as a bioweapon, further demonizing the Chinese as enemies or threats.

In response to the alarming escalation in xenophobia and racisms resulting from the pandemic, the Asian American and Pacific Islander Equity Alliance, Chinese for Affirmative Action, and the Asian American Studies Department of San Francisco State University launched the Stop AAPI Hate (SAH) coalition on March 19, 2020. From that date to February 28, 2021, the SAH reporting center received 3,795 hate incident reports. By March 31, 2021, the number of hate incidents reported increased significantly to 6,603 in a month. From March 19, 2020, to March 31, 2022, a total of 11,467 hate incidents against AAPI were reported to SAH (2020–22). The number of hate incidents reported to SAH represented only a small fraction of the number that occurred. To complement the community-based data about anti-AAPI hate, SAH collaborated with the Edelman Data & Intelligence Team to conduct a nationally representative survey with more than 1,000 AAPI respondents. The survey was administered online from September 21 to October 8, 2021. This survey estimated that nearly 1 in 5 Asian Americans (21.2 percent) and 1 in 5 Pacific Islanders (20.0 percent) experienced a hate incident in 2020 or 2021 (SAH 2021b). Nationally, this translates to an estimated 4.8 million Asian Americans and 320,000 Pacific Islanders.

SAH reports show how vulnerable AAPI individuals have been to discrimination and the types of discrimination they have faced. According to SAH data, harassment, such as verbal or written hate speech or inappropriate gestures, makes up the biggest share of total incidents reported (67 percent). These incidents are not defined as hate crimes and would not be investigated or prosecuted as such. Physical violence comprises the second-largest category of total reported incidents (17 percent), followed by the deliberate avoidance or shunning of AAPI (16 percent). Incidents that included possible civil rights violations—such as discrimination in a business or workplace—made up 12 percent of the total. The setting of these incidents was also noted: 27 percent took place in businesses, such as grocery stores, pharmacies, or big-box retail stores; 10 percent occurred online; and 9 percent occurred on public transit. AAPI individuals who are also female, nonbinary, or LGBTQIA+ experience hate incidents that target them for their multiple identities. Nearly 60 percent of incidents were reported by women and girls, who suffered from both racisms and sexism (SAH 2022). Last but not least, the Chinese reported the most hate incidents of all ethnic groups (SAH 2020–22).

Content analysis of hateful languages from the reports through June 2021 revealed five different themes that are not mutually exclusive: (1) scapegoating China, which involved blaming China or Chinese people for the outbreak of the coronavirus, deaths, and so on; (2) racial slurs: derogatory labels about Asian people were used; (3) anti-immigrant racisms: Asians were classified as foreigners forever and told to "go back to your country" or "go back to China"; (4) orientalist portraits: statements about Asians' perceived cultural orientalism were made, such as comments about dirtiness or eating habits (e.g., bat or dog eating), and similar; and (5) red-baiting: comments that connected the victims with socialism or communism (SAH 2021a).

These anti-Asian hate incidents, as well as both systemic and interpersonal racisms, negatively affected AAPI—racial discrimination experience is associated with both negative physical and mental health. SAH data show that one in five Asian Americans who experienced racism exhibited racial trauma, the psychological and emotional damage caused by racisms. Furthermore, Asian Americans who experienced racism experienced increased depression, anxiety, stress, physical symptoms, and greater stress from anti-Asian racisms than the pandemic itself. When proposing solutions, AAPI individuals and communities have identified: (1) public education, for example, ethnic studies; (2) community safety solutions, for example, victim services and preventative measures; and (3) civil rights enforcement, for example, antidiscrimination laws, as the most effective avenues to address and reduce anti-Asian racisms (SAH 2020–22).

SAH data reveal the persistence of anti-AAPI racisms and the underlying social fractures within American society. The recent demographic, social, and cultural shift of AAPI communities in the US has played an important role in producing a more active and collective community response to racisms exaggerated by the pandemic. For instance, at the beginning of the pandemic, Chinese communities in many states were mobilized to donate money, masks, and personal protection equipment (PPE) to local hospitals, police stations, and other important institutions. They did their best to build trust with the host societies (Zhang and You 2022).

Coalitions among AAAPI communities were also formed through rallies and protests after the Atlanta spa shootings on March 16, 2021, when eight people—six of whom were Asian women—were shot to death by a White gunman. In the wake of the murder, AAAPIs and their allies protested in the streets and held rallies in almost every state across the US. The eight people's names have been remembered across the nation: Xiaojie Tan, Daoyou Feng, Hyun Jung Grant, Suncha Kim, Soon Chung Park, Yong Ae Yue, Delaina Ashley Yaun, and Paul Andre Michels. Together, AAAPIs and their allies built a movement to advance social justice and civil rights for all communities of color, called the SAH movement here. SAH and other important civil rights organizations have continued to push state policymakers to take necessary steps to invest in community safety, education equity, and social justice enforcement. With collective efforts, AAAPI communities have worked together to advance equity and justice by dismantling systemic racisms, building a multiracial movement to end hate against AAAPI communities, and creating a better and safer society for all.

Racisms and sexism are always intertwined when we examine anti-Asian hate. Of the 11,467 incidents reported to SAH in two years, 60 percent of respondents identified as female (SAH 2022). AAAPI women are vulnerable and targeted again and again—from the Atlanta spa shootings to the tragedy of forty-year-old Michelle Alyssa Go who was shoved onto the tracks in front of an oncoming New York City subway train at the Forty-Second Street–Times Square station in January 2022. This increased targeting of AAAPI women is not new. Sexism and racisms have been historically mixed, resulting in AAAPIs and other women of color facing higher risks for violence and hate crimes. SAH reports found hate and violence against AAAPI women most often occurred in public places, but female respondents were also targeted in residential neighborhoods, online, and in places of worship. What the data tell us is that there are very few spaces where AAAPI women can feel safe in their everyday lives, and the impacts of anti-Asian racisms are lasting. Anti-AAAPI racisms are systemic problems that require systemic actions. AAAPI organizations, groups, and individuals have been working with policymakers at all levels to provide systemic solutions that help protect the rights of AAAPI women and communities.

AAAPI women have often been characterized as passive victims of racisms and sexism, and this portrayal overlooks their creative agencies and their collective efforts to make social changes. This study brings to light the overlooked stories, voices, and actions of these women, especially CCA women, as they combat anti-Asian racisms and build diverse communities of support to advocate for social justice.

Communities of Support, Homemaking, and Belonging

Here I create the new term *communities of support* to describe how mutual support among CCA women emerged or strengthened through coalitions and community building in response to the public health crisis, shared subjectivities, experiences of racisms and marginalization, and collective actions to make social changes. In other words, communities of support reorganize assistance in multiple directions, among immigrant mothers, international students, adoptees, and lay Buddhist women, in response to anti-Asian racisms and multiple crises of the pandemic.

This concept has been inspired by Leah Williams Veazey's (2021) term "migrant maternal online communities," Valerie Francisco-Menchavez's (2018) concept of "communities of care," and bell hooks's concept of "community of resistance" (2014). Veazey (2021) integrates important concepts in transnational migration, matricentric feminism, and Black feminism to explore "migrant maternal online communities": self-created, vernacular Facebook groups that were made by migrant mothers for migrant mothers. As those mothers brought their struggles from private life into a semipublic digital space, they drew on those digital communities to cope with loneliness, homesickness, and anxieties in transnational contexts. Francisco-Menchavez (2018, 97) creates the concept of "community of care," which is defined as "a form of reorganizing care horizontally, *from* migrants *to* other migrants informed by their transnational familial context." Examining "multidirectional care" through Filipina migrants' practice of care work among one another in New York City, Francisco-Menchavez argues that Filipina migrant mothers invested in a network of solidarity and strength in and through their shared experiences of reorganized care work with their transnational families. "Community of resistance" is articulated by Black feminist bell hooks (2014, 61) to combat racism in the US: "It is no accident that this homeplace, as fragile and as transitional as it may be, a makeshift shed, a small bit of earth where one rests, is always subject to violation and destruction. For when a people no longer have the space to construct homeplace, we cannot build a meaningful community of resistance." In my study, CCA women's agencies can be defined not only in terms of resistance, counter discourse, and subversion but also in terms of compromise, compliance, obedience, and humility. When CCA women build new homes and fight for social justice, they craft "communities of support" with other AAAPI women, activists, and broader allies. The diverse processes of community building and diverse forms of agencies show how CCA women in different professional and social roles build coalitions and combine Western and modern reasoning with Chinese values and modes of thought to achieve their own goals and agendas.

The interplay of community building, homemaking, and belonging provides an analytical lens to examine how CCA women cope with anti-Asian racisms and the multiple crises of the pandemic. Homemaking is intertwined with a sense of belonging, which is very complicated. Psychologist Geoffrey Cohen (2022, 5) defines belonging as "the feeling that we are part of a larger group that values, respects, and cares for us—and to which we feel we have something to contribute." Belonging could also be understood as "close emotional attachments to place" (Gorman-Murray 2011, 211). These spatio-emotional connections are intertwined with the confirmation of collective, interpersonal, and personal identities and invoke place-bound feelings of security and "being-at-home" (Ignatieff 1994). Senses of belonging, in a way, are the emotional bindings between individuals and groups, between subjects and spaces, facilitating comforts, identities, and becoming (Davidson and Milligan 2004). Gendered aspects of belongings have received increased scholarly attention in recent decades (Fenster 2005; Gorman-Murray 2011; Yuval-Davis, Anthias, and Kofman 2005). The existing scholarship centers on women's lived experiences of inclusion or exclusion in different scaled arenas, from the residential dwelling to public urban space and the nation-state (Domosh and Seager 2001; Fenster 2005) and in transnational contexts (Belford and Lahiri-Roy 2019).

Migration changes the concepts of "home," and the migration-home nexus has been studied through different perspectives by scholars. Shelley Mallett (2004, 68) defines home as "a 'socio-spatial system' that represents the fusion of the physical unit or house and the social unit or household." For immigrants, home is intertwined with experiences of place, space, and system and is also about memory and emotions (Chawla and Jones 2015). Sara Ahmed (2000, 90) claims, "the journeys of migration involve a splitting of home as a place of origin and home as the sensory world of everyday experience." Exploring an immigrant's "search for home" and the impact of mobility on their social experiences, Paolo Boccagni (2017, xxiv) points out that home is "both a material environment and a set of meaningful relationships, recollections, and aspirations to be emplaced." In short, home is fluid, shifting, and ambivalent (Baldassar 2002; L. S. Liu 2014; Zhu 2020), and it has been produced and reproduced through processes of adaptation, negotiation, transformation, and redefinition as we build and craft our communities based on race, nation, class, gender, religion, etc. (Belford and Lahiri-Roy 2019).

How can folklorists understand and study the home, considering it is more than just a place, a group, or a series of performances? In a 2009 address to the American Folklore Society, former president Elaine Lawless (2011,

128) discussed her own realization of a "failure of the imagination" in understanding home in her personal life. She viewed home not merely as a static location, but as a fluid place shaped and changed by memory and personal experiences. Lawless metaphorically described the home as an imaginary landscape, where perception and understanding define its reality. Reflecting on her own childhood trauma, Lawless recognized that her understanding of home consisted of layered countless maps, incorporating the perspectives and experiences of her grandmother, mother, and herself.

The definition of *home* can vary greatly among Americans: a place where one's heart is, a physical dwelling, or symbolic concepts like a castle or a money pit. Home plays an important role in identity formation and cultural validation. It is within the home that individuals learn the rules and dynamics of family, ethnicity, nationality, regional identity, and social hierarchy. The home serves as a space for transmitting recipes and showcasing festival decorations. Celebrations and performances further enhance the significance of home, and the artifacts of domestic life often accompany individuals beyond the confines of their homes. Despite their familiarity with their own homes, folklorists must recognize that the home represents a frontier in itself and a space encompassing borderlands, performances, rituals, stories, and material culture (Hutcheson 2018).

Feminists have different views of "home": some see it as a place of belonging and comfort, and some associate it with a false sense of security and safety. Celia T. Bardwell-Jones (2017) shows how it is possible to have a dual sense of home that incorporates different meanings and spans nation-states, cultures, identities, and practices. She argues that this sense of home creates a new space of possibility—the "space-between"—from which new possibilities for productive transnational dialogues and feminist solidarities may emerge.

In this study, I look closely at the process of community building and feminist agencies that emerged or strengthened when racialized and gendered experiences of being Chinese, Asian, women, or immigrants (or all of these) produced new homes as imaginary landscapes and formed senses of belonging and relationships of solidarity. CCA women's transnational lives and practices provide a deep basis for the creation and function of their communities of support, especially when they face anti-Asian racisms in the US.

Contents Map

In this book, I draw on the stories and experiences of over eighty-six contributors to examine how the COVID-19 pandemic affected CCA women in the US and how they responded to anti-Asian racisms and the multiple crises of the pandemic. I highlight how the pandemic has changed their everyday lives, (dis)identifications, and foodways and how they have created diverse communities of support and worked together to build a more diverse, equal, and inclusive society for all.

In addition to this introductory chapter, the book has six main chapters. Chapter 2 examines how Chinese immigrant mothers have demonstrated resilience, agencies, and solidarities in times of crisis and built diverse and inclusive communities of support with other marginalized groups and youth activists. I argue that communities of support have been crafted by Chinese immigrant mothers at the intersection of race, gender, politics, motherhood, and globalization, thus providing a foundation for the diverse political activisms practiced by them. I highlight the diversity and complexity of Chinese immigrant mothers' experiences during the pandemic and examine how they engaged in various forms of political activism, built broader coalitions, and practiced activist mothering to build social justice for all.

Chapter 3 presents the experiences and responses of Chinese women international students (students for short) during the pandemic when they were marginalized in multiple ways in both the US and China because of the racialization of the new coronavirus as the "Chinese virus," the deterioration of US-China relations, lockdown and quarantine policies, and various public health protocols. Affected by biopolitics and strict travel restrictions, Chinese students' journeys back home became very expensive and challenging, sometimes even impossible. The decision to stay in the US or return to China became a recurring dilemma for them, with their personal choices intricately linked to systemic racisms, public health, geopolitics, education, and economy. By showing their struggles and achievements, this chapter examines Chinese women students' resilience, coping strategies, and creative agencies during the pandemic.

Chapter 4 focuses on Chinese adoptees to examine their strategies and practices to combat racisms during the pandemic. From 1999 to 2018, American families adopted about 81,600 children from China, most of them girls, according to the US State Department (Constante 2020). Although these adoptees grew up in the US and are officially American citizens, they still became targets of racisms during the pandemic. This chapter shares the stories and voices of Chinese adoptees and illustrates how they fight against racisms, negotiate their (dis)identifications, craft broader solidarities, build communities of support, and advocate for social justice. They use narratives, arts, dance, foodways, festivals, and other forms of vernacular expressive cultural practices to articulate and exert their creative agencies in building social justice and remaking their identities, despite the feelings many had that they

Global Asian Folklore Studies, Feminisms, and Anti-Asian Racisms   33 lacked agency in their early lives. This chapter sheds light on the resilience and creativity of Chinese adoptees in finding ways to face their unique challenges and assert their visibilities and agencies in American society.

Chapter 5 presents how Chinese lay Buddhist women responded and adapted to the pandemic, how they have continued their beliefs and practices by crafting hybrid communities, how their religious practices have empowered them to go through the pandemic and other life crises, and how religion is important for their social bonding and identifications. I highlight their creative agencies in self-empowerment and self-cultivation in times of crisis through practicing Buddhism despite all restrictions and challenges.

By integrating eighty-three interviews, virtual ethnography, virtual panels, and class surveys, chapter 6 provides a snapshot of how the pandemic changed fluid foodways and everyday lives of CCA communities and explores the complicated, nuanced, and situational relationships between racisms, foodways, and gender in the US. After briefly introducing the spread of fluid Chinese foodways to the US, I present "the lunchbox incident" that CCA children often encounter in their elementary schools when their White classmates make fun of their Chinese foods. I examine how CCA young adults have developed various strategies to respond to this incident and other forms of anti-Asian racisms and how they have practiced various forms of youth activisms to fight for social justice. I also explore the fluid foodways of Chinese adoptees, dietary changes and comfort foodways of Chinese women students, and fluid foodways of Chinese lay Buddhist women during the pandemic. Overall, this chapter offers a diverse analysis of the roles foodways play in identity formation, social advocacy, community building, and personal well-being.

Chapter 7 frames racisms, antiracisms, and political activisms of CCA women; articulates decolonization and diverse voices from the margins; and points out future directions for research. Furthermore, it presents how CCA women reflect on life's meaning and envision their lives with hope after the pandemic. Every risky decision we face asks a similar question—one that "all manner of experts can never answer . . . how do we want to live?" (Beck 1999, 12). The COVID-19 pandemic has made us rethink what the meaning of life is and how we should face death and uncertainties. This is the beginning of our journey to explore the ways we want to live, at present and in the future.

How to Read This Book and Use It in the Classroom

The book was written with undergraduate students in mind, particularly for those enrolled in my courses such as Anti-Asian Racism, Women and Writing in East Asia, Health and Narratives in Global Asias, and so on. The structure of the book's chapters, with detailed introductions and ethnographic expositions, is intentional. It allows each chapter to stand alone and be assigned at different times throughout the course, providing flexibility in teaching and learning.

For scholars and students in Global Asian Studies—a field that integrates Asian studies, Asian Diaspora studies, and Asian American studies—the introduction and chapters 2–5 are particularly pertinent. Those specializing in folklore studies, anthropology, feminisms, and pandemic studies will find all chapters relevant, with the introduction providing essential theoretical foundations. For those focused on food studies, chapter 6 is especially significant. Moreover, individual chapters discussing Chinese immigrant mothers, international students, adoptees, and lay Buddhist women can be assigned separately for class discussions.

This book is written in an easily accessible style and features engaging narratives that intend to appeal to scholars and students in the humanities and social sciences as well as general nonacademic readers as we now collectively reflect on the COVID-19 years and seek to understand how diverse populations navigated them. Everyone fights their own battles in life, making this book relevant to all. Please feel free to read it in any way that suits you best.

2

BUILDING NEW HOMES

Chinese Immigrant Mothers, Communities of Support, and Political Activisms during the Pandemic

Child: I love my home
My parents and me
Love is not quarreling
Playing with me every day

Mom: I love my home
My son, my daughter, and my dear husband
Love is to endure
All the complicated things in the family

Dad: I love my home
My son, my daughter, and my dear wife
Love is giving
Letting there be no shortages at home

Together: Let my home be full of love every day
Let your home be full of love every day
No matter it is day or night
Spring, summer, autumn, or winter
Let our home be full of love with our whole hearts

Together: Let my home be full of love every day
Let your home be full of love every day

Full of happiness
Full of peace
Let our home be full of love forever

Children: I love my home
School is my home.
Teachers are like mothers
Accompanying me to grow up day by day

Children: I love my home
The green earth is my home
Everyone holds hands
To take good care of her

This Chinese song, "Home Full of Love," was presented at the Ohio Chinese Festival (OCF) on Saturday, January 28, 2023, by my five-year-old daughter, Enxi; her classmates; and some parents. The song was arranged by Enxi's Chinese teacher, Chen Laoshi (Chen), and parent volunteers at the Ohio Contemporary Chinese School (OCCS). The purpose of the song was to convey love and support within Chinese and Chinese American (CCA) families and in the Chinese school. The act of singing this song together created a strong sense of belonging and homecoming in CCA communities. Chen later remarked in our OCCS Parents Group (OPG) on WeChat that the successful OCF was a result of the remarkable collaborative efforts of numerous parents, children, teachers, organizers, committee members, and volunteers. Through their collective work, they have built new homes not only for themselves but also for younger generations of CCAs.

OCF was suspended for three years (2020–22) but made a comeback in 2023 with enthusiastic support from Ohio's CCA communities. Originally organized by Ohio Chinese Culture Link and OCCS in 2008, OCF later included co-organizers such as Cleveland Contemporary Chinese School and Greater Cincinnati Chinese School. Before the pandemic, the event was a full-day celebration, featuring art performances, cultural exhibitions, demonstrations, handicrafts, and food vendors. However, the 2023 OCF was a half-day event held at a local high school from 12:00 p.m. to 5:00 p.m., without food sales. The festival involved significant support from CCA community leaders and student leaders from the high school, with the aim to promote Chinese culture and foster friendship, mutual respect, and understanding among people in the US and China across racial and cultural boundaries.

Building New Homes   37

The 2023 OCF took place shortly after two violent incidents during the Lunar New Year in California. The first involved a seventy-two-year-old man opening fire on the Star Ballroom, a Chinese-owned ballroom in Monterey Park, killing ten people and injuring at least ten others. Two days later, only hours after news broke that another victim of the Star Ballroom shooting had passed away, Zhao Chunli, a sixty-six-year-old man, shot and killed seven farmworkers in Half Moon Bay. These acts of violence had a devastating impact on the Asian, Asian American, and Pacific Islander (AAAPI) communities, leading to mourning and collective actions. AAAPI organizations and groups called for government actions to protect AAAPI communities from gun violence while advocating for increased community safety, cultural diversity, and social justice.

This chapter centers on the impacts of the COVID-19 pandemic on Chinese immigrant mothers (hereafter mothers for short) in the US, highlighting their diverse lived experiences, struggles, actions, and achievements in response to multiple crises of the pandemic and anti-Asian racisms. I use the term *immigrant* to refer to both migrant and immigrant people. The usual distinction between migrant and immigrant is based on the permanence of an individual's stay in the host country. *Migrant* describes an individual who moves from one place to another, often to find work or better living conditions, and *immigrant* describes one who resides in a host country with the intention of permanent settlement. The immigrants in this study had lived abroad for periods ranging from two to forty-five years. The term *mother* refers to biological mothers as well as women who identify themselves as mothers.

I call the communities that I have worked with *communities of support* that have been formed or strengthened with the rise of anti-Asian racisms. AAAPIs were unjustly blamed for the outbreak of the COVID-19 pandemic and were perceived as perpetually foreign by anti-immigrant nationalists. They were subjected to xenophobic slurs, such as "Go back to your country!" or "Go back home!" Within this context, CCA families have continued to build their homes in the US, clearly stating, "We belong here!" This is particularly true for diverse Chinese immigrant mothers who have given birth or are raising their children in the US.

To collect data, I participated in three WeChat groups from 2020 to 2022: OPG (500 members), Huagen Chinese School (HCS; 374 members), and Parents and Children Education Identifications (PCEI; 112 members). In HCS, I analyzed their efforts in donating face masks to local institutions during the COVID-19 outbreak in 2020, which helped build trust within local communities (Zhang and You 2022). Introduced by Professor Ying Lu at New York

University, I joined the PCEI group in December 2021. This group organized monthly events to develop the Asian American and Pacific Islander (AAPI) curriculum and promote emotional quotient parenting within a supportive community.[1] Many core members of PCEI were also affiliated with other important CCA and AAAPI organizations, such as Make Us Visible New Jersey (MUVNJ), the Historical Record of Chinese Americans, the Chinese School Association in the United States, New England Chinese American Association, and Alliance for Impact. Being connected with these broader communities allowed me to witness key historical moments, including the passing of AAPI curriculum bills in New Jersey and other states.

Although some scholars describe WeChat as the "virtual Chinatown," Lisong Liu (2023) argues that it has been a "virtual ethnic town hall" where migrants can debate community issues, understand American society, and practice democracy. Methodologically, WeChat served as a valuable platform for me to conduct virtual ethnography with Chinese immigrant mothers across multiple states during the pandemic. Moreover, I recruited and interviewed eighteen Chinese immigrant mothers and four fathers in 2020–22. Each participant self-reported their gender identity, and all eighteen mothers identified as cisgender women married to men, with one recently divorced. Twelve mothers were born in the 1980s, three in the 1970s, and three in the 1960s. Five mothers have one child, ten have two children, and three have three children. The children's ages at the time of the interviews mainly ranged from three to thirteen years old. Levels of participants' education varied, with most mothers being highly educated (with at least a master's degree). Seven mothers were stay-at-home mothers, ten had jobs at the time of interviews, and one lost her job in March 2020. These mothers had varied family backgrounds in China, and most of them have middle-class status in the US. Interviews were conducted in Mandarin Chinese, either online or via phone calls. These interviews, along with media reports and panel discussions organized by the Parents and Children Education (PCE) Club, were analyzed thematically using NVivo.[2] Participant-chosen coding names and pseudonyms were used, and interview excerpts were translated by me from Chinese to English.

In this chapter, I examine four key themes regarding the impacts of the COVID-19 pandemic on Chinese mothers and their responses to the pandemic and anti-Asian racisms: (1) gendered pandemic and intensive motherhood; (2) diverse life and work experiences of Chinese immigrant mothers during the pandemic; (3) activist mothering and political activisms of Chinese immigrant mothers; and (4) PCE Club, everyday activisms, and communities of support.

GENDERED PANDEMIC AND INTENSIVE MOTHERHOOD

Before the pandemic, Chinese mothers frequently encountered numerous challenges during the process of cultural adaptation after coming to the US. They were confronted with conflicts and tensions between two different cultural systems about childbirth and child-rearing and had to negotiate societal and cultural norms and manage elevated demands and expectations within patriarchal family structures. Despite the political and cultural differences between China and the US, Chinese mothers are subject to similar norms of "intensive mothering" (Hays 1996), which positions mothers as the primary caregivers of their children. The pandemic imposed extra challenges and burdens on Chinese mothers, exacerbating the demands of intensive motherhood and compelling them to advocate for social justice for themselves, their children, and other children in the US.

After the declaration of the COVID-19 outbreak as a global pandemic by the World Health Organization on March 11, 2020, and the proclamation of a national emergency by the US on March 14, 2020, numerous public places, including schools, daycare centers, museums, libraries, restaurants, and bars, were closed. During the lockdowns, countless individuals lost their employment, innumerable businesses collapsed, and many deaths occurred. In fear of contracting the deadly illness, many individuals stayed at home. Hit hard by job losses and the pandemic's impacts on schooling and childcare, women in general encountered short-term difficulties and long-term repercussions (P. Cohen 2020).

UN Women (2020) collected data from thirty-eight countries to confirm that both women and men increased their unpaid workloads for household chores and care due to pandemic-related measures and lockdowns in 2020, but women were doing the lion's share and taking on greater intensity of care-related work than men. Moreover, more women than men left and are leaving the workforce, probably because of the increased care work at home or loss of jobs and livelihoods. Women and girls stand to be the hardest hit during the pandemic, but their personal experiences vary across time, space, and cultures. Women with greater resources possessed relative privilege, but they struggled in other ways. The closure of childcare facilities and the transition to remote learning resulted in an inequitable burden of household responsibilities falling primarily on working mothers rather than fathers. Patricia Cohen and Tiffany Hsu (2020) claimed that, despite the increased stress experienced by the majority of families because of COVID-19, mothers in heterosexual couples dedicated an additional fifteen hours per week on average to educational and household tasks by June 2020. They further wrote, "For many working mothers, the gradual reopening won't solve their problems, but compound them—forcing them out of the labor force or into part-time jobs while increasing their responsibilities at home. The impact could last a lifetime, reducing their earning potential and work opportunities."

The care demands and crises of additional work through and after the pandemic have been highlighted in the edited volume *Mothers, Mothering, and COVID-19* (O'Reilly and Green 2021). In the book, seventy contributors examine the impacts of the COVID-19 pandemic on mothers' care responsibilities and wage labor within the context of employment, schooling, communities, families, and the relationships between parents and children. With global perspectives and from the standpoints of single, partnered, queer, racialized, Indigenous, economically disadvantaged, disabled, and birthing mothers, the book scrutinizes the mounting complexities and demands of childcare, domestic labor, elder care, and homeschooling under the pandemic protocols. It presents the intricacies and difficulties of conducting wage labor at home, the impacts of the pandemic on mothers' employment, and the strategies employed by mothers to cope with the competing demands of care and wage labor during the pandemic.

Before the pandemic, US mothers navigated a complicated parenting terrain, facing a lack of national and state support for parenting policies (e.g., paid parental leave) and increasing demands of what Sharon Hays (1996) has termed intensive motherhood. Hays (1996, 8) coined the term *intensive mothering* to describe the "child-centered, expert-guided, emotionally absorbing, labor-intensive, and financially expensive" undertaking that motherhood had become by the mid-1990s. Hays emphasizes that intensive mothering persists because the discourse is based on the beliefs that children "need and deserve" their mothers' attention and mothers must be willing to subordinate their own needs and interests to those of their children (21). Building on Hays's research, Susan Douglas and Meredith Michaels (2004, 4) write about "the new momism," which is "a highly romanticized and yet demanding view of motherhood in which the standards for success are impossible to meet." D. Lynn O'Brien Hallstein (2010, 143) claims that intensive motherhood is "the proper ideology of contemporary intensive mothering that all women are disciplined into, across race and class lines, even if not all women actually practice it." These discourses illustrate that an ideal American mother spends considerable time, energy, effort, and resources centered on her children.

This ideal American motherhood is based on the norms of White, middle-class, cisgender, heterosexual, and ideally married women (Hallstein 2017). These norms exclude those women who are not White, who have physical disabilities, who cannot reproduce, and who give birth when they are either very young or very old. Those who are excluded from these norms may strive to meet intensive motherhood ideals, but they will rarely, if ever, be viewed as ideal American mothers. As Fiona Joy Green (2015, 198) writes, "Despite many cultural contradictions and diverse parenting arrangements and practices, intensive mothering remains the normalised cultural and political standard by which motherhood, mothering and mothers are evaluated."

White Western discourses of "intensive mothering," "work-family balance," and "mother as the main parent" emerged as byproducts of neoliberal feminism, in which a balance between pursuing career success and being the primary parent is promoted (Wall 2013). Mothers are encouraged to "have it all" and to find a balance between work and family that is hardly equalized and leaves them bearing more burdens and chasing unrealistic possibilities (Gilbert and Von Wallmenich 2014; Kornfield 2014). The isolation and stress of the pandemic created a "perfect storm" where mothers struggled like never before and continued to face long-term gender inequalities both in the workplace and at home (Cummins and Brannon 2022).

In the US, early lockdowns and stay-at-home orders led many businesses, including daycare centers and schools, to shut down or move online. The pandemic had devastating impacts on working mothers, such as increased unemployment rates, heightened health risks for essential workers required to work in-person, and a surge in working from home. Lockdowns, closures, and the need for social distancing caused mothers to lose both institutional and informal childcare support. Such losses in childcare support had significant impacts on both paid and unpaid labor of mothers (Yavorsky, Qian, and Sargent 2021). The escalated workload at home affected mothers' employment severely. In particular, mothers of young or school-aged children were more likely than men to reduce their paid work hours, drop out of the labor market, and reduce their productivity at work during the pandemic (C. Collins et al. 2021; Dias, Chance, and Buchanan 2020; Heggeness 2020).

In my study, the chaotic, complicated, and contradictory realities of mothering and motherhood both before and during the pandemic were clearly articulated by Chinese mothers. Together, they crafted diverse personal narratives to share their nuanced mothering experiences in their own words. Moreover, they have connected with other Chinese mothers who had gone through similar experiences and attempted to form communities of support with which they feel a sense of belonging and being "at home."

Diverse Life and Work Experiences of Chinese Immigrant Mothers during the Pandemic

As preventive measures against COVID-19, lockdowns and stay-at-home orders were implemented to varying degrees across states in March 2020 and did not start to lift until early May 2020. During the lockdowns, every day was a challenge for Chinese mothers, and they often encountered daily difficulties with budgeting time, energy, effort, resources, and money. Some Chinese mothers felt that they were abandoned or unsupported by their families, institutions, and governments. Despite the popular proverb that "it takes a village to raise a child," the main burdens of doing so have frequently been placed on mothers, and these are exacerbated in times of crisis. As Andrea O'Reilly (2021, 42) writes, "Mothers are most affected because it is mothers who perform the necessary carework and are responsible for social reproduction to sustain their families and communities through and after this pandemic."

The burdens of the pandemic-induced stress, losses, and recession have fallen heavily on mothers. Most of my contributors felt burned out and overwhelmed during the lockdowns when childcare centers and schools were closed. Even before the pandemic started, some mothers felt exhausted and sleep deprived and found that making time for themselves was almost impossible. Some felt that high expectations of them as "a good wife and a wise mother" (*xianqi liangmu*) in traditional Chinese culture made their lives very hard, especially when their children were small. One mother gave birth to her daughter in October 2021 and struggled tremendously as a new mother. She knew that becoming a mother was hard, but she did not expect that it would be as hard as it was; in response, she hired a nanny and asked her father to come to the US to help her.

In lockdowns, working mothers found it hard to balance work and childcare, whereas stay-at-home mothers felt overwhelmed with extra housework and homeschooling. No contributors voluntarily quit their jobs during the pandemic as many of them needed jobs for immigration status, financial stability, feeling they had a purpose in life, personal values, and independence. A few young stay-at-home mothers mentioned that they quit their jobs after they gave birth to their child or children because they found it impossible to balance work and child-rearing, and their spouses' salaries were high enough to support the whole family. Mothers who suffered tremendously during the pandemic were those who lost jobs or whose husbands lost jobs.

Loss of Jobs and Unemployment

Wu Meili (born 1972) lost her job as an accountant on March 20, 2020, after she worked from home for one week. She worked for a healthcare company, and the pandemic led to a dramatic decline in the company's revenues, resulting in budget cuts and job losses. She and many other workers in supporting roles were laid off due to the financial crisis the company faced. She expressed her complicated feelings this way:

> The hardest time during the pandemic was when I was laid off. It was very painful because it was particularly ruthless. You worked hard there and just when you had adjusted a set of accounts and felt that you could do it freely, they laid you off . . . Then I started applying for unemployment benefits. Because of my daughter and many things at home, I had accumulated a lot of things that I hadn't done while working, so I made a list every day to do something. Actually, it was no less busy than going to work even though I didn't make money. Later on, the [state] unemployment benefits arrived, and the federal ones came in, too. I have been looking for jobs every week. I think, if the economy recovers, finding a job shouldn't be difficult; after all, I've been working in this field for many years. (Interview on May 18, 2020)

Meili mentioned the devastating emotional and psychological impacts of losing a job, and she had to keep herself very busy to deal with such a life crisis. She kept looking for new jobs every week, and she eventually found a new job in September 2021; she later changed her job to work in state government in December 2022.

MY (born 1982) was a stay-at-home housewife and mother, and her husband, YZJ (born 1977), was the breadwinner in their family. Their two sons were born in 2012 and 2015. YZJ lost his faculty position on July 15, 2020, when his university superseded tenure rules and laid off ninety-seven unionized faculty members and eighty-one staff and contract professionals; more than eighty workers took voluntary resignations or retirements. YZJ had worked there for five years. It was a depressing moment for the local community, as it had tremendous impacts on individuals, the university, the region, the economy, and the surrounding areas. Faculty of color and women faculty were disproportionately affected by the layoff. Even before the pandemic, American colleges and universities had already faced financial crises due to diminishing state funding, decreasing enrollment, and concerns regarding rising tuition costs and student debts. To mitigate short-term financial losses in the spring of 2020, many colleges and universities implemented hiring freezes and offered early retirement options. However, the financial effects of the pandemic continue to deepen. It was estimated that colleges incurred costs of at least $120 billion due to the pandemic (Nierenberg and Pasick 2020).

The COVID-19 pandemic had a major impact on employment across the globe as well as in the US. In the spring of 2020, the labor market was experiencing job loss on a scale not seen since the Great Depression. In 2021 about 60 percent of jobs lost had come back, but employment was still low compared to prepandemic levels (Aughinbaugh and Rothstein 2022). The pandemic has broadened inequalities and increased poverty, and its impacts will be felt for many years to come (OECD, n.d.). The US Bureau of Labor Statistics (2021) states: "Total civilian employment fell by 8.8 million over the year [2020], as the COVID-19 pandemic brought the economic expansion to a sudden halt, taking a tremendous toll on the U.S. labor market. The unemployment rate increased in 2020, surging to 13.0 percent in the second quarter of the year before easing to 6.7 percent in the fourth quarter. Although some people were able to work at home, the numbers of unemployed on temporary layoff, those working part-time for economic reasons, and those unemployed for 27 or more weeks increased sharply over the year." According to the special supplement to the US Bureau of Labor Statistics National Longitudinal Survey of Youth 1997, from February through May 2021, the pandemic affected US men's and women's labor market experiences differently, and the differences occurred across demographic groups: those with lower education levels and poorer health, along with Black and Hispanic workers, were often affected more than others (Aughinbaugh and Rothstein 2022). The shrinking global economy affected the lives and livelihoods of people worldwide, with women shouldering a disproportionate burden due to the increases in their unpaid care work at home.

Employment and work of AAAPI women were disproportionately affected by the pandemic. According to the report "Women in the Workplace 2021" by McKinsey & Company (2021), most Asian American women reported feeling stressed, exhausted, and burned out due to combined work and household responsibilities. In particular, Asian American women experienced the greatest increase in household responsibilities among all groups (White, Hispanic and Latino, Black, and Asian American) while also balancing work. Furthermore, it is reported that 30 percent of Asian American women have considered reducing their career responsibilities, either through decreasing their work hours, taking a leave of absence, or transitioning to a less demanding job. Asian American women were 14 percent more likely to cite increased household responsibilities as a direct reason for why they were thinking about stepping back from work. The combination of existing inequities in representation and new burdens of added stresses, remote working, and household responsibilities compounds the struggles and challenges that Asian American women already faced at work and home (G. Hua et al. 2021).

Challenges of Working from Home

In our interviews, some working mothers shared the difficulties they experienced while working from home during the pandemic. PP (born 1981) was a junior professor at an R-1 research university, and she noted that the biggest changes for her were that her classes changed from in-person to online in March 2020 and that her daughter stopped attending kindergarten and stayed at home. At the time of the interview, her daughter was five years old, and her son was three. She articulated her various struggles in balancing work and life since her pregnancy:

> It is full of bitter tears. It's very difficult. Childbirth and child-rearing have big impacts on women. Pregnancy itself is not easy. When I was pregnant with my first child, I had anemia. It was very serious. I got short of breath when I walked. After my child was born, it was better. My parents and in-laws took turns coming to help me take care of my baby, so they helped me a lot. Later on, when my elder child started going to kindergarten, we were very happy. In the spring of last year [2020], we were going to send our second child to kindergarten . . . but then the pandemic came and we had to bring our elder child back home. So both children were at home making chaos.
>
> I think it's very difficult to balance work and life. On one hand, there must be support from family members. If my parents and in-laws didn't come to help us, it would be very difficult for me and my husband, as we both are faculty members. My husband is very busy. He is in the field of science and engineering and has many projects. He has meetings from morning to evening. When he is not working, he helps take care of the children at night and feeds them milk. We split our household chores equally. (Interview on June 11, 2021)

As a dual-faculty couple, PP and her husband were lucky to have positions in the same university, although on different campuses. They bought a house between the two campuses, and it took each of them about twenty minutes to drive to work before the pandemic. Many dual-faculty couples could not live in the same place, and their family lives were really challenging after they had children. PP thought that she and her husband were quite lucky for staying together. They split housework equally and maintained egalitarian relationships at home. In PP's opinion, the main solutions for balancing work and life might include having support from parents and in-laws and sending children to school. PP described her daily life when working from home this way:

> During the pandemic, my in-laws were here with us. They happened to get their green cards before the pandemic started, so they stayed here to help us. We send our children to them at around 9:00 a.m. and then take care of our children for about an hour or two during their nap time at noon. In the afternoon they help us again from around 2:00 p.m. to almost 6:00 p.m. But actually, it still has a significant impact on us. I feel like my work efficiency has dropped by at least 30 percent because the children are constantly making noise. Sometimes when you want to write or prepare lessons, your mind is very chaotic, and you would like to go downstairs for a walk, but as soon as you go downstairs, both children pounce on you and it's hard to come back up again. Before the

pandemic, we didn't cook lunch at home because everyone was working. But now everyone is at home, so work is more difficult. I used to work until 12:30 p.m. before eating lunch, but now I have to go downstairs and cook at 11:30 a.m. and after cooking I have to look after the children so my work time has been reduced a lot during this period . . . having children at home has a huge impact on young faculty members like us. It has greatly reduced our work efficiency and affected our overall efficiency significantly.

Although PP's in-laws helped her take care of her children during the day, working from home still reduced her work efficiency and productivity. PP felt lucky that she and her husband had submitted their tenure packages before the pandemic started, and they both earned tenure successfully during the health crisis.

Working from home reduced the work efficiency and productivity of PP and many other Chinese academic mothers. Remote teaching demands more time, effort, and energy in course preparation and evaluation in new digital formats. Chinese academic mothers, while they sometimes got support from their family members, generally spent more time on household work and childcare than fathers during the pandemic. Thus, they were forced to spend less time on research activities to fulfill the needs of their children. Furthermore, Chinese academic mothers had to equally respond to the quality and quantity requirements for publications and research products, as the academic productivity criteria by which they are evaluated did not change during the pandemic. Moreover, as colleges and universities have been confronted with financial crises, the pressure for research productivity and publications has become higher for many Chinese academic mothers. To keep up their productivity, some academic mothers worked at night after their children fell asleep, sometimes until 2:00 a.m., or got up to work before their children got up, possibly between 2:00 a.m. and 5:00 a.m. These mothers were hardly getting enough sleep, which had a big impact on their health and well-being. Some Chinese mothers underwent significant physical and mental health issues because of working from home and extra burdens on them. YY (born 1981), a junior professor at a liberal arts college, described her life struggles before and during the pandemic this way:

My situation is very special. When the pandemic started, my husband and I were in different places. My husband and I have had a long time apart. Right before the pandemic started, my two-year-old daughter stayed with me in [one place], whereas my five-year-old son stayed with my husband in [another]. We were only together during the holidays. I think it was OK after the pandemic began. At least my family has been united. We all moved here [near my workplace] last July [in 2020], and my husband worked remotely. We divided our household chores, and my husband was very capable and supportive. When I was teaching, he took care of our children. When he was working, I took care of our children. But I think both of us have been under great pressure. We are both in academia and have to do research and publish papers. The work pressure is very high. Our children have been at home for one year and a half, and the older one has classes online. Taking online classes drove me crazy . . . too many things have to be done and I sacrifice a lot of sleep time. I have to work during the day, take care of my children, do housework, and do many other things. I get up very early in the morning, maybe at four or five o'clock, then work. I sleep very little every day. I know this is not good for my health. (Interview on August 12, 2021)

YY did not have support from her parents or in-laws for child-rearing responsibilities and needs, and she and her husband sent their children to childcare centers several months after they were born. During the pandemic, YY found balancing work and life very difficult—especially as she tried to take care of her two children by herself at first while her husband lived and worked elsewhere. She soon asked him to help with caring for their son. Ironically, the pandemic reunited the family in one place, but it was still very hard for her to work from home while taking care of her children. To do so, she sacrificed her sleep time, only sleeping for about four to five hours a day. At the time of the interview, she realized how badly sleep deprivation had affected her physical and mental health. She sent her children back to daycare in June 2021 and tried to get back to sleeping for at least seven hours a day.

The COVID-19 pandemic negatively affected the productivity, boundary setting and control, networking and community building, and mental well-being of women in academia (Higginbotham and Dahlberg 2021). School closures and shifting caregiving responsibilities onto parents and guardians, especially mothers, had disproportionately negative outcomes for women across all sectors. Women experienced disruptions to their academic productivity and careers due to decreased ability to engage in collaborations, decreased time for networking, and increased caregiving responsibilities. The pandemic led to decreased team size, decreased representation of women in author groups, and fewer publications and citations for women. These factors may affect job stability and future funding opportunities for women. The pandemic also exacerbated existing stresses for women in academia, leading to increased burnout, sleep disturbance, and decreased motivation. The blurring of boundaries between work and family roles, increased isolation, and unequal childcare responsibilities also negatively impacted the productivity, recruitment, retention, and mental well-being of women in academia, especially women of color (ibid.).

Impacts of the pandemic on women differ depending on factors such as work or nonwork status, workplace type, career stage or focus, job rank, personal characteristics like family structure and caregiving responsibilities, health status, and so on. Understanding the nuanced ways in which the pandemic affected women could help us address any negative long-term consequences and build on any positive adaptations that emerged in the course of the pandemic.

Impacts of the Pandemic on Everyday Lives

In interviews, I asked my contributors to reflect on how the pandemic had changed their everyday lives. Some working mothers said that they had to work from home and take care of their children 24-7. Some stay-at-home mothers said that they became busier and did not have personal time for themselves. Amy (born 1981) was a "full-time housewife" who married her husband in 2007 when he was pursuing his PhD. She could not work because of her immigration status and visa restrictions, and after giving birth to her first son, she took care of him at home by herself. Three years later, she gave birth to another son. At the time of my interview with Amy on June 20, 2020, her two sons were nine and six years old. Amy said that the pandemic did not change her daily life significantly as she usually spent most of her time at home. In lockdowns, her husband and her two children stayed at home, but she still maintained her regular daily routine of doing housework and taking care of her children. She went out less frequently because of the need to limit exposure to the virus. Amy acknowledged that the pandemic more strongly affected her female friends who had to work outside the home as essential workers and take care of their stay-at-home children simultaneously. She said that she had the luxury of staying at home to care for her children, whereas her female working friends faced challenges in finding someone to look after their children during their work hours. However, Amy did mention that she had no personal time when her husband and children were at home all the time. She had to cook three meals a day, and her life was much more stressful during the pandemic.

LJL (born 1984), a mother of three children, thought the pandemic changed her daily routines and lifestyle dramatically. Before the pandemic, she could go out whenever she liked to meet friends, go shopping, or take her children to play without much preparation. During the pandemic, she had to take preventive measures and consider the risks involved anytime she left the house. She became more cautious and had to prepare more before going out or engaging in activities. This increased caution decreased the possibility of getting infected with the coronavirus.

Many contributors mentioned that they had to wear masks and wash their hands more frequently to protect themselves and their children from the virus. Mothers of young children often had to keep their children at home for much longer until the vaccines for certain age groups were released. YY kept her two young children at home for about fifteen months, and her older son took online classes during that time. She provided outdoor activities for her children in the front and back yards of her house, such as playing basketball and swimming in a small pool. She emphasized the importance of outdoor activities for her children as they could rarely play with other children during the pandemic.

A few mothers expressed their concerns about the coronavirus and the impacts of isolation on their children. The virus was invisible, and nobody knew who carried it. These mothers tried their best to protect their children by keeping them at home, but they knew that isolation would affect their social development. They found various ways of spending family time together and having fun, such as crab hunting, fishing, gardening, and so on.

The pandemic negatively changed Chinese mothers' lives in various ways, but some contributors saw "a silver lining on a dark cloud." Some mentioned that they had been spending more quality time with their children at home due to the pandemic. Although Meili was unexpectedly laid off, she then spent more time with her daughter and enjoyed their quality time together. She said:

> It [the layoff] had a big impact on my career because I wanted to work there until my daughter went to college. I was preparing to set up a career path . . . so it disrupted my entire plan . . . but it also means more family time together. What makes me happy is being able to spend more time with my daughter because she will go to college when she turns eighteen, and it will be really hard to have this kind of time together again. Our quality time together is precious. We learn from each other and exchange our cooking skills. She shares her economics and European history classes with me, which makes me feel like I am accompanying her to grow up, and I think it is quite meaningful. (Interview on May 18, 2020)

Despite being unemployed at the time, Meili thought that the pandemic provided her with a good opportunity for intimate parent-child bonding, and she valued her quality time with her teenage daughter. Similarly, Lin (born 1979) mentioned that she spent more quality time with her two young children at home during the pandemic. Lin and her husband owned a Chinese restaurant in a college town in Florida, and they often had no time to play with their children as they had to work very late every day. During the initial lockdown, their restaurant was closed from mid-March to early May 2020;

they reopened their restaurant in early May and only provided takeout service. Lin shared her unique personal experiences as follows:

> Our restaurant was closed for a month and a half. We closed in mid-March and didn't open for the entire month of April. Then in May, at the beginning of the month, we opened again because we were under a lot of pressure at that time. It was very contradictory. It was difficult to decide whether to open or not. If we opened, we were afraid. If we didn't open, we were afraid we couldn't support ourselves. So we had to open. That's how it was at that time. As for my children, they were both at home. It was OK. If we didn't go outside, I psychologically felt safer. If we went outside, I felt very unsafe and didn't dare to take the children out. We stayed at home for a long time. The children of restaurant owners are so pitiful, you know. Why? Because of their parents' work, they basically stay at home and their parents rarely take them out to play or travel because of the nature of their work. So actually this pandemic made them happy for one reason: their mother could spend more time with them. (Interview on August 6, 2020)

Lin has two young children; at the time, her daughter was eleven, and her son was seven. Her children felt that their parents were very busy every day. Her husband often came back home after their children went to bed. When their children got up early and went to school, her husband was still sleeping. Thus, although her family lived together, they spent very little time together. The pandemic unexpectedly became a happy time for their children as they finally had more time with their parents, especially their mother. Lin explained:

> After the pandemic started, I spent more time with my children at home. Even though we are just staying at home, they still feel very happy and feel that their mother is at home with them. They used to want their mother to be at home with them. My son and daughter once complained to me and said: "When will our father and mother be able to accompany us and not seem like we can't see our father and mother every day?" That's how they felt. So during the pandemic, it turned out that for me it was very happy to stay at home even though it was a bit boring not being able to go outside, but they were still very happy.

Lin appreciated her time with her children at home and thought that the pandemic gave her time to stop and reflect on the purpose of her life. She contemplated what kind of life she wanted to live and what she wanted to do in the future. Because she had been occupied with busy restaurant work every day, she had little time to think ahead about the future. She viewed herself as "only a survivor," and she wanted to live her life more meaningfully. She emphasized the importance of maintaining a positive mindset and not getting caught up in negative emotions or anxieties. She believed that staying calm and resilient could help her cope better with the challenges she faced during the pandemic. Lin demonstrated a strong sense of resilience and the ability to adjust to changing circumstances. She knew the significance of staying optimistic and focusing on finding solutions to problems, and she believed that maintaining this positive mindset could have a big impact on her children.

Online learning was a key theme discussed by my contributors. When their children attended schools online, some mothers stayed with their children during their online classes, while others let them study and attend classes alone in their rooms. Many Chinese mothers had to spend more time overseeing their children's learning to make sure that they were fully engaged in their classes and also monitor their online activities to be sure they were not downloading or uploading anything inappropriate. The need to check on their children and make sure they were coping with the new learning styles became a constant. During lockdowns in 2020, MN (born 1980) taught classes online for her university and also supervised her six-year-old son taking online classes in the same room. Her son relied on her for almost everything. After he finished his homework, MN took pictures of it and uploaded it online; she said that if she did not watch him, he struggled to figure out the learning situation and what was expected of him. Like many other students during the pandemic, the mental fatigue from this new way of learning was difficult, and MN offered her son other activities, like riding his bike, to help with this. Fortunately, MN's parents were with her, and her mother cooked at least two meals a day, thus providing MN with some extra time. MN's daughter was thirteen at the time, so MN gave her more autonomy, letting her study in her room. However, MN was worried about her daughter, noting: "As long as the elder one doesn't make any noise, I have to go over and see what she's doing. I'm very worried about what she is doing with her school. If she's always chatting with her friends and laughing, I'm not worried. Or if she's playing the violin or piano, and there's movement, I'm not worried. If she suddenly doesn't make any noise, I have to run over and see what she's doing" (interview on May 15, 2020).

Online classes were very challenging for both Chinese mothers and their children. Mothers who had two children or more had to balance the different needs and schedules of their children while also managing household chores and cooking. Amy discussed her challenges in managing her children's online classes this way:

> In March [2020], my children stopped going to school, so I think the biggest impact was that my children had to take classes at home. My older son is nine and in third grade. Because he participates in the Merit program at school, their learning progress is relatively fast, so they have to take online classes at home every day. I also have a son in kindergarten class, so his curriculum is not

as tight as his brother's. But because my two children have to study at home, their schedules interfere with each other. So for me, this part was my biggest challenge from March to the end of May [in 2020]. My older son has to follow every online class at school, and I have to arrange for my younger son to study at home. Their schedules have to be the same; otherwise, my older son will complain that he is reading and studying while his younger brother could play games or run and jump next to him. So all my time from morning to afternoon is almost blocked by my children, focusing on their homework. Their rest time is when I have to prepare three meals. So I think, for us, in addition to staying at home, self-studying at home, this is actually the biggest challenge. (Interview on June 20, 2020)

Furthermore, Amy expressed her gratitude toward her younger son's teacher, who recorded videos on five different subjects every day, such as math, reading, science, social studies, and so on. With this helpful structure, Amy followed the teacher's instructions and guidance to teach her younger son, asking him to view the teaching videos and finish his homework every day. Amy found her role in her son's online classes at home very difficult, but she was grateful to his teacher and their efforts, which made her feel less helpless.

In our interview, MN emphasized how her children and other children were struggling with sudden changes in their lives and how they adapted to their new routines. She thought children were as heroic and great as frontline healthcare workers and essential workers:

We all say that medical workers are heroes or essential workers are heroes, right? Firefighters and first responders and these people. Actually, the most heroic and greatest are our children, the little ones. Suddenly everything changed, and the whole world turned upside down, right? Like him [my son], they are the ones who are most eager to communicate with people and have close contact with people at that age. Their world has become like this all of a sudden. In a sense, they are also heroes . . . actually they are. So I said my son might have forgotten what it was like to go to school. Recently he often asks us when people can stay close together again. He can't express himself well so he asks us like this. And my daughter, besides being more sensitive, used to spend almost every day with her swimming team friends. Suddenly everyone hasn't seen each other for so long and can only do some training or something online. It's also very sad for her. (Interview on May 15, 2020)

MN viewed children's ability to adapt to sudden changes and difficult situations as heroic, and she emphasized the strength and resilience of children as well as the importance of acknowledging their experiences and contributions.

During the initial lockdown in the spring of 2020, parents and children were also faced with the uncertainty of whether schools would reopen in the fall or online classes would continue. In the fall of 2020, many schools across the US provided both in-person and online classes, and some of our contributors kept their children at home until those children got vaccines. The reopening of K–12 schools in the US varied by state and local districts, with many schools not fully reopening for in-person learning until the fall of 2021, and in most places, students were required to wear masks, with some medical exemptions, once they were back to in-person learning.

The pandemic changed Chinese mothers' lives in other profound ways. In particular, some mentioned how their travel plans were canceled or suspended. MY had not returned to China for more than fifteen years, although MY's parents came to visit her twice. She and her husband had planned to visit China during the summer of 2020 and had begun preparations for it. After the pandemic began, all of those plans went up in the air, and they did not know when they would make it back to China. PP also liked traveling, but she could not travel until 2023.

Through their diverse narratives, my contributors articulated the messy, complex, multifaceted, and contradictory challenges and realities of mothering and motherhood. These narratives reflect the nuanced experiences and coping strategies of Chinese mothers during the pandemic. The degree to which and manner in which individual mothers' agencies are expressed are contingent on their specific circumstances, and it is imperative to comprehend the intricacies, complexities, and ambiguities at play in these expressions, as they may not always manifest as overt resistance or compliance but may rather come across in subtle and nuanced forms.

The COVID-19 pandemic posed unprecedented challenges and opportunities for Chinese mothers in the US. On the one hand, they faced various difficulties in living through early lockdowns, balancing work and family responsibilities, adapting to new modes of communication, and coping with stress and isolation. On the other hand, they developed diverse strategies to overcome these hardships. With the surging anti-Asian racisms, some mothers started to engage in political activisms, which are the focus of the next sections, where I examine how these mothers practiced activisms in their everyday lives, how they have connected with other mothers and activists through collective actions, and how they created and sustained diverse communities of support to contribute to social justice.

ACTIVIST MOTHERING AND POLITICAL ACTIVISMS OF CHINESE IMMIGRANT MOTHERS

The discriminatory incidents and hate crimes targeting Chinese and AAAPI people during the pandemic have not only sparked outrage but have also highlighted the urgent need for systemic changes and increased awareness of anti-Asian racisms. Chinese mothers, as part of the broader AAAPI communities, have been directly affected by these acts of racisms. They witnessed their children, loved ones, friends, and fellow community members face verbal and physical assaults, discrimination in various spheres of life, and harmful stereotypes perpetuated by the media. These experiences have ignited a deep sense of injustice and a determination to challenge and eradicate racisms. Chinese mothers have taken to various platforms, including social media, grassroots organizations, and community initiatives, to amplify their voices and advocate for social justice.

Chinese mothers, empowered by their own experiences and driven by empathy for others, have become vocal advocates against anti-Asian racisms. They have sought to educate all children about the diverse experiences and contributions of AAAPI individuals and communities, dispel stereotypes, and promote solidarity and diversity. Moreover, the intersectionality of gender, race, and ethnicity adds another layer to their advocacy. Chinese mothers, facing both gender-based discrimination and racial prejudice, have been at the forefront of addressing the unique challenges and barriers faced by AAAPI communities. They seek to amplify their voices and push for greater inclusion and equity in education.

Nancy Naples (1992) coined the term *activist mothering* when analyzing how the community organizing of African American and Latina women living and working in low-income urban neighborhoods has contributed to our understanding of the social construction of gender and mothering; Naples's work also highlights the importance of cross-generational continuity of activist mothering for their communities. Naples used the community workers' descriptions of the various activities they participated in as mothers and defined *activist mothering* in the broader scope of mothering practices, which are not limited to their own biological or legally related children but also include those outside their kinship groups, encompassing "a broad definition of actual mothering practices" (448). For those community workers, "good mothering" is defined to "comprise all actions, including social activism, that addressed the needs of their children and community" (448).

Patricia Hill Collins's (2009, 192) concept of "othermothers," defined as women who assist bloodmothers or biological mothers "by sharing mothering responsibilities," emphasizes the centrality of fictive kin in African American communities in the 1970s as continuities of African traditions. Collins points out that African American women's experiences as "othermothers" have provided "a foundation for conceptualizing Black women's political activism," and she writes, "Experiences both of being nurtured as children and being held responsible for siblings and fictive kin within kin networks can stimulate a more generalized ethic of caring and personal accountability among African-American women" (205). Similarly, Chinese mothers not only feel accountable to children within their own families and communities but also experience a bond with all the children in the US.

Chinese mothers practice diverse forms of political activisms, and their political activisms are often rooted in their collectivist orientations and sense of investment in the well-being and education of not only their children but also all the children in America. They draw on their bicultural identifications and experiences to advocate for social justice and equity for themselves and their broader AAAPI communities. By doing so, they challenge the stereotypes, prejudices, and structures that have historically marginalized and excluded them and their communities.

For Chinese mothers in my study, what began as the daily expression of their obligations to their children has developed into full-fledged actions as activists and leaders in AAAPI communities and broader society. Since 2020 the rise in anti-Asian violence has prompted an increase in attention to the issues of anti-Asian racisms and public policy solutions to address them. AAAPI activist mothers and community leaders organized protests, rallies, and vigils for lives lost and required teaching AAPI histories in the K–12 curriculum through legislative actions and grassroots movements. In May 2021, President Joe Biden signed into law legislation aimed at addressing the rise in anti-Asian hate crimes, which Congress passed with broad, bipartisan support (Vazquez 2021). In my study, I draw on the activities and actions of MUVNJ, a coalition of students, parents, educators, legislators, professionals, and New Jersey community members advocating for thoughtful and comprehensive inclusion of AAPI studies into the K–12 curriculum for New Jersey public schools, and the PCE Club to analyze activist mothering in global Asian communities and the intersections of antiracisms, politics, and mothering during the pandemic.

Recently Chinese mothers and AAAPI activists have collaborated with teachers, students, state legislators, and education officials to make important progress toward establishing AAPI studies requirements for students in the US, although the paths toward establishing those requirements vary from state to state. According to Committee of 100 research (2023), as of July 1, 2023, eleven states, including California, Colorado, Connecticut, Florida, Illinois, Nebraska, Nevada, New Jersey, Oregon, Rhode Island, and Utah, have codified AAPI studies requirements, and sixteen states have recently introduced legislation that would create such requirements.

On July 13, 2021, Illinois became the first state to enact the Teaching Equitable Asian American Community History (TEAACH) Act, a stand-alone bill that requires schools to include Asian American history in the social studies curriculum (Shivaram 2021). Jennifer Gong-Gershowitz, the second Chinese American to serve in the Illinois General Assembly after Theresa Mah, sponsored the legislation, noting, "Asian American history is American history. Yet we are often invisible. The TEAACH Act will ensure that the next generation of Asian American students won't need to attend law school to learn about their heritage." She further said, "Empathy comes from understanding. We cannot do better unless we know better. A lack of knowledge is the root cause of discrimination and the best weapon against ignorance is education" (Shivaram 2021). Gong-Gershowitz has become a role model for many CCA mothers and activists and has inspired AAAPI communities to advocate for AAAPI visibilities in education, media, and public institutions.

New Jersey is the second state to pass AAPI curriculum bills. On January 18, 2022, Governor Phil Murphy signed S4021/A6100 and S3764/A3369, which ensure the inclusion of the contributions, history, and heritage of AAPI in the New Jersey Student Learning Standards for Social Studies for students in kindergarten through Grade 12 (State of New Jersey 2022). In particular, S4021 requires schools to implement AAPI curricula, while S3764 establishes the Commission for Asian American Heritage within the Department of Education. This historical moment brought unprecedented joy to activist mothers in MUVNJ, PCE Club, and broader AAAPI communities.

Professor Ying Lu (Ying) is a key activist mother in the PCE Club and a board member of MUVNJ, one of the key organizations that successfully advocated for the passage of the AAPI curriculum bills in New Jersey. Ying was born and educated in China before coming to the US in the 1990s. She earned a PhD in public policy and demography from Princeton University in 2005 and a PhD in statistics from the University of North Carolina at Chapel Hill in 2009. Originally, Ying focused her efforts on researching political issues rather than advocating for the rights of AAAPIs. Despite this, she experienced various forms of microaggressions in her daily life. For example, while traveling by train from New Jersey to New York City for work, several people sitting near her noticed her presence and began to loudly discuss China-related topics, making derogatory remarks about Chinese people and restaurants. After these individuals disembarked, some surrounding passengers approached Ying to offer comfort and apologies. This experience made Ying realize that relying on the kindness of others was insufficient and that it was important for her to speak up for herself. Before the pandemic began, she joined a book club at Princeton University that would later become MUVNJ. Initially comprising only five or six members, the group's primary activity was to read books about AAPI history. Through her participation,

Ying discovered many previously unknown stories about AAPI and became deeply interested in AAPI history. The book club grew in size and eventually established a website to promote books on AAPI history.

In early 2020, as the COVID-19 pandemic surged, AAAPI individuals and communities were subjected to waves of discrimination and hate incidents when they were scapegoated for the initial breakout of the virus in Wuhan, China. According to MUVNJ, there was an 82 percent increase in incidents of discrimination against AAAPIs in New Jersey between 2019 and 2020 (Alan Z. 2022). The tragic shootings in Atlanta and the brutal attacks on elderly Asians in San Francisco galvanized Ying into action. She realized that she could make a difference and do more for AAAPIs in the US. This realization motivated her to become involved in creating and developing AAPI curriculum bills with other activist mothers.

On Saturday, February 5, 2022, Ying and several of her colleagues and book club members, including some second-generation Chinese American student leaders, were invited to share with PCE Club parents and children the process of advocating for the legislation of the AAPI curriculum bills and discuss their active involvement in the implementation of the bills. During the panel, Ying invited Dr. Kani Ilangovan (Kani), a psychiatrist and the founder and core leader of MUVNJ, to share her personal stories and experiences. As an Indian American who grew up in the US, Kani has experienced racial discrimination throughout her life. In her elementary school, she was the only student of Indian descent. She recalled an incident in art class where students were instructed to draw self-portraits. While the White children used peach crayons to depict their faces, Kani struggled to find a suitable color for her darker skin. After much hesitation between brown and peach crayons, she ultimately chose the latter because she did not want to be perceived as different by her classmates. Confronted with her "bleached" self-portrait, Kani felt a sense of both amusement and helplessness.

Kani is now a mother of two daughters. To prevent them from experiencing the same situations she faced, she enrolled them in a school where 70 percent of the student body was Asian American. She shared her story with her daughters and was pleased to see that they used brown crayons to draw themselves. However, during a visit to the school to view the students' artwork, she was disheartened to discover that 70 percent of the children with Indian names still used peach crayons to draw themselves, despite being surrounded by peers who looked like them. It seemed to Kani that those children still felt compelled to present themselves as White. In her work as a psychiatrist, Kani frequently encountered patients who had been severely traumatized by racial discrimination. Reflecting on her personal experiences and recent hate incidents, Kani—who had never been politically active—decided that it was time to take action. Kani said: "They [Asian American children] are not seen in the curriculum that they're taught. They don't read about people like them. They don't know their history just like I didn't when I was growing up. If our stories aren't taught, then we'll continue to be invisible" (panel on February 5, 2022).

Drawing on their collective experiences in the book club, Ying, Kani, and other members of MUVNJ resolved to advocate for the inclusion of AAPI history as a mandatory component of the public school curriculum in New Jersey. They presented their proposal to the state legislature, arguing that only through such education would future generations be able to fully appreciate the contributions of AAPI to American history and recognize them as integral members of American society.

Both Ying and Kani believed that education was the antidote to hate and discrimination. They collaborated with sixty-three civil organizations in advocating for the AAPI curriculum bills' passage in New Jersey. Diverse activists from across the state, representing a wide range of ages and backgrounds, contributed to the joint efforts, including reaching out to lawmakers and disseminating information about the significance of the bills for AAPI through multilingual channels (Chao 2021). After Governor Murphy signed the AAPI curriculum bills on January 18, 2022, Kani said: "All children deserve to know they belong. All children deserve to feel safe. This law will help ensure Asian Americans are represented in our great American story. According to the latest Stop AAPI Hate report, 1 in 3 AAPI parents stated that their child experienced a hate incident in a school in this past year [2021]. With the rise of anti-Asian violence, education is the best antidote to hate" (State of New Jersey 2022).

The experiences of racism motivated AAAPI mothers to become activists fighting against its debilitating and demoralizing effects, along with structural oppression. They have worked together to create a just society and better future not only for their children and the other children in their communities, but also for all children in America. With their actions to advocate for broader social justice, AAAPI mothers have broadened our understanding of the intersections of activist mothering, diverse community coalitions, and political activisms on the ground. Their diverse antiracist mothering practices have served as the base for future generations of AAAPI communities to move forward and broaden their space in American society.

Both Ying and Kani are AAAPI activist mothers and leaders who participate in building broader coalitions with legislators, community advocates, schools, allied organizations, and individuals. Racisms have been serious structural problems for centuries in the US, but the pandemic has provided opportunities for AAAPI mothers to build antiracist solidarities, craft communities of support, and advocate for social changes. Moreover, AAAPI activist mothers have influenced many Chinese mothers who have decided to take small actions in their everyday lives to make this world a better place for all. In the following section, I present how Chinese mothers in PCE Club practice everyday activisms, build diverse communities of support, and make important social changes within and for their communities.

PCE Club, Everyday Activisms, and Communities of Support

As a national volunteer-run 501c(3) nonprofit and nonreligious organization, PCE Club was founded in September 2003 by five Chinese families during a family gathering in New Jersey. In March 2004, Gao Jingbo (president), Zhang Yingting (executive vice president), Wang Zhe (secretary), Wu Jianhua (treasurer), and several Chinese parents decided to formally register PCE Club in the state of New Jersey. The goal of the PCE Club is to provide a learning and sharing platform for Chinese-speaking parents to develop the social and emotional intelligence that is crucial to effective intergenerational communication.

Chinese mothers are the key founders and leaders of the PCE Club, and many of them were born and educated in China. After immigrating to the US, they had to navigate different educational, cultural, and political systems. Their children were often born and raised in the US, resulting in not only a generational gap but also a "cultural wall" between them. These mothers encountered difficulties in reconciling cultural differences and effectively communicating with their children to establish mutual respect and understanding. They wanted to understand their children's real needs and support them in a way that their children would appreciate. Due to the significant lack of resources available to them, they were compelled to devise their own strategies and solutions to overcome the challenges they faced.

Since 2004, the PCE Club has organized monthly events focused on parenting and children's education. These events combine expert lectures, experience sharing, and practical exercises designed to provide CCA parents with a forum for exchanging ideas and insights on education and personal growth. Participants have the opportunity to discuss topics of pressing concern and offer mutual aid to form communities of support. Children also take part through talent performances. In 2020 the PCE Club expanded its reach through the establishment of WeChat groups that now serve over three thousand families across the US. PCE Club's programs improve feelings of inclusion, belonging, and overall well-being for CCA families and communities.

In early 2021, in response to the widespread anti-Asian hate and sentiments, PCE Club organized parenting seminars on racial identification and cultural confidence that successfully increased awareness and civic engagement in CCA communities. On Saturday, January 30, 2021, PCE Club activist mothers Liu Ying and Xu Lei convened a special panel titled "Two Generations of Chinese: Identity Belonging & Confidence Growth" to address the challenges encountered by CCA parents in their relationships with their children. Ying was invited for the first time to attend PCE Club's events and soon built strong communities of support with its members based on shared antiracist understanding, empathy, and solidarities. In that first panel on identification, Ying and experienced educational experts Duan Lian and Tai Jinqiang presented how self-confidence, sense of belonging, identification, and overall well-being of CCA individuals were influenced by cultural and educational differences between China and the US, the social and cultural status of CCA communities, and the structural barriers they face in American society. They presented how CCA parents could help their children improve their self-confidence and cope with identity crises. They encouraged CCA parents and children to work together to fight against racial prejudices and discrimination and ask their local schools to include AAPI history in the curriculum and discuss racial issues starting from elementary school.

The panelists successfully mobilized the enthusiasm of CCA parents and children, and many mothers then became dedicated to supporting their children in their schools and actively interacting in those spaces. They supported Ying and her allies in their efforts to advance AAPI curriculum bills in New Jersey and other states. They also organized a variety of activities in their children's schools and communities to promote AAPI culture and visibilities. These activities included but were not limited to advocating for school districts to increase the contents of the AAPI history in the K–12 curriculum, donating and recommending AAPI-themed books in elementary and middle schools, advocating for school districts to increase Chinese language classes, celebrating AAPI festivals, and organizing AAPI Heritage Month celebrations in May. Between January 30, 2021, and March 21, 2023, the PCE Club organized about fourteen virtual panels to discuss various issues related to Asian American identities and shared the panel recordings on YouTube. Many CCA mothers, scholars, student leaders, and young activists were invited to share their experiences and insights with CCA communities. These events connected CCA families to advance the influence of AAPI culture, strengthen their sense of belonging, and make positive impacts on local communities.

The slogan "Belonging is an ACTION!" was created by CCA mother activists to empower themselves, their children, and other children. During various panels, CCA mothers and children discussed their struggles with identifications and the challenges they faced in their daily lives. These challenges included school bullying, inadequate attention to AAPI children in American educational systems, microaggressions, and unfair treatment experienced by CCA adults and children in schools, workplaces, and society. CCA mothers and children also shared their actions and achievements in actively coping with these complex situations. These actions included volunteering at schools, communicating with teachers and parents from diverse backgrounds, participating in advocacy efforts, educating those around them, working with teachers, principals, and neighbors to improve support for AAPI students, writing letters to media and educational organizations to urge them to provide more coverage of AAPI culture, speaking out, developing leadership skills, and more.

AAPI activist mothers have built diverse communities of support to advocate for social justice during the pandemic. For example, MUVNJ has actively engaged with local communities and constructed diverse coalitions in New Jersey. Its board exemplifies both cultural and religious diversity, with members from China, India, South Korea, and other countries, and members representing Christianity, Buddhism, Hinduism, Sikhism, Taoism, and atheism. Despite their different cultural and religious backgrounds, MUVNJ board members are united by their shared common goals to advocate for the integration of AAPI contributions, experiences, and histories in K–12 classrooms. They all self-identify as AAPI and share a deep love for their children, and their coalitions encompass AAPI spanning across generations, from the first to the fifth generation.

The long-existing systemic racisms and surging anti-Asian racisms during the pandemic compelled AAPI mothers to become passionate advocates for social justice. Their experiences, combined with a desire for change and equality, motivated them to challenge racisms, educate children, and work toward a more diverse, equitable, and inclusive society for all, including partnering with and being inspired by local Black, LGBTQIA+, and other marginalized communities. The Amistad Commission Bill is what initially inspired MUVNJ (2022) to advocate for an AAPI Curriculum Bill in New Jersey, and the AAPI Curriculum Bill was modeled after the LGBTQ and Disability Bill.

MUVNJ partnered with Garden State Equality (GSE), New Jersey's largest LGBTQIA+ advocacy organization, to enhance education diversity in the state. Established in 2004, GSE has become a prominent civil rights organization, with over 150,000 members. Their services encompass advocacy, policy initiatives, and training to promote safe environments for youth, improved healthcare for the LGBTQIA+ community, and respectful treatment of seniors. GSE also supports New Jersey's activist communities by bringing an LGBTQIA+ perspective to the shared struggles for justice. Their work is informed by concerns for racial, economic, and disability justice. They envision a vibrant and diverse Garden State with full equality in the law where all LGBTQIA+ residents experience equality in their lives.

Communities of support highlight diverse forms of building support by Chinese women in global contexts. Although Chinese mothers in this study are living or working in the US, they actively craft their subjectivities within their transnational families and build solidarities and strengths in global Asian communities and beyond. Communities of support are crafted by Chinese mothers at the intersection of race, gender, politics, motherhood, and globalization and provide a foundation for the diverse political activisms practiced by them.

CONCLUSION

In this chapter, I have examined how Chinese mothers in the US experienced and responded to anti-Asian racisms and multiple crises of the pandemic. I have explored various aspects of their lives and activisms, including how they created a sense of home, belonging, and support among themselves and others; how they challenged gendered inequalities and intensive motherhood; how they dealt with various challenges and opportunities in their work and life situations; how they engaged in activist mothering and political activisms to combat racisms; and how they practiced everyday activisms and crafted diverse communities of support.

This study aims to illuminate the often overlooked voices and stories of Chinese mothers, whose experiences during the pandemic have been largely absent or marginalized in existing scholarship on motherhood and COVID-19 (O'Reilly and Green 2021; Boche 2022). Through a focused exploration of their unique challenges and coping strategies, this research has brought much-needed attention to their voices and stories, highlighting the intricate interplay of cultural, racialized, and gendered dynamics that shape their experiences. The pandemic has had far-reaching impacts on diverse families and communities, but these impacts are not equal. As this study demonstrates, Chinese mothers faced unique challenges rooted in their multiple identities as Chinese, Asian, women, immigrants, and mothers. Their struggles were compounded by racisms as well as the pressures of intensive

Building New Homes   63

motherhood within a pandemic that disrupted traditional support systems and imposed new burdens, particularly in childcare and education. This research has amplified the voices and stories of these mothers, allowing their experiences, resilience, resourcefulness, actions, and contributions to be recognized and appreciated. By centering their stories, the study not only fills significant gaps in the academic understanding of motherhood during times of crisis but also challenges and enriches the broader discourses on family dynamics, political activisms, and social justice. Their stories provide invaluable insights into the complexities of navigating motherhood and anti-Asian racisms during the pandemic.

Anti-Asian racisms coupled with experiences of isolation, traumas, and losses formed integral parts of Chinese mothers' experiences in the US during the pandemic. These were key components in their building of and participation in diverse communities of support and their advocating for social justice with other mothers, their children, and allies. They initiated and reciprocated support through these communities as they drew from their transcultural identifications and experiences as immigrants in the US and built broader coalitions to make AAPI visible. Chinese mothers in this chapter transformed their lives within their communities from devastating circumstances to historical moments in AAPI civil rights movements.

The personal narratives in this chapter highlight Chinese mothers' diverse creative agencies in dismantling systemic racisms and other structures of oppression. The multidimensional repercussions of the pandemic on Chinese mothers reveal that COVID-19 was not only a public health crisis, but also a problem with complicated impacts on employment, livelihoods, work, life, race, gender, politics, and social justice. The surging anti-Asian racisms have put "invisible" AAPI at the center of social justice actions and achievements. The diverse lived experiences and actions of Chinese mothers underline the need for improved policies on social justice. Based on this examination, I propose several solutions and policy recommendations to support Chinese mothers and all mothers in the US.

First, I suggest that we shift our focus to the significant work involved in child-rearing and to the roles and responsibilities that all community members have in parenting, regardless of gender. Furthermore, we should move away from the unattainable and impossible White Western paradigms of patriarchal institutionalized motherhood toward articulated mothering practices that collectively conceive of parents, parenting, and parenthood beyond conventional assumptions and expectations of what it means to be a "good mother" (Green 2015). By recognizing the tremendous work involved in raising children, I intend to challenge the patriarchal norms and structures that oppress and exploit mothers under capitalism, racisms, colonialism, and heterosexism. I also aim to celebrate the agencies and creativities of mothers, especially Chinese mothers, who practice mothering as individual, collective, and political acts, and call for a change in our society that values and supports all forms of care work and nurtures the well-being of all community members.

Second, I recommend that all US mothers should have full access to affordable comprehensive healthcare and childcare. If working mothers have to take care of their children at home due to school closures or other reasons, they should enjoy paid family leave with full employment benefits, which would allow them to balance their work and family responsibilities without compromising their income or career prospects. Ideally, all US mothers should have access to the resources and services they need to care for themselves and their children. These benefits are essential for mothers' physical and mental health, as well as their economic security. This is not only a matter of human rights, but also of public health and social justice.

Third, the US government needs to address the challenges faced by Chinese mothers and AAAPI mothers by including them in health services, childcare cash or credit transfer, and other social programs. Chinese and AAAPI mothers face specific challenges that are often overlooked or ignored by mainstream policies and programs. These include language barriers, cultural differences, legal status issues, economic hardships, social isolation, and racial discrimination. The US government needs to address these challenges by including Chinese and AAAPI mothers in diverse social programs that are culturally sensitive and responsive to their needs. Moreover, the US government should protect them and their children from various kinds of discrimination and racisms that increased during the COVID-19 pandemic. The US government should uphold the human dignity and rights of Chinese and AAAPI mothers as valued members of society.

Fourth, US workplaces should expand flexibility and support to ensure employee well-being and improve inclusivity policies, especially for Chinese and AAAPI mothers. During the pandemic, AAAPI mother workers struggled to balance their work and household responsibilities. Providing workplace benefits such as extended paid sick leave, concierge services, and childcare support can greatly help AAAPI mother workers. The pandemic pushed us to rethink the way we work. After working from home for one to two years, some employees didn't want to go back to the workplace of the past. This is particularly true for some mother workers who now want to work for employers that prioritize cultural changes that improve work environments. Employers that meet these demands would attract and retain mother

Building New Homes   65

workers and leaders, leading to a better workplace for everyone (McKinsey & Company 2021).

Last but not least, in support of the efforts of AAPI activist mothers, it is crucial for the US government to enact national AAPI curriculum bills that require teaching AAPI history in all public schools. Incorporating AAPI history into the K–12 curriculum is essential not only for promoting inclusivity but also for fostering critical thinking, cross-cultural understanding, and civic engagement among students from all backgrounds. By learning about the struggles, actions, achievements, and contributions of AAPI individuals, groups, and communities, students can develop a more accurate and nuanced understanding of American history and society. Moreover, teaching AAPI history can help combat stereotypes, prejudices, discrimination, and racisms that AAAPI have faced from the past up to the present.

NOTES

1. The activists use the term *AAPI curriculum bills*, rather than *AAAPI curriculum bills*, aligning with their focus on AAPI history and communities in the United States. It is important to note that the term *AAAPI*, which I introduced, is utilized broadly to include Asian Diasporas and AAPI communities worldwide.

2. NVivo is a qualitative data analysis software that allows me to organize, analyze, and visualize data.

3

TO RETURN OR TO STAY

Chinese Women International Students and Their
Transnational Experiences during the Pandemic

YINUO, A STUDENT FROM SHENZHEN, was studying at a US liberal arts college when she saw the first tweets about the coronavirus. She warned her uncle in China, which led him to cancel a trip to Wuhan in December 2019. Her college quickly shifted to online classes when COVID-19 cases emerged in the US in March 2020. Yinuo purchased air tickets and arrived in Hong Kong on March 17, 2020. She was not required to take any COVID tests, and the trip was very smooth for her. She quickly passed through customs at one of eleven "ports" or border control areas between Hong Kong Special Administrative Region and Shenzhen. Afterward, she took a bus to Shenzhen and was quarantined in a hotel for fourteen days before going back home.

During the pandemic, Yinuo's family didn't face food shortages but changed their cooking habits. They avoided eating out or ordering takeout for the initial months, and Yinuo's mother became an excellent cook, as did their neighbors' mothers. The community began sharing homemade foods, strengthening neighborly bonds. Yinuo's mother started baking bread at home and cooked delicious dishes like sweet-and-sour pork. As the pandemic subsided, the family returned to dining out and ordering takeout, and they celebrated important festivals and events. Yinuo thought that the pandemic allowed her to reflect on the good and bad aspects of living in China, and she felt grateful that she had stayed healthy and had been able to spend quality time with her family during the crisis.

However, the pandemic affected Yinuo's study profoundly. In the 2020–21 academic year, she attended online classes from home. Her college required students to return to campus in the fall of 2021, implementing vaccine and mask mandates. Yinuo flew back to the US with college friends in August 2021, and travel restrictions and lockdown policies in China made it challenging for her to return home during this time.

Yinuo's F-1 student visa expired after her graduation in May 2022. Fortunately, the ban on non-Hong Kong residents entering Hong Kong was lifted on May 1, 2022, and Yinuo was able to purchase air tickets to Hong Kong on May 31, 2022. She fulfilled the entry requirements by being fully vaccinated, providing negative polymerase chain reaction (PCR)–based nucleic acid test results before departure, and reserving a quarantine hotel room for seven nights in Hong Kong. Prior to her departure, she flew to San Francisco, stayed overnight, and took the required test near the airport. After arriving in Hong Kong, Yinuo stayed in the quarantine hotel for seven nights, enjoying delivered meals.

Before returning to Shenzhen, Yinuo had to undergo another nucleic acid test for COVID-19 and make an appointment with a Shenzhen Health Station. She stayed an extra night in Hong Kong to wait for the test result. On June 10, 2022, she passed the Shenzhen Health Station and traveled to a hotel in Shenzhen for a fourteen-day centralized quarantine followed by seven days of home quarantine.

During the coronavirus outbreak in 2020, Xinyan, a high school student from Jiaxing, Zhejiang, experienced significant disruptions during the Lunar New Year, or Spring Festival. With shops closed and people staying at home, traditional celebrations were replaced by virtual gatherings on WeChat. Xinyan and her family stocked up on convenience and easily storable foods since online food delivery services were unavailable. They followed a simple meal plan, occasionally enjoying instant noodles and frozen dumplings. Recognizing the importance of a healthy diet for immunity, they prioritized nutritious foods.

In early 2020, Xinyan discovered the "Rice Cooker Cake" challenge on TikTok. The cooking method in this challenge made cake-making easier and more accessible for those without ovens. Despite more failures than successes, many enjoyed the process and connected with others. Xinyan found the challenge meaningful, bringing excitement to people's isolated lives and impacting the market by increasing flour and baking tool sales. Inspired, she began baking daily, receiving praise from her parents and gaining a sense of accomplishment.

The pandemic prompted individuals to rethink various aspects of their daily routines, including work, study, leisure, and rest. Diverse national policies in response to the pandemic led individuals to develop various strategies in navigating travel restrictions, transitioning to remote work or virtual learning, and adhering to social distancing measures. Xinyan experienced a year and a half of online study. She concluded her final year of high school from home and completed her inaugural year of college remotely.

Xinyan observed and reflected on the rise of hatred and attacks targeting Asian, Asian American, and Pacific Islanders (AAAPIs) during the pandemic. She identified three key moments that highlighted and perpetuated racisms toward Chinese and AAAPIs. First, some Americans blamed the Chinese for the outbreak, fueled by misinformation that linked the virus to Chinese dietary practices, particularly the consumption of bats. Second, Chinese international students faced physical attacks and discriminatory remarks, with demands for them to return to China. Third, President Trump's use of the term *Chinese virus* allowed his supporters to direct their frustrations toward AAAPI communities, leading to significant harm. Xinyan recalled incidents such as the assault on a Singaporean international student in the UK, where racial slurs related to the coronavirus were used. Though she did not personally experience discrimination, these reports made her contemplate the anti-Asian racisms amplified by the pandemic. She wrote, "As Asians, we are being viciously labeled, scapegoated, and selectively ignored for our strengths by other countries. Therefore, we should not fight against other races but fight against discrimination itself and look at the world with a dialectical view" (class survey, on March 7, 2022).

Ruohan from Nanjing, Jiangsu Province, had anticipated celebrating her eighteenth birthday with friends in early 2020. However, the outbreak of COVID-19 caused panic, leading to the scarcity of essential items like masks, and Chinese local governments implemented strict control measures in public spaces. Therefore, Ruohan had to stay at home and celebrate her birthday with her parents instead. Even after her parents returned to work, she continued taking online classes from home during her first year of college in the US, similar to Xinyan's experience. Due to the time zone differences, Ruohan's classes often took place in the middle of the night, with some classes as early as 5:00 a.m. This disrupted her sleep schedule, and she only interacted with her parents during dinner. The prolonged delay in experiencing real college life due to the pandemic caused her to feel increasingly depressed.

Ruohan encountered instances of racisms upon arriving in the US, such as insulting gestures and curses being aimed at her. Another incident took place in one of her classes when her teacher failed to comprehend her question and simply dismissed it. However, her empathetic classmate, recognizing the ignorance displayed, became upset as he viewed it as a form of discrimination. Adjusting to life in the US was a new experience for Ruohan, requiring her to adapt quickly. In 2022, she played a key role in co-organizing the inaugural AAAPI Arts Festival with her classmates. This festival served as a platform to celebrate AAAPI identities through live performances and visual arts, functioning as both an educational resource and a space to honor AAAPI culture. It also provided an opportunity to showcase the achievements and contributions of AAAPI students within her college.

The stories of Yinuo, Xinyan, and Ruohan are snapshots of the diverse lived experiences of Chinese international students (hereafter referred to as Chinese students), especially women students, in the US during the pandemic. The pandemic and associated responses—such as border closures, lockdown measures, flight curtailment, anti-Asian racisms, and escalating geopolitical tensions between the US and China—led to multiple marginalizations and exclusions of Chinese students from both home and host societies. As the largest body of international students, 1,061,511 Chinese students studied overseas at a tertiary level by April 8, 2022 (UNESCO 2022). According to the Institute of International Education (IIE 2022), the number of Chinese students studying in the US decreased from 317,299 in 2020–21 to 290,086 in 2021–22. With deteriorating US-China relations, racisms, gun violence, visa bans, and travel restrictions, the US is losing its ground as the most popular place for Chinese students to pursue higher education abroad. Data from the US State Department reveals a significant decrease in F-1 visas issued to Chinese students, with only 31,055 issued in the first half of 2022 compared to 64,261 during the same period in 2019 (Hua, Hao, and Korn 2022). This decline in student enrollment has had financial implications for colleges and universities across the US.

Historically, Chinese students were highly educated and privileged compared to other Chinese immigrants (Ye 2001). Initially, only a few chose to stay and integrate into American society after completing their studies, and their experiences remain significant in Chinese American history and culture. In the past, Chinese students also faced anti-Chinese discrimination, and many visited and some even developed strong connections with Chinatowns despite their elitist views of the residents therein. In later years, particularly after 1949 when 5,000 Chinese students were granted refugee status, more students began to immigrate and stay in the US (Zia 2019). After Presidents Ronald Reagan and Deng Xiaoping signed significant agreements in the early 1980s, promoting exchanges in science, technology, and culture, Chinese students recognized the opportunities offered by studying in the US and responded enthusiastically, fueling a "study abroad fever." Many of these students eventually settled in the US, adjusting their immigration status to become permanent residents and citizens. By the late 1980s, more than 80,000 Chinese students had immigrated to the US, forming a large wave of Chinese scholars arriving in America (I. Chang 2003). After the Tiananmen Square incident in June 1989, President George H. W. Bush issued executive orders allowing Chinese nationals to stay in the US. In 1992, the Chinese Student Protection Act granted over 50,000 students and scholars permanent resident status in the US (I. Chang 2003). In the twenty-first century, a wave of Chinese undergraduate students came to study in the US, and undergraduate enrollment from China rose from under 10,000 to over 135,000 from 2005 to 2015 (Ma 2020). However, Chinese undergraduate student numbers dropped from 125,616 in 2019–20 to 109,492 in 2021–22 (IIE 2022).

Situating these complicated contexts, this chapter examines how Chinese women students in the US experienced and reflected on racisms, discrimination, (im)mobilities, mental health issues, COVID tests, and quarantines during the pandemic. From May 2020 to June 2022, my collaborators, research assistants, and I conducted structured, narrative virtual interviews with twenty-three women students and five male peers using platforms such as WeChat, Zoom, Tencent, and phone calls. Moreover, we interviewed two overseas Chinese leaders who supported Chinese students during the pandemic. Our contributors were recruited from thirteen universities and liberal arts colleges across the US, encompassing both major cities and small college towns. Originally, twenty-five contributors were undergraduate students, but as the research spanned over two years, nine graduated and pursued graduate studies in prestigious research universities. In 2020, we also recruited two female and one male graduate student who later successfully graduated and sought careers in the US. All interviews were conducted virtually in Mandarin Chinese, with each lasting between one and two hours. Pseudonyms were used to protect participant confidentiality, and I translated the interviews from Chinese to English. Moreover, social media postings and two class surveys conducted in 2021 and 2022 were integrated into the analysis.

The lived experiences and responses of Chinese women international students during the pandemic reflect multifaceted marginalizations exacerbated by the racialization of the coronavirus as the "Chinese virus," deteriorating US-China relations, and stringent health policies. While COVID-19 tests and quarantine measures were universally applied, the intersectionality of gender, race, and nationality uniquely positioned Chinese women students in compounded states of vulnerabilities. The biopolitics and strict travel restrictions were not exclusive to Chinese women students; however, their impacts on this group were heightened due to existing gendered and racialized structures, stereotypes, biases, and expectations. This chapter's focus on Chinese women students is critical in highlighting how these overlapping layers of discriminations have uniquely affected this demographic.

In *Dreams of Flight*, Fran Martin (2022) explores the significance of transnational educational mobility in the lives of young, middle-class Chinese women students (especially those born in or around the 1990s) to elaborate and embody diverse forms of subjectivity and feminine gender via her multisite fieldwork conducted between 2015 and 2020. Notably, 60 percent of Chinese students studying abroad were female, and Martin presents the highly gendered dimensions of transnational educational mobility, emphasizing that overseas study could provide women with temporary liberation from societal and familial expectations surrounding marriage, enabling them to explore alternative ways to reflect on life paths, relationships, and sexuality. Furthermore, transnational mobility more broadly could foster independence and facilitate the development of "mobile enterprising selfhood" (286). However, gendered discrimination within the Chinese labor market also serves as a driving force for mobility, and Chinese women encounter new gendered and racialized discrimination and challenges in Western countries like Australia. Martin sensitively examines how Chinese women students abroad negotiate conflicting demands of neoliberal individualism and neotraditional femininity, which signifies the resurgence of regressive gender norms and illuminates how they forge translocal belonging despite facing spatial and social exclusion.

Martin completed her book manuscript in late 2020 when she observed how the global pandemic shed light on the heavy reliance of the Australian higher-education system on international students. The severe impacts of virus-induced border restrictions caused a significant decline in the enrollment of international students, causing financial losses and uncertainty about the future of higher education. Although there might be a revival of international education markets after the crisis, numerous problems remain. Will Western countries fundamentally shift away from relying on international student fees to support public higher education? Is neoliberal globalization undergoing a crisis that will change the world we know? The answers to these questions remain open (Martin 2022).

The rapidly changing pandemic presented Chinese women students with numerous challenges, leaving them feeling unsure about where they belonged. They faced the dilemma of whether to stay in the host country or return to China, with their personal choices influenced by issues of racisms, public health protocols, geopolitics, education, and economy. This study seeks to understand how Chinese women students responded to racisms and public health protocols during the pandemic, as well as their perceptions of their roles and agencies, which offer valuable insights for institutions to evaluate their (non)interventions and develop better strategies for future crises. Moreover, this study aims to provide a critical assessment of top-down approaches to public health measures and policies. The analysis will culminate in practical recommendations for governments, higher education institutions, and policymakers. In particular, I illustrate how the US government should avoid implementing visa restrictions on international students; how American colleges and universities should build toward cultivating a more welcoming, caring, supportive, inclusive, and engaged campus community to recruit and retain not only Chinese students but also international students in general; how both Chinese and American governments should collaborate to advance cultural and academic exchanges among diverse scholars and students globally; and how we should resist the neoliberal logic of operating higher education institutions and rather advocate for running them for public well-beings, global engagement, and social justice.

Chinese students are the largest group of international students in the US, accounting for 31 percent of the total in 2021 (IIE 2022). They often face various difficulties in adapting to different academic and cultural environments, such as language barriers, academic pressure, social isolation, racisms, discrimination, and mental health issues (Su et al. 2021; Yan and Berliner 2011; Zhang-Wu 2018). They used to be viewed as a privileged group, but the COVID-19 pandemic and associated responses, such as border closure, lockdown measures, flight curtailment, quarantines, anti-Asian racisms, and deteriorating US-China relations, made them marginalized and excluded in multiple ways in both home and host countries.

When discussing the class statuses of Chinese international students, it is crucial to move beyond the oversimplified narrative that portrays them as a uniformly privileged group. In reality, these students come from diverse socioeconomic backgrounds that significantly influence their access to resources such as travel, language proficiency, technology, and financial support. Some may hail from affluent families with extensive global exposure, allowing them smooth transitions into Western educational systems. Others, however, might come from modest or even economically disadvantaged backgrounds, where obtaining an international education requires significant sacrifices and resourcefulness. In China, disparities in regional development also mean that students from metropolitan areas like Beijing, Shanghai, or Shenzhen might have better educational preparation and access to technological advancements compared to their peers from rural regions. In the US, these differences continue to manifest in varied levels of support networks, financial stability, and cultural adaptability. Recognizing these nuances is essential in understanding their diverse lived experiences and addressing their unique challenges and needs.

"Overwhelmed on Both Sides"

Xin, an undergraduate student in a liberal arts college who took online classes in China during her first year of college, articulated the pain suffered from being excluded in both the US and China:

> In addition to the pain brought by the virus, the discrimination and prejudice between people are just as miserable. The accusations between governments and the abuse between people on social media make me feel helpless. I was in China in the early days of the pandemic and did not experience much hatred, but my relatives and friends overseas were not spared.
>
> Personally, being part of the international student community, I was being cyberbullied on social media at the beginning of the pandemic. Foreigners think we passed the virus out of China, my friends who stayed in America during that time got yelled at when walking on the sidewalk or [were] mistreated in other public spaces; Chinese people are unfriendly to us as well, they think that international students' returning increases the burden on China. Compared to my friends' experiences, I have been very lucky to stay at home and stay away from these malicious behaviors. (Class survey, March 2022)

Xin's account underlines how unprecedented tensions between the US and China exaggerated marginalization of Chinese students on both sides.

Yue, an undergraduate at a fine arts college, also summarized her dilemma as feeling "overwhelmed on both sides":

> I think some [Chinese] people have stereotypes about international students. Some may think, when you study abroad, you go abroad to enjoy yourself. International students at home feel that they are spontaneously promoted by some people, not by us. We do not do anything, but we are promoted, and then targeted. Some people start to have erroneous assumptions about us. I do not know if this reveals people's hatred toward the rich or some class tensions. I feel quite helpless about this. But when we come to the US, international students have to face some racist or other problems. Anyway, I think it is quite difficult for international students to be on both sides, and we are overwhelmed on both sides. (Interview on June 23, 2022)

Yue highlighted the various forms of discrimination encountered by Chinese students in both the US and China. In China, negative stereotypes were prevalent, while in the US, they faced racial discrimination and other challenges. Navigating two distinct social, political, economic, and educational systems proved to be incredibly difficult, especially when both sides implemented unfriendly policies targeting Chinese students. Yue's observations were reflected in the accounts of some other contributors who said that they also felt "unwanted" or "abandoned" on both sides.

Chinese women students, grappling with feelings of being overwhelmed, unwanted, or abandoned in both the US and China, experienced identity crises and "belonging uncertainty" (G. Cohen 2022). Qing, who graduated from the College of Wooster (CoW) and began her graduate studies at New York University in 2020, underwent a sudden shift in her worldview and questioned the safety of her position as a Chinese student in the US. She felt she was treated like "an enemy" by the US government and likened her return to China in May 2020 to that of a refugee fleeing during wartime. The contentious policies between the US and China further complicated the lives of Chinese women students.

EXPERIENCING ANTI-ASIAN RACISMS IN THE US

For generations, AAAPI communities have been blamed for various economic challenges, national security threats, and systemic failures that are out of their control. In early 2020, AAAPIs were scapegoated for causing the COVID-19 pandemic, with political leaders leading the charge and circulating the anti-China rhetoric responsible for increasing anti-Asian racisms on- and off-line. Within these contexts, Chinese students suffered from the double harms of COVID-19 and racisms worldwide, and many had their first racist encounter during the pandemic. Some Chinese students heard terrible slurs being yelled at them on the street by people in passing cars, and some felt terrified to walk alone, especially at night. Some found themselves being subjected to verbal or physical harassment, and others were told to go back to China. With the media coverage of anti-Asian hate crimes, including mass shootings and singular cases of physical assault, many Chinese students felt depressed and angry.

Stop AAPI Hate (SAH) data indicates that nearly 60 percent of hate incidents were reported by Asian American and Pacific Islander (AAPI) women and girls, and my research revealed that Chinese women students in the US were particularly vulnerable to racisms and sexisms. Among our contributors, consisting of twenty-three women students and five men students, twelve women and three men shared personal experiences of racist incidents. Moreover, one woman student mentioned that her Chinese women friends had also encountered racisms. While ten women and two men did not personally experience acts of racism, they were aware of their occurrence. Out of the twelve Chinese students who did not encounter racist acts, six women and one man were in or had returned to China in 2020, residing in a relatively safe environment. Moreover, four women and one man stayed protected and isolated in college dorms or rented apartments. Two women students noted that their colleges actively fostered a welcoming and inclusive environment, taking action against students who made racist remarks.

Among the fifteen students who personally experienced racist encounters during the pandemic, three mentioned that they and their Chinese friends were discriminated against when they wore face masks in early 2020. After Wuhan lockdowns on January 23, 2020, Chinese health experts recommended face masks as a fundamental means to protect people from infections, and the Chinese government mandated its citizens to wear masks. As suggested by their family and friends, many Chinese students in the US started to wear face masks in February 2020. However, before April 2020, the US Centers for Disease Control and Prevention (CDC) emphasized that masks were only for the sick and health professionals. As the pandemic ravaged the US in March and April 2020, the CDC finally recommended the use of face masks by ordinary people in public (Ma and Zhan 2022). However, masks were in short supply, and there was not sufficient personal protection equipment (PPE) even for healthcare workers. Hu, an undergraduate student, described his personal experiences in early 2020:

> Especially at the beginning, when we [Chinese students] wore masks first, the US didn't have a lot of cases and Americans didn't take it seriously, they didn't wear masks. When they saw us wearing masks, they deliberately stayed away from us. Of course, I think I can understand it, and one might think of it as a cultural difference. Because in Western culture people think that they only have to wear masks when they get sick, they may think that you have an infectious disease or something like that [if you wear masks].... For instance, when I wore a mask and took an elevator, the person who came after me waited for me to go first, and some people stayed far away from me when we passed each other. (Interview on May 30, 2020)

To mask or not to mask was a dilemma for Chinese students in the US due to the contradictory policies about masks in their home and host countries in early 2020, and this issue was not resolved until the CDC revised its guidelines on wearing masks between March 30 and April 3, 2020 (Ma and Zhan 2022). Yue described a similar experience to Hu: "When the pandemic started, my friends ... spontaneously wore masks, and they were all criticized by local people. Why do you create panic? Why do you wear a mask? Are you sick? Lots of things like this happened, I think this kind of environment was depressing" (interview on June 23, 2022).

In addition to public shunning and critique, our contributors experienced some "stares" and "looks" in public places, especially at urban universities.

Xu, a graduate student, went through the dark moments of the first wave in March and April 2020 in New York City. He isolated himself in his small apartment, took classes online, and did his internships virtually. He described his worries this way: "It was in March and April [2020], I saw something about Asians being attacked in the news, I became very nervous and worried. Unconsciously, I thought if it would be dangerous or threatening for me to go outside. I noticed that some people gave me this look, for example, they stared at me. Because I wore a mask at that time, because almost all Asians wore masks at that time, while others didn't" (interview on June 5, 2020). Xu insisted on wearing masks when he went outside to throw out the trash and buy groceries. He moved at least thirteen times in 2020–21 due to uncertainties and changing plans.

Overall, Chinese women students' racist encounters occurred both in public places and on campus. Ting, a senior in a liberal arts college, shared two racist encounters that occurred in a public park in August 2020 and at a shopping center in January 2021:

> I once took a walk with my host family sister. . . . There was a place in the periphery, close to the trail, and there was the main road. I was just walking there, and then suddenly, a car slowed down, and someone [in the car] shouted "Trump!" at me, certainly not at my sister because she is a White girl. Then another time I went shopping with Li and Guo [two Chinese students], a car stopped, and someone [in the car] shouted something at us. We didn't hear it clearly, but we knew that it must be those things, and he was a child. Anyway, we felt differently about what had happened. Guo and Li were relatively calm, and they thought that this kind of thing was normal, but I could not bear it. I could not believe how this had happened. It is racial discrimination. (Interview on May 31, 2021)

Ting's undergraduate major was psychology, and she knew how traumatic it was for her to experience those racist incidents. She was a golf athlete in her college and experienced another "traumatic" moment in April 2021 when she attended a game at another college: "Audiences booed me once. I didn't play well, so I was booed and heckled. I was really scared at that moment. When I played the next day, I was extremely scared and extremely nervous. I recalled what happened the day before. But fortunately, my teammates continued to support me. They had never said that it was China's fault that the pandemic occurred. They said that it was a disaster, and nobody could control it. So they are very nice, otherwise, it would be very difficult for me to stay in the US." Ting had built her support system, and her main allies included her teammates, host family, and her American boyfriend. She was cautious not to walk alone and told herself that some people were racist, but not all of them. Her teammates and boyfriend were very supportive and tried their best to make her feel safe.

Miao was an undergraduate student at a liberal arts college, and she was studying abroad in Germany when COVID-19 broke out in early 2020. One day, when she and her Asian friend were walking home, a man sitting in a café shouted "virus" at them. She left quickly with her friend without looking back. Another day, she dropped her friend at a train station. A White woman shouted at them: "Where do you come from? Are you from China?" Miao felt weird, and said: "Yeah, so what?" The White woman then shouted: "Go back to China!" That woman also uttered some curse words in English. Miao ran away quickly. She soon bought air tickets to go back to China and then felt that she was discriminated against by her own people.

Discrimination against Chinese International Students in China

In addition to racist encounters abroad, Chinese students experienced discrimination at home during the pandemic. Our contributors mentioned that there were negative stereotypes of Chinese students in Chinese media. For instance, they were characterized as being bad at studying and choosing to study abroad to avoid the highly competitive Chinese college entrance examination known as the Gaokao. These negative stereotypes were not grounded in reality. Chinese students choose to study abroad in the US for complicated reasons, such as dissatisfaction with the Gaokao system, disappointment with the quality of higher education in China, beliefs in the high quality of American higher education, the perception that American degrees have high value, and so on. Sociologist Yingyi Ma states that Chinese parents often motivate their children to study abroad to transmit and solidify their resources and status across generations and to make their children acquire "cosmopolitan capital" in the US, "which is perceived as the epicenter of globalization and a place where higher educational resources are concentrated" (Ma 2020, 37). Many of our contributors are top students in their classes, and they have worked hard to pursue their goals and dreams. The stereotypes of viewing Chinese students as being bad at studying are biased, but these stereotypes were exaggerated in Chinese media and social media during the pandemic.

In early 2020, when Chinese students went back to China, they were blamed for "spreading the virus from a thousand miles away" (*qianli toudu*). Ming described what happened to him and its effects:

> During the pandemic, the most hurtful words were not "Chinese Virus" but from our fellow countrymen. There was a time after I went back to China [in July 2020], a lot of comments on the internet accused students studying abroad

of returning home. Even some of those reports excluded students that were studying abroad from the list of building the country and called us "poisoners." What made me more upset is that these comments were not [supported by] a minority [of people,] and were supported by most people. What could be more distressing than being hurt by people you think are close to you? (Class survey, March 2022)

The idea of "spreading the virus from a thousand miles away" came from a short video by a domestic broadcaster condemning a few returnees' violations of the COVID-19 protocols. The video went viral on Chinese social media in early March 2020 and unexpectedly targeted Chinese students and overseas Chinese. The broadcaster said in the video: "When we were building our homeland, you were nowhere to be found. Now you come rushing back from a thousand miles away, spreading the virus all around" (R. Ye 2020). At that time, China reported fewer new domestic cases, and some new imported infections were identified. Some people then viewed returnees from overseas as harbingers of infection. On March 18, 2020, during a press conference, Beijing's health authorities said that "students abroad should suspend their trips coming back to the country unless absolutely necessary," quoting the risk of becoming infected while traveling (R. Ye 2020). To contain the spread of COVID-19, many provincial-level and municipal-level governments imposed strict quarantine measures on all travelers arriving from overseas. Returning passengers were often required to self-quarantine for fourteen days either at a designated hotel or at home, depending on local regulations. However, a few returnees did not follow the rules, and these stories went viral on social media. For example, a Chinese Australian woman went jogging outside during her mandatory quarantine in Beijing, and a Chinese female student asked for "purified water" at a hotel during her quarantine. Those incidents sparked outrage online, and overseas Chinese and Chinese international students were thus blamed for "spreading the virus." Like Ming, many Chinese students felt hurt by these virtual attacks.

Fei, a political science major, also experienced discrimination when she went back to China. In our interview on June 29, 2022, she said: "I think it is very normal for us to go home . . . it is basic human rights. When everyone is willing to be quarantined and take expensive nucleic acid tests, but the flight is still restricted, I do not think it is very reasonable." She felt very happy to go home, but she could not share her feelings on social media because she was afraid of being attacked. Indeed, she was attacked by some netizens on Weibo because she supported her fellow international students:

When I came back in May [2020], when I first came back, many international students said something on Weibo that seemed to me very reasonable, that is, it was a very normal thing for us to go home, and then everyone was willing to be quarantined and to take nucleic acid tests, there was no need to expose and attack us online. Then I seemed to support them or do something at that time, I can't remember, maybe I commented. Then people started to attack me crazily. My Weibo reminders kept ringing. I wondered what had happened, so I opened my Weibo account. Then I received tons of messages from many people who scolded me badly. I was very scared, so I changed my Weibo settings to private. (Interview on June 29, 2022)

Fei had never experienced such animosity before and became very scared. She was aware of the increased digital surveillance in China, but she did not know if the people who attacked her were random internet users. She was terrified and did not know what to do.

In 2022, the Chinese government's "zero-COVID" strategy came at increasingly high costs and was questioned by many people who suffered from food shortages, limited access to medicine and healthcare, travel restrictions, and other problems during full or partial lockdowns. From the Spring Festival in 2021 to late 2022, Chinese local governments had issued strict travel regulations, and Chinese citizens were asked to stay wherever they were. The return of Chinese students was not a problem until China faced the high social and economic costs of lockdowns, soaring youth unemployment, collapsing small businesses, supply chain shifting of overseas companies, a slow-down of economic growth, and political repression in 2022 (V. Wang 2022a).

CHINESE WOMEN STUDENTS' STRATEGIES TO FIGHT AGAINST RACISMS AND DISCRIMINATION

Chinese women students have been passive victims in neither the US nor China during this time—rather, they have become active agents of social change on their own terms. Based on my participant observation and interview data, I find that Chinese women students have developed three main strategies to fight against racisms, multiple discriminations, exclusions, stress, and the pain that came from facing a global pandemic: (1) speaking out and making oneself visible; (2) strengthening empathy and building broader coalitions; and (3) changing the stereotypes of Chinese international students.

Strategy One: Speaking Out and Making Oneself Visible

The first main strategy that Chinese women students have articulated and practiced is to speak out and make oneself visible. Tian, who graduated from a liberal arts college with a math degree in 2022, emphasized that it was important for Chinese students to tell their stories and share their experiences with broader audiences. She believed that when Chinese students shared their stories, people learned more about what the students had experienced and what challenges they had faced during the pandemic. According to Tian, by making themselves seen and heard, Chinese students would make people really understand their struggles, suffering, and achievements and thus help create a more inclusive and equal environment in both host and home societies.

Meng expressed her opposition to the accusation made by certain internet users that Chinese students were responsible for "spreading the virus" in China. She pointed out that many Chinese students in the US chose to stay wherever they were and only returned to China once they were fully vaccinated or had taken necessary precautions to protect themselves and others. If some students did return home due to homesickness or other valid reasons, it was understandable. Meng believed it was unfair to blame Chinese students for being the sole cause of virus transmission, as there were confirmed cases within the country as well and not all imported cases could be attributed to Chinese students. She acknowledged that some internet users held negative stereotypes about Chinese students, assuming they came from wealthy backgrounds, and criticized their decision to return to China during the pandemic. Meng hoped that these individuals would get more education to understand the challenges and difficulties Chinese students faced, leading to a more open-minded perspective.

Hang emphasized the importance of voicing her opinions, stating, "I feel compelled to speak up and express my thoughts," and she strongly advocated for Chinese students to stand up for themselves (interview on June 3, 2020). Hang actively made herself visible and audible, hoping that her actions would discourage further attacks on international students and encourage the attackers to exercise restraint.

Rong, who graduated from her US college in the spring of 2021 and pursued graduate studies at another US university, referred to individuals who launched online attacks against Chinese students as "cyber mobs." She highlighted how these groups had become increasingly aggressive since the COVID-19 outbreak, disregarding societal norms and freely engaging in harmful speech. During our virtual interview on May 19, 2021, Rong shared a heartbreaking story. She recounted the experience of a male Chinese friend studying at an American university who faced conflicts with others during the pandemic and tragically took his own life. Following the news spreading online, some "cyber mobs" claimed that he deserved such a fate due to his belief in the superiority of American higher education and his decision to study abroad. The level of vicious attacks was shocking to Rong. She acknowledged

To Return or to Stay 81

that the Chinese media failed to adequately cover the real experiences of Chinese students, thereby perpetuating negative stereotypes. Rong expressed her hope for greater accountability among internet users concerning their online speech and actions.

Strategy Two: Strengthening Empathy and Building Broader Coalitions

The second strategy that Chinese women students have developed is strengthening empathy and building broader coalitions. This strategy is intertwined with the first strategy of speaking out and making oneself visible. Meng explained it as follows: "I think it is very important to facilitate communication between us and other people, because many people do not know us, they do not know what happened to us and what we went through. They only see what they could see, and do not see what they can't see. They do not know what we are doing. So I think it is necessary to facilitate communication and tell people what happened to us. In this way, people would have empathy for us and understand why we have done what we chose to do" (interview on May 19, 2021). Meng believed that people would strengthen their empathy and understand Chinese students' sufferings and pains if they listened to their true stories. In her opinion, successful communication among people is the key to cultivating empathy, and strengthened empathy would further facilitate productive communication among people.

Strengthening empathy and building broader coalitions are crucial strategies for Chinese women students to change systemic racisms in the US. For instance, some demonstrated empathy and coalition toward those involved in the Black Lives Matter protests in the summer of 2020. Following the tragic Atlanta spa shootings in March 2021, Chinese and Chinese American communities collaborated with their allies to orchestrate the SAH rallies in nearly every state nationwide, with many Chinese women students taking up leadership roles.

Coco Liu, the president of the Chinese Students and Scholars Association (CSSA), coled the March for Asian Lives at CoW on March 26, 2021. She felt that AAPI communities had always faced racisms and unfair treatments, and the pandemic had just amplified them. She shared her personal stories in public and gave a powerful speech at the march. She began her speech by sharing her lived experiences during the pandemic:

> In 2019, the third year after I came to the US, the COVID pandemic started in my home country. My family's health was seriously threatened, but my worries were ignored and even taunted by someone. My flight home was canceled, without a choice. Starting from the spring of 2020, the school halted. At the beginning, the campus dining had limited options for vegans. On my few trips for

groceries down the street, there were people staring at me, spitting next to me, or shouting "go back to China" from their cars. There were [taunts like] "Chinese virus" and "Wuhan flu." Someone dumped trash on the Chinese flag in the Chinese language suite of Luce Hall . . . my dearest cousin studying in New Jersey was physically attacked. With sorrow, insecurity, fear, worries, homesickness, imposed guilt, hopelessness, and anxiety, I lost 22 percent of my body mass in two months. My lowest weight record was seventy-six pounds. Panic attacks and fainting haunted me, and I cried alone in bed, saying "I don't want to be here. I don't belong here. I want to be home." I was severely depressed, though I was able to flourish again during the summer with faith and love from my host family.

Coco said that she chose to be silent to avoid conflicts at the beginning, but she soon started to speak out. In her speech, she recalled that over 3,800 hate incidents were reported to SAH in a year, including an eighty-nine-year-old woman who was hit on the street and Tadataka Unno, a professional pianist, who was beaten so badly that he could no longer play the piano. She also referenced what happened to Chinese Americans during the plague outbreak in San Francisco in the 1900s. Because the first person to die of the plague was a Chinese American, they were blamed for the outbreak even though the disease was traced back to an American-Australian ship. She also mentioned the Chinese Exclusion Act of 1882 and the Japanese internment camps during World War II. She further said: "Today, there is still a threat of death to 23 million AAPI, 1.1 million international students from Asia, and 11 percent of faculties and professors who are identified with Asian origin. Some of us in the USA came with a choice as global citizens, some just feel more and more like foreigners in their own country. When you see polling results of elections broken down by race, Asian Americans are rarely listed as a separate category. Because Asian Americans are considered statistically insignificant, it literally means that this group does not matter."

After reviewing the history and current situations of anti-Asian racisms in the US, Coco tried to provide some solutions to the problems. Her recommendations included promoting love among people and making AAPI history required in the curriculum. She also recommended that the government and the public improve data collection and reliable reports for hate crimes, provide counseling for the victims of those crimes, and make their services available in multiple languages. She also asked the government to stop arresting people who were fighting against voter suppression. At the end of her speech, she shared her big "dream" with the audience: "I have a dream that one day not only this nation, but the world will rise up and live out the true meaning of its creed: 'We hold these truths to be self-evident, that all people are created equal.'" She continued: "I dream for an ever-better place where, regardless of our appearance, age, gender, regardless of our beliefs, culture, and identity, we have equal voices. We are contented with the present, and we belong where we are." Coco's dream for a diverse, equal, and inclusive world is rooted in the American dream, and by articulating her dream, she expressed her desire to unite AAAPIs together and build broader coalitions with Black, Indigenous, and people of color communities. By working with other AAAPI students, faculty, and staff, she created a historic moment and crafted spaces for follow-up curricular changes and policy changes at her college and beyond.

Strategy Three: Changing the Stereotypes of Chinese International Students

The third main strategy that Chinese women students have developed is to change the stereotypes of Chinese students. Qin, a PhD student in biology, told me that she saw many virtual attacks on Chinese students and overseas Chinese in early 2020. She did not want to waste her precious time arguing against "cyber mobs"; instead, she preferred to "do whatever one can" to "change the stereotypes" of Chinese students. She said: "As for changing the stereotypes, I think it will be great if every Chinese student can do a great job. Of course, this is an ideal situation. After all, everyone's cultural background is different. Some students are spending money like water, and some study very hard. Everyone's situation is different, and there is no way to make a general statement. But in general, at the individual level, we can do what we can and change the stereotypes" (interview on June 16, 2020).

Qin is an exemplary figure for Chinese students, exhibiting diligence, intelligence, and resilience. Born in Wuhan, she grew up in a family that operated a small store near a prestigious university. From a young age, Qin developed a keen interest in biomedical science. She pursued her undergraduate studies in bioengineering at Central China Agricultural University. As a senior student, she embarked on a study abroad program as an exchange student in the US, fully supported by the China Scholarship Council, an organization facilitating international academic exchange. Inspired by her experience, Qin applied and was accepted into the PhD program at her American university, and she decided to remain in the US for several years. During the COVID-19 outbreak in Wuhan, she anxiously monitored the well-being of her parents, who fortunately remained in good health. Despite the challenges, Qin persevered in her studies and research. In June 2021, she successfully defended her dissertation and obtained her PhD. Subsequently, she began her postdoctoral research at Harvard Medical School. On August

14, 2021, Qin married her Chinese American husband, a fellow scientist, and they happily resided together in Boston. Qin's journey exemplifies the remarkable achievements that Chinese students can attain, following in the footsteps of outstanding Chinese scientists and scholars trained in the US who have made significant contributions worldwide.

Qing was the CSSA president when she was a senior, and she thought that it was important for Chinese students to improve their capabilities, prove themselves, and change the stereotypes against them. Chinese students are often regarded to be "rich second generation," the sons and daughters of the Chinese nouveaux riches. Qing said that not every Chinese student came from a rich family, and the family backgrounds of these students were very diverse. In addition, Qing opposed the habit of calling Chinese students "white-eyed wolves," a term used to describe ungrateful people who show no thanks to those who help them or refuse to pay back the kindness of others. Qing concluded: "We are ambitious, and we are fighting! Not everyone is wasting their lives, and not everyone agrees with what the American government said. I think we should bravely express our opinions online" (interview on June 4, 2020).

During our interview, Rong shed light on why there were many negative stereotypes about Chinese students in both the Chinese media and on social media platforms. She highlighted how a few influencers or internet celebrities falsely claimed to have studied abroad, only for the truth to be uncovered later, revealing their attendance at fake universities, their lack of dedication to their studies, or their use of supposed educational backgrounds for commercial gains. This deception left many internet users feeling deceived, leading to the development of biases against the entire group of Chinese students. Moreover, certain TV dramas and movies portrayed Chinese international students indulging in hedonistic lifestyles and prioritizing sensual pleasures over their academic pursuits. Thus, these unfavorable depictions swiftly permeated the media, further contributing to the negative perception of Chinese students.

Rong emphasized the significance of portraying positive images of Chinese students in the media. She emphasized that the majority of these students opt to go abroad to advance their studies and pursue their dreams. Regardless of whether they choose to return to China or remain in their host nations, many Chinese students have made significant contributions to our society. Rong proposed the idea of highlighting and celebrating their accomplishments and positive impacts, aiming to create a more widespread recognition and appreciation of these students, which in turn would help foster positive perceptions and representations of Chinese students.

The three main strategies developed by Chinese women students are intertwined rather than separate, and they employed different strategies in different contexts and sometimes integrated all three to advocate for social change. In their everyday lives, many Chinese women students achieved remarkable accomplishments and built strong reputations. They actively participated in civil rights protests, collaborated with diverse allies, spoke out, and fought for social justice. For example, during the nationwide SAH movement in March 2021, Chinese women student leaders, such as Coco Liu, publicly shared their personal experiences, built broader coalitions to combat racisms, and collaborated to build a more diverse, equitable, and inclusive society for all.

To Return or to Stay

To return or to stay was a very difficult decision for many Chinese students during the pandemic, especially women students and their families, as their mobility was seriously hindered by changing border and quarantine policies, visa policies, transport provisions, geopolitical tensions, and economic resources. When COVID-19 spread quickly worldwide in early 2020, more and more countries opted to take the strictest measures possible to contain it. More than one hundred countries had instituted either a full or partial lockdown by the end of March 2020, affecting billions of people; many others had recommended restricted movement for some or all of their citizens (BBC 2020). The surging anti-Asian racisms aggravated the vulnerability and marginalization of Chinese international students (Ma and Zhan 2022), and the severe disruption of transnational migration infrastructure during the pandemic hindered the transnational social space, resulting in the exclusion of Chinese international students in a variety of nations (Y. Hu, Xu, and Tu 2020).

While the rising anti-Asian racisms prompted them to return home, Chinese students encountered unexpected barriers when they tried to go back to China. Many were prevented from returning home by China's tightened border control, quarantine policies, and flight constraints. On March 26, 2020, the Civil Aviation Administration of China (CAAC) announced significant restrictions on both inbound and outbound international air travel to China to allay concerns over rising coronavirus infections. The so-called Five-One policy allowed each Chinese airline to "maintain one route to any specific country with no more than one flight per week"; each foreign airline was also allowed "to maintain one route to China with no more than one weekly flight" (CAAC 2020). This policy affected Chinese students as air tickets back to China became rare and expensive, and therefore, many

Chinese students had to stay in their host countries. Even though some could get air tickets, the transnational trips became very long and challenging with public health protocols and infection risks.

As the pandemic evolved quickly, the boundaries between disaster and "safe" zones were blurred, with everywhere being affected by COVID-19 to varying degrees. However, different countries were in different phases of the pandemic at different times, and China was depicted as a "safe haven" amid "global chaos" in March 2020 (e.g., Xinhua News 2020). As infections and deaths mounted in the US during the first wave, many Chinese students wanted to go back to China. However, the Chinese government cut international flights—almost 99 percent of flights to and from China were canceled in an effort to keep infected travelers from reigniting the contagion there—and any available flights were breathtakingly expensive (May 2020). Before the pandemic, economy-class round-trip air tickets between the US and China were about $900, but the price of a one-way flight to China went up to $16,000 or more in April 2020.

The decision by Chinese students to stay in their host countries or return to China was influenced by factors such as their families' economic resources, cultural capitals, and social connections. The first-year, second-year, and third-year Chinese college and graduate students with valid F-1 student visas could remain on campus. Those who had graduated and whose F-1 student visas had expired had to return to China, sometimes embarking on adventurous journeys.

After graduating in 2020 and facing sold-out nonstop flights and flights with transfers in Mexico or European countries, Hang found available air tickets home via London and Finland, sending emails to key institutions to confirm the viability of her chosen route. On May 20, 2020, she and her boyfriend flew from Columbus to Chicago, then Chicago to London, and finally London to Finland. However, they faced a challenge at both the Chicago and London airports, as their layover in Finland exceeded the regular transfer time limit of twenty-four hours. Hang provided written records of her communications and, with the assistance of airport crews, received special permission to continue their journey. Upon arrival in Finland, Hang encountered other Chinese travelers who had taken a similar route due to the absence of nonstop flights from the UK to China at that time. They all boarded the same flight from Finland to Shanghai. Hang fell asleep during the flight and woke up upon arriving at Pudong Airport in Shanghai. The entire trip lasted fifty-three hours and cost her approximately $10,000, significantly longer and more expensive than the prepandemic nonstop flight from Chicago to Beijing, which took around thirteen hours and might cost $900.

The COVID-19 outbreak in March 2020 left about 1.4 million Chinese students stranded worldwide, with around four hundred thousand in the US (May 2020). Out of fear and desperation, a group of parents publicly petitioned the Chinese government to facilitate their children's return home. They requested the consulate general of New York to arrange affordable flights (Parents of Chinese Students 2020). In response to the petitions, Chinese embassies globally reached out to Chinese students, sending them health kits. Two of my contributors, Rong and Mai, volunteered to assist Chinese embassies in sending health kits to Chinese students in the Greater New York area and provided support through WeChat groups. They said that many Chinese students were smart, independent, and positive and knew how to take care of themselves.

Starting in early May 2020, the Chinese government arranged a limited number of flights to get some Chinese students and overseas citizens back to China. NA, another contributor, told me that only those whose I-20 or DS2019 forms expired or would expire soon and those teachers who worked for the Confucius Institute could apply for a seat on the officially arranged flights from the US to China. Based on her calculation, about twenty such flights were running from May to June 2020, and there were about two hundred seats on each plane. However, about forty thousand Chinese students and citizens submitted their applications, and only 10 percent of applicants secured the air tickets. The price of each air ticket ranged from 23,500 yuan (about $3,357) to 60,000 yuan (about $8,571). NA was stuck in a small college town and desperately waited for two months. She finally got an air ticket by the end of May.

Qing graduated in May 2020 and applied for a nonstop flight back to China upon seeing the government's notifications. In the early morning of May 23, she received an email from China Eastern Airlines (CEA) informing her of a scheduled flight from Chicago to Shijiazhuang on May 25, just two days later. Unsure of how CEA selected passengers, Qing speculated that it might be based on the order of applications or other considerations like I-20 expiration dates. CEA assured her that they would call each passenger. Spending a full day packing and discarding unnecessary items, Qing eagerly waited for the phone call from 9:00 p.m. to 12:00 a.m. but received none, making her anxious that she had not been selected. Seeking clarity, she reached out to fellow recipients of the email and discovered that a student from Duke University was experiencing the same wait. CEA promptly replied, reassuring them that calls were still being made and advising them to wait without worries. Finally, at 12:30 a.m. on May 24, Qing received the awaited call, but technical issues hindered communication. Frustrated, she hurried to the lobby on the first floor of her dorm with essential documents in hand, where she obtained a strong signal. Despite initial difficulties, Qing persisted, and after three calls, she successfully confirmed her ticket purchase with CEA. Some of her female Chinese friends who couldn't return to China kindly provided her with PPE, including goggles and an N-95 mask. Qing took meticulous precautions during the thirteen-hour flight and experienced great joy upon reaching Shijiazhuang. Following COVID testing, she spent fourteen days in a designated hotel before her mother picked her up to return home in Beijing.

Hang and Qing were among the fortunate ones who managed to return safely to China, but many Chinese students were unable to do so. Many contributors shared their unsuccessful attempts to purchase air tickets, which were frequently canceled. The inability to secure tickets left some women students feeling desperate and hurt, and they also faced criticism from "cyber mobs" blaming them for "spreading the virus" in China. The negative experiences led some to abandon their plans to return home. Meanwhile, some fourth-year college students, like Xia, opted to apply for graduate schools in the US rather than return to China.

Xia had pursued a double major in computer science and sociology at a liberal arts college. When her college transitioned to online classes in March 2020, she decided to remain on campus rather than return home. At that time, her understanding of COVID-19 was limited, and she harbored concerns about the potential risk of infection during her journey. Xia attempted to purchase masks from local stores, but they were consistently sold out. Eventually, she managed to obtain a box of medical masks from the wellness center. Xia found herself confined to her small dorm room, facing her personal computer, and the online learning experience proved to be challenging, leading her to experience a temporary loss of motivation in her studies.

Staying isolated in her dorm room was depressing for Xia, and she often felt lonely. Although some Chinese students lived in the same dorm, they did not see each other regularly, though they sometimes went to the dining hall together to get meals. In the summer of 2020, Xia's adviser in computer science passed away. There was no funeral for him, and instead, she had to commemorate him online. It took her a while to process her deep grief. One day, she went to Walmart to buy groceries and saw a flower bouquet on sale. She bought it, and after bringing it back to her dorm, she cut the withering flowers and kept the beautiful ones. After she arranged the flowers in a vase, she felt better. Then she knew that it was time for her to move forward.

In the fall of 2020, after the initial months of the pandemic, Xia's college used a wide range of flexible, hybrid approaches. In particular, her college used a multilayered strategy to create a safe campus and classroom environment: (1) high-accuracy testing for COVID-19 for all students upon arrival, as well as for staff and faculty; (2) daily temperature and symptom self-checks; (3) rapid and accurate tests on campus; and (4) detailed quarantine and isolation plans. In addition, her college used social distancing, mask mandates, and other strategies based on CDC guidelines to prevent the transmission of COVID-19.

Xia's college also provided significant support for international students during the pandemic. In 2020, a series of limitations on both work and student visas was enacted by the American government. On July 6, 2020, new regulations were issued by the Immigration and Customs Enforcement Agency, which oversaw the F-1 visa process through which international students went to colleges in the US. These regulations required that international students in the US take courses in-person or through a hybrid format. If students took only remote or online courses, their visa status would lapse and they would be required to leave the US. American colleges and universities strongly opposed it, and they worked together to get it rescinded.

Xia's college offered mostly in-person and hybrid courses in the fall of 2020, whereas many American universities decided to teach most or all courses remotely. After Xia's school started, two second-year Chinese women students moved to the same dorm, and another Chinese female student who studied abroad came back. Xia was very happy to be with them, and they had a wonderful time together sharing a hotpot dinner every Friday, working together to purchase and slice the beef and making noodles and steamed buns.

After two months of good public health on campus, Xia's college faced surging COVID-19 infections and therefore started remote classes for one week. Despite extensive testing, contact tracing, quarantine, and many other efforts, new cases continued, most of which were connected to social-event clusters. The local public health department then recommended that the college pivot to a longer period of remote learning, lasting for the remaining five weeks of the fifteen-week semester. The college accepted the recommendation in the best interest of public health. Some Chinese women students flew back to China afterward, though Xia remained on campus.

Xia's life became very busy after she worked on her senior thesis and applied for graduate school. Her thesis topic was related to COVID-19, and she got tremendous support from her interdisciplinary advisers. She changed her research questions during the winter break and managed to continue her research with dedication. She successfully defended her thesis and graduated in May 2021 and went on to pursue her PhD at a top research university in the fall of 2021.

Although most Chinese women students experienced homesickness and longing for home, in 2020–22, many could not start their journey because of uncertainties in flight scheduling, border closures, quarantine policies, soaring inflation, and exaggerated tensions between the US and China, no matter how desperately they longed for home and grieved in their host countries.

Caiwei and Wanru came to the US in the fall of 2019 and studied at a top public research university. When the pandemic hit, Caiwei's mother wanted her to go back to China, but Caiwei wanted to stay; meanwhile, Wanru wanted to go back home, but her mother did not want her to travel. They both moved out of their dorm in early 2020 and rented an apartment together. Caiwei explained why she wanted to stay in the US: "The air tickets were too expensive, and there were high risks of getting an infection on a flight. Originally, the quarantine policies were not very strict, but they became very strict some time ago, and returnees might have to be quarantined for twenty to thirty days. I said that I did not want to spend money on anything that turned out to be unsatisfactory or even disastrous. The costs were high, the infection risks were high, and quarantines were mandated. I said [to my mom]: 'I'd better stay here'" (interview on June 17, 2022). Caiwei discussed her situation with her mother for about two months, and her mother finally accepted her decision to stay. She stayed in her apartment every day, attended her classes online, cooked three meals a day, cleaned her room, talked with her roommates, and chatted with friends online. She was satisfied with her student life in the US.

Wanru could not go home as she wished, and she suffered from depression from the fall of 2020 to the spring of 2021. She described her experiences this way:

WANRU: At that time, I could not fall asleep at night, and I cried on my bed alone. I had a very bad time and lived a very hard life. But I was eager to stay strong and did not want my parents to know about it. I did not want them to worry about me, so I carried all the burdens by myself. It was very difficult to live at that time.

INTERVIEWER: At that time, you were crying, and you could not fall asleep, what made you suffer the most? Did you see the people around you dying or anything?

WANRU: I thought life was repeating itself day after day, and I lived a similar life every single day. Every day, I repeated similar things from the previous day, and you could predict that you would live a similar life the next day. You didn't even know what day in the future this kind of life would end. It actually brought a big problem, and I repeatedly asked the question: What is the purpose? What is the purpose of living such a life every day? I came all along to this place, but as a result,

I did not see American society and culture. I was isolated in a small room every day. What is the purpose of doing this? (Interview on June 23, 2022)

Wanru started to feel better when scientists learned more about COVID-19. Her university reopened with vaccine and mask mandates in the fall of 2021, and she began to rebuild her connections with the outside world. She made friends with many amazing Chinese professionals who were often older than her, and she built strong networks to support herself. She was grateful to those friends who made her more open-minded and provident. Although she did not know when the pandemic would end, she knew what kind of person she wanted to be in five years, which achievements she wanted to obtain in ten years, what she could do to achieve those goals day by day, and which choices that she had to make in the present that were most reasonable and useful for her. She learned to differentiate between what she wanted to do and what she had to do. She knew that she had to do lots of things in order to do what she wanted to do in the future.

The decision to return or stay presents a complex dilemma for Chinese students, involving weighing personal, social, political, and economic factors. On a personal level, students consider their academic pursuits, career prospects, family ties, and sense of belonging. Sociopolitical climates, China-US relations, systemic racisms, public health protocols, immigration laws, and potential career opportunities also shape their decision-making. Economic developments in both countries further complicate the decision. The decision to return or stay is a multifaceted issue encompassing individual aspirations, cultural identifications, educational systems, political dynamics, and economic developments in the US and China.

Mental Health of Chinese International Students during the Pandemic

The COVID-19 pandemic posed unprecedented challenges to the mental health of people around the world, especially for vulnerable groups such as international students. Chinese international students faced multiple stressors during the pandemic, such as travel restrictions, social isolation, academic pressure, financial difficulties, racisms, and exposure to traumatic events. These stressors might increase their risks of developing depression and anxiety symptoms, which could impair their academic performance and quality of life.

Mental health is defined by the World Health Organization (WHO) in its World Mental Health Report (2022, xiv) as "an integral part of our general health and well-being and a basic human right," and "having good mental health means we are better able to connect, function, cope and thrive." The report further notes that the impacts of the pandemic on mental health are lasting: "The COVID-19 pandemic has created a global crisis for mental health, fuelling short- and long-term stresses and undermining the mental health of millions. For example, estimates put the rise in both anxiety and depressive disorders at more than 25% during the first year of the pandemic. At the same time, mental health services have been severely disrupted and the treatment gap for mental health conditions has widened" (xiv).

The pandemic had a profound impact on people's lives, causing loss of life, livelihoods, and separation among families and communities. Children and young adults worldwide experienced disruptions in learning and socializing. Chinese women students faced many of these challenges, including anxiety and depression, and had to seek ways to recover and heal. Wanru, for example, built her support system and sought advice and help from older Chinese friends. In our interview, I asked if she had seen a doctor to help with her mental health, and she said she had tried it but found it ineffective. She described her struggles in this manner: "Because English is not my mother tongue, I can only roughly express myself to the doctor on many issues. I can't use my second language to delicately articulate the real emotional changes that I experienced at that moment" (interview on June 23, 2022).

Other contributors expressed similar sentiments to Wanru. Some were hesitant to seek help from American counselors due to language barriers and concerns about being fully understood. They felt that expressing their complex emotions in English might be challenging, and that American counselors might not fully grasp their experiences or provide the necessary support. Thus, some women students turned to Chinese counselors, either online or in-person when they returned to China. Others persevered in their search for the right counselors in the US until they found one who understood and could offer the assistance they needed.

Z experienced depression and often felt a sense of despair and hopelessness, believing that her ongoing research on COVID-19 had no positive impact on society. These feelings led her to contemplate suicide. Fortunately, her university offered free counseling services. After initially seeing one doctor who referred her to another, she felt that the new doctor lacked genuine care and decided not to continue the visits. However, when the university doctor recommended another doctor for online sessions, Z found that this doctor sincerely listened to her and provided practical advice. She began seeing this doctor every week, initially crying during their conversations but gradually transitioning to happier and more open discussions.

To Return or to Stay   93

Under normal circumstances, women are at a higher risk than men for anxiety and depressive disorders, though the specific biological factors and mechanisms involved remain largely unknown (Kundakovic and Rocks 2022). The global pandemic exacerbated the risks of anxiety and depression, particularly among women. In addition, increased instances of anti-Asian racisms have been linked to increased risks of depression, anxiety, nonsuicidal self-injury, binge drinking, and suicidal thoughts among AAPI university students (Zhou, Banawa, and Oh 2021). Based on my interviews, I found that many Chinese women students experienced mental health issues during the pandemic but rarely sought formal treatment.

Chinese women students faced numerous challenges in maintaining their mental health during the COVID-19 pandemic and beyond. Even in normal circumstances, international students in the US are more prone to mental disorders, struggle with local medical systems, and are less motivated to seek psychological services than their domestic peers (Brunsting, Zachry, and Takeuchi 2018). The pandemic put them in a more isolated position abroad with less access to public resources due to financial, informational, language, or cultural barriers. Chinese women students who returned to China encountered obstacles such as closed borders, reduced international flights, expensive airfare, and potential exposure to the virus during travel. Those who remained in the US experienced unmet psychological needs stemming from physical separation from loved ones and a lack of social support in their local environments. Anti-Asian racisms targeting Chinese students further compounded their challenges, as they were often scapegoated for spreading the virus or were attacked for wearing masks or responding differently to the pandemic due to cultural differences. Juliet Honglei Chen and colleagues (2020) call for colleges and universities to proactively engage with international students and address their needs in a culturally sensitive manner. I endorse these recommendations and believe that tailored measures are urgently required to foster unity among local governments, educational institutions, and communities, creating a more inclusive, caring, and supportive environment for international students, especially women students, during and beyond the pandemic.

The Long Journey Back Home: COVID Tests and Quarantine

The pandemic posed significant challenges for Chinese students in the US, including anxiety, depression, and feelings of isolation. When confronted with intense homesickness, some students made the difficult decision to return to China to reunite with their families. Others opted to take a gap year or semester to recuperate and readjust their lives. However, obtaining an air ticket proved to be a daunting task, and even after securing one, their journey back to China was arduous and time consuming.

As the pandemic progressed, there were increasing requirements for COVID-19 testing for passengers flying to China in 2020–21. The CAAC, the General Administration of Customs, and the Ministry of Foreign Affairs of China issued guidelines to reduce the spread of COVID-19 across borders. The Embassy of the People's Republic of China in the United States of America (2020–22) issued several notices based on these guidelines. For instance, starting from September 15, 2020, passengers were required to provide a certificate of negative COVID-19 nucleic acid test result issued within three days before boarding. Starting from November 6, 2020, passengers bound for China were required to take nucleic acid and IgM antibody tests and apply for a green health code with the "HS" mark or a certified health declaration form before boarding the flight. Starting from December 23, 2020, the Chinese embassy and consulates general only accepted the nucleic acid RT-PCR and IgM serum antibody test reports from their designated laboratories within forty-eight hours before passengers' boarding. After the vaccines were approved, requirements were adjusted according to passengers' vaccination status.

After Shanghai lockdowns or "silent management" in early 2022, it became very hard for Chinese students to go back to China. Starting from April 22, 2022, changes that were made to the requirements for passengers included but were not limited to "the last nucleic acid test shall be taken within 24 hours, instead of 48 hours, before boarding, and an antigen test taken within 12 hours before boarding" (Embassy of the People's Republic of China in the United States of America 2022). There were also changes to the requirements for passengers with an infection history or transiting in the US. One important requirement was that passengers traveling to China must get their samples for the nucleic acid RT-PCR and IgM serum antibody tests collected at the departure city of their direct flight to China. Starting from July 1, 2022, the Chinese embassy or consulates general issued a health code according to new test requirements: passengers were required to take two nucleic acid tests, separated by an interval of twenty-four hours, with different test reagents at different laboratories with Clinical Laboratory Improvement Amendments certification in the US within forty-eights hours of departure. Knowing that the requirements for passengers became very stringent, many Chinese students gave up their plans to go back to China. For those who flew back home in the summer of 2022, their long journey was exhausting.

Between June 3, 2020, and June 29, 2022, I conducted interviews with seven Chinese women students while they were in quarantine in China.

These interviews shed light on the evolving situations and health protocols for travelers. Hang and Qing, who returned to China in May 2020, did not need to take COVID tests before their departure but were tested upon arrival and quarantined for fourteen days. Over time, the requirements became stricter, requiring flexibility from Chinese women students. Tian initially planned to return in late 2020 but faced new requirements for nucleic acid and IgM antibody tests, leading her to reschedule her trip for May 2021. With guidance from Chinese internet users on platforms like Xiaohongshu, Tian successfully obtained her green health code and flew back to China. While she found the process demanding but manageable, she recognized the complexity it could pose for old people traveling alone. The return journey took a toll on her physically and emotionally.

In the summer of 2021, Chinese students faced some easing of travel restrictions for their trips between China and the US due to the availability of COVID vaccines. However, traveling across borders was still not as convenient as prepandemic times. Ting, who graduated in May 2021 and had received two doses of the vaccine, found an opportunity to return to China. She purchased a discounted air ticket from Los Angeles to Shenzhen for $2,300, along with a ticket to fly to Los Angeles for around $500. During her stay in Los Angeles, she booked a hotel for two nights at $138 per night. Ting visited a designated laboratory near the airport and underwent nucleic acid RT-PCR and IgM serum antibody tests, which cost her approximately $350. In total, her expenses amounted to around $3,426. With her vaccine records, negative COVID test reports, and green health code, she successfully boarded the flight back to Shenzhen.

In the summer of 2022, Chinese students faced renewed challenges in their journey back home due to lockdown measures in China. While many countries started reopening in the spring of 2022, China maintained its "zero-COVID" policy, which had been successful in controlling the virus in 2020 and 2021 when the US and Europe struggled with high death and infection rates. China's approach, viewed as evidence of the effectiveness of its top-down governance model (CSCIO 2020), involved continued implementation of lockdowns, mass testing, and quarantines, even as other countries adapted to living with COVID. With many Chinese cities implementing partial or full lockdown measures, returning to China became extremely difficult for Chinese students.

Xin completed her first year of study in China before traveling to her American college in the fall of 2021. Feeling homesick, she decided to book a flight from New York to Fuzhou on May 23, 2022. Initially, she had to undergo three nucleic acid tests within specific time frames (seven days, forty-eight hours, and twenty-four hours) before departure. However, on May 17, 2022, the Chinese embassy changed its policy, no longer requiring a negative test within seven days. The antibody test, self-isolation, and self-testing requirements were also canceled, with two nucleic acid tests now required within forty-eight and twenty-four hours before departure. Despite the policy change, Xin still underwent three nucleic acid tests, incurring costs of around $200 per test. Due to lockdown measures in Shanghai, her flight was redirected to Fuzhou City in Fujian Province. Following arrival, she completed a fourteen-day quarantine in a designated hotel. Xin then traveled by high-speed train to Guangzhou, where she had to undergo a seven-day home quarantine and an additional seven days of health monitoring. In total, she endured twenty-eight days of quarantine and isolation. While Xin went through these challenges to reunite with her family, she did not want to do it again in the summer of 2023 if the mandatory quarantine was not canceled.

For students who went back to China between the spring of 2020 and the summer of 2022, the quarantine time varied from fourteen days to twenty-eight days or more based on various local public health protocols. Among my twenty-eight student contributors, ten female students and three male students went back to China at different times and had mandatory hotel quarantine for at least fourteen days at their own expense before going back home. Their quarantine sites included Changchun, Tianjin, Shijiazhuang, Qingdao, Shanghai, Fuzhou, Guangzhou, Shenzhen, and Hong Kong. Each city had its different public health policies at different times, and our contributors experienced their hotel quarantine differently. Some could order food for delivery by using online apps, and others could only eat meals provided by the hotel. Our contributors who could freely order meals online often had a happier time than those who could not.

On May 14, 2020, and June 21, 2022, Fei embarked on two trips back to China. During our interview on June 29, 2022, she reflected on the differences between the two journeys, noting that the first trip was comparatively easy despite having a more expensive air ticket. In 2020, she purchased a ticket for approximately 60,000 yuan (about $8,571), but she did not need to undergo any nucleic acid tests before departure. Following a fourteen-day hotel quarantine, she went home directly. In contrast, for her second trip, Fei bought her air ticket well in advance, costing around 20,000 yuan (about $2,857). Her flight was from Seattle to Shanghai. Before her departure, she traveled to Seattle two days in advance and underwent two nucleic acid tests at a designated laboratory. The cost of one nucleic acid RT-PCR test amounted to around $300, and an IgM serum antibody test cost $80. Unfortunately, her international student health insurance did not cover the expenses incurred from these tests.

Each of Fei's trips back to China presented its own set of difficulties. In the summer of 2020, securing an air ticket proved to be extremely challenging, causing Fei to experience anxiety and depression as multiple flights were canceled. In the summer of 2022, Fei felt fortunate that her flight was not canceled and took all necessary precautions for her journey. While undergoing nucleic acid tests at a laboratory, Fei encountered other Chinese women students who were in similar situations. Some students had recently graduated, sold their belongings, and were determined to return to China. Luckily, their flights were unaffected, but Fei encountered a Chinese girl in a dire situation. The girl's mother had a sudden cerebral infarction, and she had to spend a large sum of money to get the same air ticket as Fei. Unfortunately, upon arriving in Shanghai, the girl tested positive for COVID-19 and had to endure an extended quarantine period. Despite her efforts to gain permission to visit her hospitalized mother, she received no satisfactory response, causing immense heartbreak for her and her family.

Fei thought that China's COVID control policies should be more "human-oriented" (*yi ren wei ben*), especially after scientists had learned more about COVID and developed the vaccines. In her opinion, the virus will never disappear, and humans have to live with COVID and move on in their lives. Ultimately, she wanted to live a life with "freedom of entry and exit" or "freedom of movement" (*jin chu zi you*). When Fei told her father that she wanted to go back to China, he thought her decision was made because she lived a hard life in the US. However, Fei said that she lived a very good life in the US, and her life was back to normal in early 2022; she just wanted to go back to China to see her mother.

Fei's dream of having "freedom of movement" was shared by many Chinese students during the pandemic. When the pandemic swept across the world in early 2020, many governments were quick to shut their borders. The reopening in many parts of the world was smooth in early 2022, but it was a grinding and slow process in Asia. Many Asian governments were concerned about the vulnerability of their older populations and the sustainability of their health systems, but the isolation became difficult to bear. COVID cases spiked in many parts of Asia in 2022, but hospitalizations and deaths fell as more recent strains of COVID-19 proved to be milder. When the vaccination rates increased and economic headwinds worsened, many governments in Asia opened their borders and learned to live with COVID as the rest of the world did in September 2022 (Stevenson and Dooley 2022).

Fei's dream came true in late 2022 when China stopped its "zero-COVID" policy. In late November 2022, a fire resulted in the deaths of ten residents in Xinjiang. With many people suspecting that a COVID lockdown had hampered rescue efforts, protests erupted across China. Fearing that the protests posed an unprecedented challenge to the ruling Chinese Community Party, the government began loosening restrictions and largely abandoned the rules requiring mass testing, lockdowns, and mass quarantines within days. It also lifted the bans on the sale of cold and flu medication—a policy enforced in some places to prevent residents from using over-the-counter drugs to reduce fevers and avoid supervision (Bradsher, Che, and Chien 2022). However, with a 180-degree change in policy, the virus quickly spread like wildfire all over the country as the government failed to plan adequately, adopt the most effective vaccines, get shots in the arms of the most vulnerable citizens, or give health workers enough time to prepare for the surge of the patients (Che 2022; Qian and Pierson 2022). Across many cities, pharmacies sold out of the most common cold and fever medicines, and a huge surge in hospitalizations and deaths stressed healthcare facilities and workers to the breaking point. Social media users resorted to dark humor to cope with the crisis, twisting the Chinese government slogan under "zero-COVID" that reminded Chinese people "anyone who should be transferred for quarantine will be transferred for quarantine." The new version became "Anyone who can have COVID will have COVID" (Pierson et al. 2022).

On December 26, 2022, China's National Health Commission announced that the Five-One policy and other COVID quarantine policies for travelers from overseas would be abandoned from January 8, 2023. International travelers would no longer be required to enter quarantine upon arrival and would be required to show only a negative PCR test within forty-eight hours before departure. The end to the Five-One policy and the international COVID quarantine measure was part of a broader announcement that China would downgrade its classification of COVID-19 from a Category A infectious disease, a category that includes cholera and the bubonic plague, to a Category B disease, which is the same category as AIDS and bird flu (V. Wang 2022b). COVID mass quarantine ended, but our reflections on quarantine continue.

Quarantine in Critique

Since the time of its first major application during the plague of the fourteenth century, quarantine has been a controversial public health measure; its use entails a period of total suspension of social, economic, religious, and ordinary political activities (Bashford 2020; Pellecchia 2017). Philosopher Giorgio Agamben's (2003) definition of a "state of exception" seems to grasp at once all implications of such severe infection-control measure—Umberto Pellecchia's (2017, 20) interpretation of this concept notes: "As for an extraordinary state of emergency, whose causes and consequences remain unexplored or unexpressed to the general population, the political power subordinates the political life to a paradigm of government for which normal rights are suspended." Quarantine during the pandemic assumed some features of Agamben's "state of exception": ordinary people's movements were restricted, their normal rights were suspended, and their everyday activities became interrupted and subject to scrutiny. China imposed strict public health measures in various ways, such as the use of health codes, frequent mass testing, and restriction of mobilities, whereas the US gradually relaxed its measures.

In public health, the main critique of quarantine is the one based on the abuse of state power (Bashford 2020). The term *quarantine* is often used to describe the state-enforced and coercive isolation of individuals following exposure to the contagious virus or close contact with someone known to have the virus for an incubation period. The CDC distinguishes between "isolation" as the separation of sick people after confirmed infection and "quarantine" as the separation and restriction of movements of those exposed to the virus (CDC 2021). As the Omicron variant continued to spread throughout the US, the CDC (2021) reflected the ongoing science on when and for how long a person was maximally infectious and shortened the recommended time for isolation for the public to five days in general, starting from December 27, 2021.

The dilemma of quarantine policies exists in states' changing capacity to compel behaviors of both citizens and noncitizens. The key issues include but are not limited to: How should states balance the rights of individuals with infectious risks to populations? How should risks be calculated and rights infringed for collective benefits? Who decides? How could quarantines be minimized so as not to endanger individual livelihoods, well-being, and economic wealth, which depends on the freedom of movement and exchanges of goods, people, technologies, and ideas across borders (Bashford 2020)?

My research contributes to the idea of bringing a bottom-up approach that sees the concrete struggles, actions, responses, and reflections of Chinese students, especially women students, as the main object of study. What I observed is that within policymaking that utilizes quarantine and other coercive public health measures, those who were subjected to these measures were not involved as participants or stakeholders. When traveling or not traveling across the world, Chinese students are perceived by institutions and agencies as homogeneous and rigidly defined entities that must be controlled for the sake of their own lives. Such an approach recalls Michel Foucault's idea of biopolitics, based on which power is exerted through mechanisms of discipline and control over the health of populations. In this sense, quarantine and other coercive measures to curtail the pandemic become devices of political control and power. They were politicized and brought into the realm of social, political, and historical dynamics. To depoliticize them is to bring those who were, are, and will be affected by them to the table, engage them in the process of decision-making, and acknowledge their agency and contribution to providing alternative and diverse ways for pandemic control.

CONCLUSION

The COVID-19 pandemic and associated responses, including border closures, lockdowns, quarantines, anti-Asian racisms, and geopolitical tensions, marginalized and excluded Chinese students, especially women students, in both host and home countries. When combating racisms and multiple discriminations, Chinese women students have developed three overlapped main strategies: (1) speaking out and making oneself visible; (2) strengthening empathy and building broader coalitions; and (3) changing the stereotypes of Chinese students. When facing "belonging uncertainty," Chinese women students' sense of home became fragmented and ambiguous. To return or to stay was not only a personal choice but also intertwined with the issues of racisms, public health, geopolitics, economy, and education. Chinese women students had to make sense of their situations and make their decisions based on individual agendas and structural restraints. By highlighting their lived experiences, narratives, struggles, and actions, I intend to make several policy recommendations to support them to succeed and thrive.

First, the American government should refrain from imposing future visa restrictions on international students. Previously, there have been instances where laws and regulations limited the entry of Chinese immigrants, students, and scholars into the US, including an order by President Trump in 2020 that prevented Chinese graduate students and postgraduate researchers linked to military-related institutions from entering the country. Although the Biden administration resumed visa processing for Chinese students in May 2021 and expressed openness to their presence, the previous order was not reversed. American university officials acknowledged that such restrictions on individuals with suspected ties to military programs dampened the interest of Chinese students overall, making it challenging to reverse this sentiment (Hua, Hao, and Korn 2022).

American higher education benefits greatly from its global intellectual community and the international students who play a vital role in fostering inclusivity. As esteemed members of this community, international students demonstrate exceptional dedication by overcoming numerous obstacles, including distance from loved ones, language barriers, and navigating complex visa and immigration systems. Their intelligence, talents, perspectives, knowledge, courage, and commitment deserve recognition and the opportunity to flourish. Whether they decide to remain in the US or return to their home countries, their choices should be respected, as they deserve to belong and thrive in their educational pursuits.

Second, American colleges and universities should strive to create a more inclusive and supportive campus community that welcomes and retains not only Chinese students but also international students in general. In my research, I sought input from my contributors regarding the support they received from their institutions and their suggestions for improvement. Apart from promoting inclusivity and combating racisms, our contributors highlighted specific actions from their schools and professors that made them feel valued and supported. They expressed gratitude for accommodations provided during the lockdowns in March 2020 when some international students faced homelessness due to canceled flights. Certain colleges allowed these students to stay in dorms and ensured they had access to food services. Moreover, professors demonstrated support by making special arrangements for Chinese students attending online classes from different time zones, such as recording lectures and discussions, offering flexible scheduling, and addressing anti-Asian racisms through course content. These professors became role models, inspiring our contributors to advocate for social justice and amplify their voices. •

Our contributors had two recommendations for American colleges and universities to better support Chinese students, particularly women students. First, they suggested recruiting Chinese women counselors at student wellness centers to assist Chinese women students during mental health crises. These students faced racisms, isolation, and exclusion during the pandemic, and they struggled to convey their deep anxiety and depression in their second language. Having professional counselors who shared their backgrounds and spoke their native language would provide a safe space for them to express their feelings. Second, our contributors proposed creating platforms that facilitate connections among Chinese students in the US. The feelings of loneliness and isolation had a lasting impact, and Chinese women students desired more opportunities to connect with their peers. While smaller liberal arts colleges naturally facilitated interactions, larger universities required diverse platforms to foster deeper connections. Existing CSSA could serve as a starting point, but additional support from colleges and universities to organize significant events and activities for AAAPI communities on campus and beyond would alleviate the burden on CSSA student leaders and promote inclusivity.

Third, both Chinese and American governments should collaborate to advance cultural and academic exchanges among diverse scholars and students globally, instead of competing with each other in unhealthy and unproductive ways. The intellectual exchanges between China and the US have contributed to many breakthroughs in science and technology, and benefited students and scholars in both countries. However, in recent years, American universities and researchers have faced conflicts and controversies in their collaboration with Chinese counterparts. The situation has resulted in academic engagements between the two countries being depicted in negative discourses in the media (Franceschini and Loubere 2022). Both the Chinese and American governments should stop treating each other as enemies and deepen and broaden their exchanges and collaboration to solve various problems that we all face today, including climate change, economic recession, wars, food shortages, gender inequality, and racisms, among many others.

Finally, we should resist the neoliberal logic of operating higher-education institutions and advocate for running them for public well-beings, global engagement, and social justice. Recent studies have shed light on the neoliberalization of universities as overly hierarchical "dark academia" (Fleming 2021) and the degeneration of universities into "zombie institutions," churning out generations of "the thinking dead" (Murphy 2017). This has had complicated implications for international students as they face commercialization, mental health problems, the rise of managerialism, and the competitiveness that divides programs, departments, and individuals through countless rankings and evaluations. Within these contexts, it is clear to see how key principles of academic life such as "academic freedom" have come to be substantially subverted (Franceschini 2021; Franceschini and Loubere 2022). All of these issues have been exaggerated by the pandemic, and more problems have emerged on the ground, such as fiscal deficits, financial crises, deteriorating mental health issues, surging anti-Asian racisms, and so on. It is time for us to change the paradigms; advocate for running colleges and universities for public well-being, global engagement, and social justice; and empower our international students, especially women students, to make positive changes not only in the US but also across the globe.

4

COMING OUT OF "THE FOG"

Chinese Adoptees, Antiracist Solidarities, and Remaking Chinese/Asian American Identities

CALLIE, BORN IN HUANGSHI, HUBEI Province, in 1997, was adopted by a White American family in 2000, and she grew up in Ohio with her parents and older siblings. In college, Callie began to explore her Chinese identity by joining an Asian club, participating in cultural events, and connecting with other Asian and Asian American students. As an Asian adoptee, she struggled with her sense of belonging, unsure if she was more Asian or American. People often asked her, "Where are you from?" and she would answer: "America. I'm from Ohio. I've lived here all my life." But people would then ask, "Where are you really from?" Callie had to learn how to deal with these questions, too often a common experience for Asian people or people of color in the US.

Callie faced systemic racisms and indirect racial discrimination during her upbringing. The American education system focused mainly on European and White American history, neglecting the contributions of Asian, Asian American, and Pacific Islanders (AAAPIs). In elementary school, Callie encountered microaggressions related to her appearance, with classmates mocking her monolids and making sarcastic comments about being Chinese. Furthermore, China was often joked about and assumed to be a poor country. Growing up, Callie lacked role models who looked like her, but she found a connection with her Chinese math teacher in her senior year of high school. Despite stereotypes about Asians excelling in math, Callie didn't feel additional pressure based on her ethnicity but simply aimed to do well in general.

During the pandemic, Callie faced the challenge of people—even her own family—not understanding the harm in calling COVID-19 the "Chinese virus" or "Kung flu." She explained that associating the virus with a particular group contributed to anti-Asian hate crimes and negatively impacted how Asians were perceived. Callie shared an occasion when a local politician who retweeted a story referring to the virus as the "China virus" or "Wuhan virus" received backlash for his insensitivity following the Atlanta spa shootings. She emphasized the need for politicians and everyone to be mindful of their language and use neutral terms. Callie believed that COVID-19 was a global issue and that no individual or group should be blamed or ostracized.

In addition to the "Chinese virus" rhetoric and the Atlanta spa shootings, some other key moments impacted Callie tremendously, including the incident where Vicha Ratanapakdee, an 84-year-old Thai man, was pushed down and died in January 2021 in San Francisco, California, and the beating of a 65-year-old Asian woman that was witnessed by two New York doormen who simply closed the doors rather than intervene to help, on March 29, 2021. She thought that the doormen's behavior reflected the larger narratives and responses of how the US treated Asian Americans and their pain: they simply shut the door, ignored it, and did not do anything about it. This led to strong actions from AAAPI activists, who organized bystander and self-defense training and strongly advocated for AAAPI rights.

Zoe Seymore was born in Guangxi Province in November 2000 and adopted by a White American single mother in October 2001. In 2005, her mother adopted her younger sister, who was also from Guangxi Province but from a different orphanage. Her mother sent them to Chinese school and celebrated Chinese festivals with them. Zoe has been a part of some adoptee organizations in an effort to figure out who she was. After learning about a potential twin sister through Brian Stuy's twin research, Zoe's family connected with the other family, finding similarities in their dynamics. Zoe had always contemplated searching for her birth family, but she had mixed feelings after attending the College of Wooster (CoW). Despite this, she started a birth parent search to uncover her medical history and find her biological parents in 2021.

During spring break in 2020, Zoe's family had initially planned a college tour for her younger sister but had to cancel due to the rising COVID-19 cases. As CoW extended the break and transitioned to online learning, Zoe found herself staying at home. She had to adjust to online learning, watch videos, participate in discussion forums, and submit her finals online. In July 2020, she was unexpectedly hospitalized due to severe and persistent leg pain. Despite receiving medication, the pain persisted, and a nurse noticed other symptoms. Zoe was then taken to urgent care and underwent a sonogram, revealing blood clots in her leg. Admitted to the emergency room, she underwent a COVID test and multiple CT scans. Surgery was performed to remove the blood clots, and she remained in the hospital for nineteen days without visitors. Upon returning home, she relied on a walker and had a home health nurse. Due to her immobility, Zoe took online classes at home in the fall of 2020 and resumed in-person attendance in the spring of 2021.

After the Atlanta spa shootings in March 2021, Zoe felt very dissatisfied when she read the email from the president of her college, who had also sent emails to the campus community in June 2020 in response to the Black Lives Matter protests and in January 2021 after the Capitol riot. Zoe felt that it was great for the college president to provide messages of condolence and sources of support, but it was not enough. She said, "We need to do something because we can't just keep sending emails and keep sharing stories, and then not have anything get done" (interview on May 23, 2021).

Zoe coled the March for Asian Lives with Coco Liu at CoW on March 26, 2021, which marked a historic moment in the college as about three hundred people from diverse backgrounds came together. Zoe and Coco gave very powerful speeches at the city square. Zoe's speech started with her personal experiences during the pandemic, and she expressed her anger when someone called her "a virus." She said:

> We are not a virus. I am not a virus. Hatred is the only virus in this country, and it starts with all of us. It starts with what we are taught, what we teach others, and how we behave. In order to turn hate into love, we must want to turn hate into love. It is important to not stay silent. Be proud to be Asian. We belong here. We deserve to be safe, to feel safe, and to be unafraid. . . . Now is our time to start building a new future for us and our children. Things are not going to change overnight. One march and one speech won't change systems. It will take time and all of us working together. With the right people and the right stones, I believe we can begin to make this world a better place.

Zoe felt proud of the successful march and the support she received from the community. She believed that being Asian American entailed preserving generational history, sharing personal stories of both hardships and achievements, and advocating for changes to create a just and equal society.

Callie and Zoe's personal experiences are unique in many ways, but their struggles and achievements echo those of thousands of Chinese international transracial adoptees during the pandemic. The quickly evolving public health crisis and rising anti-Asian racisms affected them physically, mentally, and spiritually. In this chapter, I examine how the pandemic affected Chinese adoptees in the US and how they have exerted their creative agencies in

106 Impacts of the COVID-19 Pandemic on Chinese and Chinese American Women

combating racisms, remaking their (dis)identifications, and advocating for social justice.

Here "transracial adoptees" refers to individuals who are adopted into families where at least one parent is of a different race or ethnicity than the adoptee's birth family (Ferrari et al. 2017; Park 2012; Seymore 2023). "Chinese international transracial adoptees" specifically refers to individuals born in China and adopted by families in the US where at least one parent is of a different race or ethnicity (Seymore 2023). While not all Chinese adoptees may personally identify with these labels, for this study, they are referred to as "Chinese adoptees." These adoptees have diverse personalities and family backgrounds, but they share the experiences of being adopted from China and facing surging anti-Asian racisms during the pandemic. The politicization of terms like *Chinese virus* or *Kung flu* intensified anti-Asian racisms, leading to verbal harassment, physical assault, and online attacks against Chinese and AAAPIs in the US and other countries. The increased media exposure of hate incidents and crimes during the COVID-19 pandemic has brought greater social awareness to Chinese adoptees and AAAPI young adults, leading them to form alliances with other marginalized communities and advocate for social justice for all.

From February to August 2021, Zoe and I conducted interviews with twenty-six Chinese adoptees across the US. Zoe reached out to Chinese and Asian adoptee groups on Facebook, receiving enthusiastic responses. Among our contributors, twenty-four were identified as women, one identified as nonbinary, and one was unsure. Their birth years ranged from 1993 to 2001. Their age at adoption ranged from six months to three and a half years. Twenty-four were adopted by White American parents, while two were adopted by an Asian American father or mother. In terms of education, sixteen were college students, six were college graduates, and four were graduate students. Twenty-two were single, and four were married with one contributor having two young children. Their locations at the time of the interviews included Arizona, California, Colorado, Florida, Idaho, Illinois, Indiana, Kentucky, Maryland, New Jersey, New York, South Dakota, Ohio, Oklahoma, Oregon, Pennsylvania, Texas, Washington, and Wisconsin. For confidentiality, some states are represented by codes as requested by certain contributors.

The particular diaspora of Chinese adoptees is often perceived to be the result of China's One-Child policy, the traditional preference for a son in a Chinese family, and the international adoption program. From 1979 to 2015, China implemented its One-Child policy for population control. In 1991, China began its international adoption program, and 120,000 children, mostly girls, left China, including more than 85,000 to the US (K. A. Johnson 2016), comprising nearly one-third of all international adoptions to the US (Bureau of Consular Affairs 2019). Chinese adoptees represent the second-largest subgroup of Asian adoptees after Korean adoptees, and the peak period for adoptions from China occurred from the late 1990s to the early 2000s. Most Chinese transracial adoptees (83 percent) are now young adults, and this population is predominantly female (98 percent) (AAF 2014), reflecting a cultural preference for males in China and the resulting abandonment of baby girls (Hesketh, Lu, and Xing 2005).

To trace the earliest adoptions of Asian children, scholars often point to the first wave of Korean War orphans as foundational for South Korea's participation in international adoptions for over seven decades and for establishing the transnational adoptions of Asian children to the US. However, Chinese children from Hong Kong also entered the US in the 1950s and 1960s. Before these adoptions, mixed-race Filipino children were adopted following the Spanish American War, and mixed-race Japanese children were adopted following World War II. The history of Asian adoptions thus reflects US militarism, intertwining with US empire and expansion, as US servicemen played a crucial role in the transnational adoptions of mixed-race children (Catherine Choy 2013; Hamilton 2013; Molnar 2017; Oh 2015).

Adoptions from Asia continue into the twenty-first century, and the ongoing impacts of adoptions tell complicated Asian American stories. Catherine Ceniza Choy writes (2013, 7), "In Asian American studies, the word 'adoption' is increasingly significant for elucidating the breadth and depth of Asian American demographics, cultural expression, contemporary issues, and history." The Asian adoption studies subfield considers how adoption profoundly shapes Asian American communities and histories of belonging, citizenship, and kinship (McKee 2022).

Korean adoptees were one of the largest immigrant groups from South Korea to the US in the mid-twentieth century. By the mid-1990s, adoptions from China had surpassed those from South Korea, and the mass movement of Vietnamese children during Operation Babylift in 1975 was one of the most notable transfers of Asian children to the US in modern history. Although South Korea, China, and Vietnam were, and are, not the only nations sending Asian children for adoption, adoptees from these three countries are disproportionately represented in memoirs, documentaries, and scholarship on Asian adoption due to significantly lower adoption rates from other Asian nations (McKee 2022).

In the US, transracial adoptees are often depicted as passive recipients of the "transracial adoption paradox" (Lee 2003, 725). For instance, many studies focus on adoptees' racial/ethnic self-designations, their subjective comfort with their races and ethnicities, or their perceptions of discrimination and racism. Far fewer studies investigate how transracial adoptees navigate and reconcile racial and ethnic differences (Meier 1999). Scholars need to better understand transracial adoptees as active agents of change in their own lives. For example, there is a need for studies on how adoptees personally negotiate their identities and sense of belonging in society (Grotevant et al. 2000; Meier 1999). Moreover, it is crucial to examine how transracial adoptees cope with discrimination and racisms in healthy and adaptive ways.

Chinese adoptees have been significantly impacted by China's previous strict birth-planning policies (K. A. Johnson 2016; Carter 2022) and transnational adoption practices, but their voices are not emphasized enough by scholars who study family planning policies in China and those who study transnational adoptions and Chinese diasporic communities in global contexts. My research addresses this gap by integrating Asian, Asian American, and Asian Diaspora studies into Global Asian Folklore Studies and highlighting the lived experiences, narratives, voices, actions, and achievements of Chinese adoptees during the pandemic. My goal is to demonstrate Chinese adoptees' creative agencies and strategies in fighting against racisms, negotiating and remaking their identities, and advocating for social justice.

In the contexts of adoptions from China, scholars such as Ann Anagnost (2000), Sara Dorow (2006), Heather Jacobson (2008), and Andrea Louie (2015) critically examine adoptive parents' claims of kinship and their influence on the identity formation of adoptees. Leslie K. Wang (2016) critiques reductive interpretations of orphanage use in China, and Lili Johnson (2018) provides a nuanced analysis of Chinese adoptees' involvement in birth search processes. In this study, my focus is on the young adult Chinese adoptees who have come out of "the fog," understand the impacts of adoption and anti-Asian racisms on their lives, explore their cultural roots and heritage, reevaluate family and friend relationships, fight for social justice, and remake their (dis)identifications during the pandemic.

Coming Out of "the Fog"

"The fog" is an important term describing the situation when adoptees begin to understand how adoption impacts their lives. Helen, adopted by a White single mother in 1997 when she was almost one year old, mentioned this important concept as follows:

> There are many different perspectives from adopted people about their life circumstances and for me, there's this term called "the fog," which is the idea [of] when adopted people start to understand how adoption impacts their life.

Because I think before when you're still in "the fog," it's kind of this feeling of knowing you're adopted, or maybe even not knowing you're adopted and thinking that "Oh, I am, but it has no impact on my life." But then coming out of "the fog" would be understanding your origins, your roots, being more curious about where you come from, really exploring how the adoption worked with the legal aspects of it, being curious about all that, and really seeing some of the pitfalls and actually a lot of negatives within the adoption community. (Interview on March 10, 2021)

For many Chinese adoptees in the US, being Chinese or Asian is to experience racisms as "a rite of passage" (Turner 1967, 1969; Van Gennep 1909). The moment that they come out of "the fog" is the moment they realize where they came from, who they are, and how adoption and racisms have impacted their lives. Within this, they have to learn how to face their traumatic past, uncertain present, and unknown future, and explore their roots and identities as well as what kind of life they want to live. They have to have very challenging and uncomfortable conversations with their loved ones about race and racisms. After that, they sometimes have to split with their racist friends and family members no matter how painful the splitting is. Meanwhile, they have learned to build broader connections with their true supporters and allies. They have made new friends through social media and connected with other adoptees online. They have formed their important communities of support and led the trends to make important social changes in the US.

During our interviews, the first key question was to ask Chinese adoptees to share their personal stories of adoption at individual comfort levels. All of them talked about their adoption stories, and many said that they were abandoned shortly after birth; put in front of a hospital, a police station, a government building, a train station, or a bus stop; and then sent to an orphanage by the police or someone in authority. A few had foster parents, and some stayed in the orphanage. Our contributors were primarily adopted between six to eight months and one to two years old. Most of them were adopted by White American families. Their adopted parents were often at least forty years old when pursuing the adoption route. Some Chinese adoptees shared their adoption stories as follows:

I was born approximately on March 13, 1993. That's what the government says, but I don't know my real true birthday. . . . I was supposedly found in front of a government building in China. We don't really know a lot of information. They said around Niansanli town in Yiwu. I guess I was taken from that area and taken to Yiwu Social Welfare Institute at around three months old, or approximately, we don't know; the paperwork says that but we're not sure. I spent three and a half years in the orphanage in Yiwu, and then I was adopted by an American, Christian, middle-class couple with their older biological son. Since then, they raised me and loved me. A few years after that, they diagnosed me with Asperger's, [which is] autism spectrum disorder, but I'm very high functioning. They didn't get any more children because they thought I was pretty challenging behavior-wise. I've been interviewed by people like Jenna Heath from *Our China Stories*, I've been to Adopteen, [and] I've done a lot of other adoptee activities like Families with Children from China. I'm [currently] studying Chinese and I'm hoping one day I can go back to China when COVID is over and find my birth parents. (Ni Zhuhua, interview on February 21, 2021)

My birth year is 1993 . . . I was adopted in 1995 through Holt International Agency. I'm from Nanning, Guangxi. My birth name is Jihong Yuan. I was told that I was found at a bus stop and taken to the orphanage. I lived with a foster family, so, at the time of my adoption, I was actually not in the orphanage, I was with the foster family in China. I was two years old and everyone else in my group of adoptees was also female, but they were infants. So, I was like the only older child, I guess. . . . My adoptive parents got married in their early thirties. My father had testicular cancer, and so, they chose to not pursue fertility treatments and they decided that they wanted to go the adoption route. My sister, who is not biologically related to me, is of Chinese Filipino ancestry and she is from the United States. Yeah, that's us. My dad is Japanese American, third generation. My mom is Caucasian. (Daisy, interview on March 5, 2021)

Both Ni Zhuhua and Daisy were born in 1993, and they were adopted by American families when they were two or three years old, whereas many adoptees in their groups were adopted when they were infants. They both have some information about where they were found in China but are not sure about the accuracy of the information. They also both have connections to adoption organizations and communities. Daisy mentioned Holt International Agency, a Christian organization and adoption agency based in Eugene, Oregon, known for its international adoption and child welfare work. Operating in seventeen locations across five continents, including countries like Bulgaria, Cambodia, China, Colombia, Ethiopia, Haiti, India, Mongolia, Philippines, South Korea, South Africa, Thailand, Uganda, Vietnam, and more, Holt International aims to provide care and support to vulnerable children worldwide. Since pioneering modern international adoption practices in 1956, the organization remains a prominent leader in adoption and family support (Holt International, n.d.).

In my study, eighteen of twenty-six contributors were born in the 1990s, five were born in 2000, and three were born in 2001. Their American adoptive parents had various reasons for choosing to adopt, including medical issues that prevented them from having one or more biological children. Some adoptees have siblings who were also adopted from China or Asia. The American adoptive parents often went through an "extensive process" of interviewing with the international adoption agency, going over financial records and signing lots of paperwork. They also signed an oath pledging their life to unconditionally love and nurture Chinese adoptees as their own.

In general, Chinese adoptees were often adopted by a White "American, Christian, middle-class" couple with or without children. Most American adoptive parents did not hide the adoption stories from Chinese adoptees and began gradually telling adoptees as soon as they could speak and start to understand. The personal narratives surrounding Chinese adoptees' adoptions primarily draw on photographs, videos, emails, journal entries, and official documents in both China and the US as most adoptees were adopted at an early age, and they could not recall any memories in China. These adoptees are often told that their adoption stories have historical and individual significance so they should be shared and remembered. Jade mentioned that her adoptive parents made her feel very comfortable talking about being adopted:

> I was born in 1998. . . . I was adopted when I was eleven months old from Anhui Province, specifically the city Hefei. And before that, I lived with a foster family—I don't know too much about that; I just know that I did. My dad is White. He's mostly Anglo-Saxon, [those] kind of roots, and my mom is Puerto Rican and Spanish. And my mom is American and my dad is Canadian, so there is that difference [between] them. I don't know too much about why I was put up for adoption and stuff like that, that's usually the typical thing with Chinese adoptions. I've always known I was adopted; there wasn't a time when my parents didn't want to tell me. I feel like I never "found out," it was just there. So, I've always felt very comfortable talking about being adopted. It's never been a "no" subject at home. And even with my friends and stuff, like any of my peers, it's one of the things I just mention eventually, like, "Yeah, I'm adopted." I know some people it's a very personal thing for them, so they don't like to tell everyone they know. But I was really "that kid" that was like, "Yeah I'm adopted. Yeah, whoo." I'm pretty much the same [now]. It's not necessarily an exciting topic. It's just like that's my identity; I identify as an adoptee. (Interview on February 24, 2021)

While Jade is comfortable with her adoptee identity and her family always felt comfortable talking about her adoption, the differences in physical features between her adoptive parents and herself sometimes created awkward moments in public places. In our interview, Jade said that some people could not connect her with her White father, and there had been some jokes about it. One day, she fell at an ice-skating rink and slammed her head into the ground. She could not move for a second, and her father immediately came over. The person who was in charge on the ice said: "Who are you? You can't be here!" Jade had to tell him in her pain: "This is my dad!" This situation was not uncommon for Chinese adoptees. Similarly, before Zoe could drive, when giving rides home to friends, she said: "Oh, by the way, my mom is White, so you're not getting kidnapped." She understood that her friends might expect an Asian parent to drive them home. She had to say: "My mom is White, so you're not getting into a stranger's car. She just doesn't look like me."

Many adoptees tried to find their birth parents in China, but it is very difficult for many reasons. Among my twenty-six contributors, only two had found their birth parents by 2022. Rose is one of those who succeeded. Adopted in 1996 by a White single mother in Ohio, Rose, not having any siblings and not having a father, became curious as she grew up about her experience of being adopted. She became interested in learning where her physical features came from. Her mother asked her if she would like to look for her birth family, and Rose replied, "Sure! I would love to do that!" Rose thought that she needed to know her birth family to fill what she felt was a hole in her heart and that doing so would help her move forward. She and her adoptive mother started to look for Rose's birth family and put up posters in China for five years. They found a family, but after they did a DNA test with them, they found the family was not a match with Rose. In 2014, when they were about to give up, Rose's adoptive mother suggested doing a commercial. They ran a commercial for two weeks in Rose's birth city and received many responses. The TV producers helped them narrow the responses down to ten people. The first person Rose contacted was a girl, who told Rose, "I found out I had a sister a year ago, and I think it might be you." They started talking and ended up doing a DNA test with the girl's parents, and they matched. In China, Rose had a father and a mother; her sister was a year older than her, and her brother was ten months younger than Rose. Rose found them when she was a freshman in college. She did not speak Chinese; however, a translator helped her, and they used WeChat to communicate. Rose visited her birth family that summer and saw them again three years later. Her adoption made her very interested in genetics. After graduating from college, Rose went to graduate school to study genetic counseling.

Every Chinese adoptee's experiences are unique and personal. They often experience a variety of emotions related to their adoption, their birth parents, and their adoptive families. Some contributors felt that they were abandoned by their birth parents and felt anger toward them. Some felt curious about their birth parents and wanted to learn more about them. Chinese adoptees made individual decisions about whether or not to search for their birth parents in China or to meet them in person if they found them. Rose was very fortunate to have a positive experience, finding and meeting her birth family in China. The process helped her build strong connections with her roots, understand her past, and know where she came from and where she would go.

Experiencing Anti-Asian Racisms during the Pandemic

The pandemic was a very difficult time for Chinese adoptees—probably the most challenging one. It became "a rite of passage" for young adult Chinese adoptees when they realized that anti-Asian racisms had been a serious problem in the US as they felt it a lot more acutely during the pandemic than probably at any other time of their life. Even though most of them were raised by White American families, and all are officially American citizens, their family backgrounds and citizenship have not protected them from the harms of racisms. Emma, who was adopted by her White parents when she was thirteen months old in December 1997, articulated her complicated feelings this way:

> I feel like it [the pandemic] opened up a whole world to me, I guess. When the discrimination against Asians ramped up due to COVID and the rhetoric around it, it really made me look into like being an adoptee. *Not just like an adoptee, but like a Chinese adoptee being adopted by someone who's White.* And it made me think about how I felt guilty that I was nervous or scared around people who were being judgmental towards me or other Asians because I didn't have the full Asian experience, because I don't have Asian parents or elders to be nervous for, because mine are White. But that doesn't negate how I felt for my own personal safety. *There was the first time in my life that [I] ever felt unsafe due to my ethnicity.* I'm a typically pretty anxious person, and so, like, I take self-defense. And that was originally because I'm a small woman, and so I'm very easy to kidnap, and there are people out there who want to do me harm. But now it encompasses even more than that because I think the statistic was Asian hate and violence has gone up like 1,000 percent or something crazy just with COVID, and I was nervous. And because I felt guilty about being nervous, even though visibly I am Chinese, but I feel very White. I like Starbucks and I like leggings and all that stuff that's very typical to a White girl and a White woman, but that doesn't change how I look to anyone who doesn't know my family or my situation. And so, it's really made me dive into my own heritage and roots, and dive into adoption and looking into like adoption trauma and stuff like that. And it's opened up a can of worms and Pandora's box. But it's been really, really good to work through that. (Interview on May 20, 2021)

For Emma, even though she felt like "a White woman" in many ways, her assimilation into American culture did not change how she "looked" to people who knew nothing about her background, and it did not protect her from the harms of racisms. It was her first time feeling unsafe because of her race and ethnicity. These feelings have been common among Chinese adoptees during the pandemic. For Chinese adoptees adopted by White American parents, they probably did not have to worry about whether their White adoptive parents or grandparents might be attacked, but they were as deeply concerned about their own "personal safety" as other AAAPIs. The feelings of being unsafe due to one's race and ethnicity were commonly shared by AAAPIs during the pandemic, even though anti-Asian racisms are nothing new in America. Some Chinese adoptees also had to carry the extra burden of facing racisms in their adoptive families and exaggerated identity crises in their lives.

In my study, nineteen out of twenty-six adoptee contributors shared their encounters with racisms amid the pandemic. All of them demonstrated a keen awareness of the prevalence of anti-Asian racisms in media and social media platforms. The racist incidents they recounted were not limited to specific environments, occurring in both public and private spheres, whether online or off-line. Racisms were perpetrated not only by strangers and acquaintances but also by friends and even family members. Some Chinese adoptees discussed their racist encounters in various settings as follows:

> A lot of the time, I would feel personally attacked just because there have been so many negative things going on about Asians, specifically East Asians, around the coronavirus. Over break [in 2020], I was in a very rural area of Pennsylvania, and I just heard a lot of kind of insulting things about eating bats and how the Chinese were responsible for everything, and it was just—I can't find the word—but it just was not a fun experience. It made me feel really bad and made me question who I was friends with and everything. . . . These are people I had respected and cared about, and I still do, but it was just really upsetting to hear those things from those people. (Melody, interview on February 26, 2021)

> When the former president called it the "China Virus" and the "Kung flu" and all that really bad [stuff], it's not that there wasn't racism towards Asians before, it was just that he was giving people more permission in a way to be more outwardly racist towards people. And again, hate crimes against Asians are heavily underreported, [but] it felt like all of a sudden, Asians were being attacked more than usual, which might be the case, but also, there was more attention on it, so the media felt like, "Oh, we should probably put this in the news because it's a thing that's happening now." I guess Trump really emphasized those problems that we were having but it's made known to the public more now, I think. (Jade, interview on February 24, 2021)

> I go to a predominantly White college, and it's small, about 3,000 students, mainly undergrad, and last semester [in 2020] there were these little stickers popping up that were . . . they said, "tyrannical moxie." And then it said "mask

Coming Out of "the Fog"   115

up shut up 2020" with the Chinese flag in the background. They also said, "Do as I say sheep." So those were popping up, and my school didn't really, actually, they didn't do anything about it. I mean I took some down and people were slowly taking them down, but they didn't ever release any statements condemning the stickers, or I don't think they—I mean it would be hard to figure out who did it, but it's probably someone in graphic design. My school is small. And then around, I know at the beginning of March [in 2020], I never really had anything said to me, but when COVID-19 first came out, I had started hearing about anti-Asian discrimination. And around that time, since COVID-19 was kind of relatively new to the US that was kind of the time where it was like you only need to wear a mask if you have the virus. So, I had heard stories of Asians getting targeted and getting weird looks if they wore a mask. . . . I know I have friends who had other things happen. (Grace, interview on March 12, 2021)

Our contributors experienced discrimination against them in various contexts and also witnessed anti-Asian violence and hate crimes on media and social media. Some felt very angry when they saw the violence against AAAPI communities, especially against the older population. Yang Ji said that it was very cowardly to just randomly walk up to some old Asian people and push them or hurt them. To her disappointment, these incidents were often not considered as hate crimes at the beginning and were instead downplayed. Melody, adopted from Guangdong Province by two White parents in Pennsylvania, reported an incident at her college:

I remember last semester [in the fall of 2020], I was walking down the street, [and] it was maybe around 9:00 at night, so it wasn't extremely late, but it was kind of dark. I remember I was coming up one sidewalk, and I passed this man under a streetlight and we kind of saw each other, just because we were in passing. And then later, I was going down the sidewalk the other way. And he saw me again, and he started shouting at me like: "You don't belong here. This isn't your country." And in that specific moment, I just kind of walked away as quickly as I could, because I personally didn't want to confront that, because I was by myself, I just didn't know where it would end up. But I think if I experience discrimination from a casual remark that people will say, like on social media or just talking with my friends, I'll try to kind of correct it and just gently say, "Hey this is actually really offensive because . . ." and explain that, but I think harsher discrimination that's more intentional, I try to just disassociate myself with that just because there is such a violent connection with a lot of the discrimination of that type. (Interview on February 26, 2021)

During this incident, Melody was shocked and did not know what to do. She remembered that the young White man was not a college student, and that he did not wear a mask, but had a long and thin black case on his back, possibly a gun. Melody was very scared, and she went back to her dorm very quickly. She did not report the incident to her college, but since then, she has become very wary and almost fearful walking at night. Whenever she thought about this moment, she felt the panic and fearfulness that she experienced that night. Helen also experienced two incidents, one on Facebook and the other at a coffee shop:

At the very beginning of January 2020, officially before anyone in the USA had gotten any of the cases, I was in Israel, in Palestine . . . that part of the world. The very last day of my trip there, I was with my school—it was a school trip—[and] I [was doing] some excavating, so that meant I was down in the dirt digging for fossils and artifacts from ancient people, and I found this really cool figurine. In ancient times there for Greeks, not Greeks, but Jewish people, ancient Jewish communities, they had little figurines of, not gods, but it was something really cool that I found. And so, the excavation company that I was doing the project with, took a photo of me and posted it on their Facebook page like, "Look at what Helen found. What do you think this is?" And I was so proud of myself; it was a really exciting moment. And a bunch of people online, a lot of the people mostly responding on the Facebook page were local Israeli people who lived in Israel, were saying, "Oh, did she find COVID? Is that what she found?" So instead of trying to actually guess [and] trying to actually answer the question more practically, it was more of like, "Oh, we don't really care what she found. She's an Asian person. She looks Chinese. So, let's just poke fun of that and say that she found COVID. That's what she found." So yeah, that was a big blow. It was not fun to have a really proud moment of myself and to be happy about something and then have it be taken away, have that moment be taken away by prejudice. That was one instance, one experience.

And another experience was in Chicago, kind of in May/June of 2020, I think I was walking around in my neighborhood, and I went to a coffee shop. I was sitting down—and you know how the restaurants spread out the seating and everyone wears their masks, and they only take off their mask if they're about to eat a bite of their sandwich or have a drink of coffee—and so, it was me sitting in the corner and one of the managers, or someone of the employees who was working there [approached me]. I had my mask off because I was drinking my coffee, and just knowing that the employee went out of their way to tell me to put my mask on when other people in the restaurant also didn't have it on either, I don't know. For me, it felt that, "Oh, you're picking me out because I'm Asian." But other people in the restaurant also have their masks off because they're eating too, and it's not like I was being defiant of the rules because I was still following the rules. (Interview on March 10, 2021)

Helen felt hurt on both occasions, and she also felt like she had to carry pepper spray when walking on the streets. She articulated the importance of being cautious and taking measures to protect herself. She did not fight back on both occasions because she had to choose her battles carefully. She did

Coming Out of "the Fog"   117

not know those people who made comments on Facebook and the employee at the coffee shop, and thought it was not worthwhile to change their minds if she did not have close relationships with them. But if it was a close friend or family member who made jokes about Chinese or Asian people, Helen would have a good reason to confront racism. She continued:

> I think there are moments where I hold it in and I don't say anything, and other times where I'm trying to stick up for myself and actually put myself in the position to stand up, whether or not it'll be received well or not. But I think overall, the impact is that it reminds me that I'm not invisible, because I think people like to say, "Oh, Asian Americans, they're not really Americans," or the idea that we're foreigners; we're perpetual foreigners. And yeah, I think it just reminds me that I have work to do. I think Asian Americans have work to do to tell people that we're not going to stay silent and we're not going to allow people to walk all over us. It's something that we need to start fighting for.

Helen's accounts represent the heightened awareness among young Chinese adoptees and their determination to make important social changes through breaking the silence, standing up against racisms, and demanding respect and equality.

Frequently, when US racisms have been discussed, the focus has been on Black and White, and AAAPI voices and stories have often been overlooked. This invisibility was partially due to the view of AAAPI individuals as "perpetual foreigners" as well as the pervasiveness of the myth of the "model minority," with its numerous distorted images of AAAPI academic and economic success. These stereotypes lost their meaning when AAAPI individuals experienced racisms every day during the pandemic. The harsh reality has made AAAPI young adults speak out and actively combat racisms, discrimination, and structural inequality within US society.

Alongside Facebook and coffee shops, public retail spaces posed challenges for Chinese adoptees. For instance, while in Target, Emma noticed that she kept getting "dirty looks and dirty stares" from people. Some adoptees also noticed that people started to avoid them in public places, and some people had particularly strong reactions to seeing Chinese adoptees in March and April 2020. Two incidents were shared as follows:

> I haven't had too many because I've been staying home. But right when it [COVID-19] was really bad, like when it first started popping up a lot in New York, which was last March [in 2020], I went grocery shopping with my dad, and I remember—I've never felt this way before—but, I didn't want to be alone wherever we were going. I was hyperaware about how Asian I was all of a sudden. I've always known obviously, but I was like, "Oh." And of course, I'm Chinese, so that's even more concerning. We went into a CVS together, and

I walked in ahead of him [my dad]—but he was right behind me—and this older woman happened to see me. And I wouldn't have thought anything of it if we had been like a little too close together and she's just concerned about social distancing, but she looked right at my face, into my eyes, and made a little sound and quickly just ran off in the other direction. [And] no one else had that same reaction; it was just her. At that moment I was like, "Oh. Was that a situation?" I don't know if I'm reading too far into it, but it felt weird, and it didn't feel good. I don't think anyone running away from you feels good anyway. (Jade, interview on February 24, 2021)

One time I was at Kroger with my dad [around April 2020]. I was adopted by a Caucasian family. And my dad's a six-five White guy, so normally when I'm with my family, I have "White privilege" kind of; people are less likely to say stuff to me. But I was at Kroger in Cincinnati, and I sneezed once. And this lady who is next to us, this Caucasian lady, she was next to us in the checkout line, and she was like, "Why'd you come here if you know you're sneezing?" and she's like, "Can you stand six feet away?" And I was like, "I am," and my dad said, "She's fine where she is." And the lady just kept going off on me [to] just stand further away, and she was like, "I have a grandpa with Alzheimer's" and I was just like, "What?" because that doesn't make you more susceptible to COVID. (LiEllen, interview on February 28, 2021)

These two incidents were not uncommon among our contributors. AAAPIs often had similar encounters in public places during the COVID-19 outbreak. They were treated like "a virus," and people might avoid them or run away from them. That public avoidance hurt Chinese adoptees' feelings when they were also facing the fear and uncertainty of the new coronavirus.

Chinese adoptees not only had to deal with their own mistreatment in public places but also had the extra burden of dealing with conflicts with and discrimination from their White friends. Some adoptees' friendships with White people were affected by the pandemic. Eva, born in 1998 and adopted from Wuhan by a White family at fourteen months old, discussed how her friendships with White people were broken and how she crafted her new friendships:

I think I've always got comments in society, "Go back to China once your green card expires" [and] stuff like that. But I could just brush it off as just people being generally jerks. But it was different on campus when certain friends of mine who, race had never really been a conversation we had, [and they] didn't want to hang out anymore or didn't want to have conversations with me, or were afraid like I would give them COVID, even though there was only one case by that point in the US. So just the change in [the] nature of my friendships to an extent, because I'm mostly friends with White people; it's just the demographic that I hang out with the most. It's just moments like that [I] was like, "Oh, OK.

[I] wish I had these conversations with you guys sooner so that I knew who is racist and who isn't." ... At least with the friendships that have since dissolved, the way I dealt with it, I ended up leaning on other people who like weren't racist and problematic. I just began having more conversations about race to try to sort out who is problematic in my life and who's not. Because we hang out with less people now, I was more ready to just cut people off if they were going to be racist towards me or have biases about who I was. (Interview on February 17, 2021)

Eva's account demonstrates the fragile relationships between Chinese adoptees and their White friends as well as her own creative agencies to find real friends and allies. Another adoptee, Emma, also lost a couple of her closest friends in 2020 because she did not want to put up with racisms from them. Those friends did not understand what happened to Emma and did not have empathy toward her suffering. Similarly, Daisy lost her closest White girlfriend because their stances became very conflicting, and there was no common ground for them to stand up together.

When facing racist comments and treatment from White friends, Chinese adoptees did not keep silent or repress their feelings. Instead, they faced the problems honestly, walked away from their racist friends, and made new friends who understood and supported them. Another Chinese adoptee, LiEllen, even discussed how she broke up with friends who did not follow mask mandates and had participated in big parties at bars without wearing masks. LiEllen did not want to be friends with people who did not take responsibility to care for other people.

Broken relationships were commonly experienced by many adoptees during the pandemic. Racisms have split American society, and political ideologies also divided Americans. Many Americans decided that organizing their lives around COVID-19 or not was core to their political identity as progressive or conservative, even as pandemic isolation and disruption affected everyone, fueling mental health problems, drug overdoses, and violent crimes; increasing health issues; and growing educational, social, economic, and gender inequalities. The huge partisan divide affected many Americans' decisions about if they should wear a mask, keep social distancing, or get vaccinated. Katara, adopted by her White parents in 1998 when she was six months old, reflected on the splitting world on March 3, 2021: "I think it also surprised me how quickly it became an 'us versus them' kind of world." One Chinese adoptee felt that America was broken in a variety of ways, with a dysfunctional medical system, systemic racism, inability to ensure a livable wage, rising unemployment, and similar issues. The divide occurred globally, nationally, regionally, and locally. Sometimes that divide even happened within one's own family.

Facing Racisms within One's Own Family

Probably the most painful discrimination that some Chinese adoptees faced came from their own families as they became aware of how racist some of their relatives were. Mia (nonbinary, pronouns: they, them, their) was born in 1998 and adopted in 1999 by a White couple. They were a graduate student of architecture at a state university and noticed that their adoptive family was more blatantly racist than they realized. Mia had relatives on Facebook who posted "Chinese flu" and "Kung flu" rhetoric. One uncle said that he would never eat at PF Chang's again as a joke. Mia got more sensitive about racisms, and it was painful that relatives had fun heckling Mia about it every time they saw them. Mia tried to connect with other adoptees and Asians and studied Asian American history by themselves. Mia also tried to talk to family members about racisms, but it was too painful. Mia thought that their "Asianness" was erased—their family members forgot that Mia was Asian and they were not, so they made jokes and assumed that they did not hurt anyone. In reality, all those racist jokes and rhetoric hurt Mia deeply. Mia shared more stories about their painful encounters:

My sister recently graduated from high school and she's from Vietnam, so she wore the traditional Vietnamese clothing underneath her graduation robes. And my aunt said that she looked like Mulan, which it's a bit problematic because there's a difference in traditional clothing. And so, when I told my aunt, "Mulan is Chinese and [my sister] is wearing Vietnamese traditional clothing," my aunt pretty much said, "Oh, Asians are all the same. It all looks similar enough." To which I said, "That's really not OK." And then throughout the rest of my stay, my aunt would continually bring up that Asians are all the same just to get on my nerves. So that was another thing. Which just at the beginning, I was trying to be educational and be like, "They're different so let's treat them differently." And then by the end, it was just my aunt trying to annoy me about this because I've made a deal about it at the beginning. And rather than trying to understand where I was coming from and trying to, I don't know, learn, she'd rather just stay willfully ignorant. Which is painful for me. It's difficult to try to share something about myself, or just being Asian, and have it so willfully ignored.

And then also, there was a case where a distant relative of mine posted to Facebook like, I don't know one of those typography things that was like, "I'd rather get COVID-19 than have . . ." or well, no, it was, "I'd rather get Kung Flu than have Biden for president," something along those lines. And it made me very sad and angry. And I then replied to it, against my mother's advice, because my mother was like just leave it alone. I just replied to it, "I'm very disappointed to see this. Please remember that you have Asian relatives, and that the pandemic has caused them a lot of pain and a lot of fear." To which I was replied with a . . . this relative replied to me saying pretty much, "I don't think anyone

Coming Out of "the Fog"   121

was in trouble during Trump's presidency." And pretty much vote for Trump. And that was also painful and again, an erasure of my experience. (Interview on May 28, 2021)

Mia pointed out that racisms and White supremacy were everywhere, within one's family and in public. She continued: "Just all of these events that happened between me and my relatives, is just an erasure of my Asianness, an erasure of my sister's Asianness, an erasure of the differences between our Asianness, our Asiannesses. And that's painful to experience, especially because even though they're going to erase it, no one else will. When I go out in public, I'm still perceived as Asian."

Mia felt that the Asiannesses of them and their sister were erased in their White adoptive family, just as the history and voices of AAAPIs used to be erased from US textbooks. Furthermore, AAAPI communities are very diverse, but they are reified as the same in the eyes of some White people. The erasure of Asiannesses and the reification of diverse Asiannesses demonstrate various forms of anti-Asian racisms that exist at systemic and individual levels. The paradox of Chinese adoptees' invisible Asiannesses at home and visible Asiannesses in public illustrates the prevalence of anti-Asian racisms and injustice in multiple forms and contexts. For Chinese adoptees, the erasure of their Asiannesses within their families was as painful as the discrimination they experienced in public. These distressing experiences of being marginalized in multiple contexts have heightened their awareness of injustice and prompted them to advocate for social justice for all marginalized communities.

Emma, who commented that the pandemic was the first time in her life when she ever felt unsafe due to her ethnicity, painfully experienced discrimination from her racist parents-in-law. A professional photographer living in a small midwestern town, she married her White husband in November 2019 and moved out of her White adoptive parents' house for the first time after living there for about twenty years. Before she started dating her husband, he showed a photo of her to his father, who said, "Oh, this is like Asians are us, like bridesareus.com. Where did you find her?" The comments hurt Emma, but she just brushed it off at the beginning. One day in the car, her husband suddenly realized something and said, "You know, I think my parents are racist." Emma then said, "Yes, they are." She then explained a couple of scenarios that had been painful to her that he had mostly forgotten. Emma later decided to limit contact with her parents-in-law, choosing not to talk to them except on holidays. Emma was aware that her parents-in-law were racist against not only Asians but also other minorities. Moreover, they did not agree on politics. Emma regularly saw a therapist, and they talked about how they wanted to approach the conflicts and whether it was worth educating her parents-in-law on certain things, deciding that some were worth confronting and others weren't.

Fortunately, Emma's husband was not racist, and he was very supportive of her. She could bring up uncomfortable conversations with him, and he tried his best to be empathetic and caring. However, Emma understood that her husband, as a White man, was not necessarily going to understand her challenges as someone who was Asian living in a predominantly White world. Before they went to see his family, her husband always discussed their game plan of what were absolute boundaries—what topics or issues and expressions or phrases would they get up and leave over, if her parents-in-law brought them up or said them. Emma felt grateful to her husband for having her back and telling his parents to stop saying what was not appropriate. Emma said that if she could do it over again, she would still marry a White man, but she would speak up more about her own heritage, beliefs, and political views. For a long time, she was so silenced and unable to share what she believed because her White adoptive parents' belief systems were very much the opposite of her own. She felt like she was not allowed to speak up about anything. Gradually, she learned to stand up for herself and had those uncomfortable conversations with her loved ones.

It is challenging for Chinese adoptees to talk about race and racisms within their own White families. Emma learned how unwilling her family and in-laws were to learn about what it was like being Chinese in America and how unwilling they were to even hear about her personal experiences. Emma felt unwelcome, especially with her in-laws. No matter how she phrased what she wanted to say, her in-laws seemed unwilling to listen. They wanted her to say: "I am White, I am American!" She just could not do that. Although they knew her as a family member, they were unwilling to learn and empathize. Emma also felt shocked to hear some anti-Chinese comments from her White adoptive father with two adopted Chinese daughters. He had expressed some anti-Chinese sentiments for years, but she just brushed them off. It was not until the pandemic that Emma started to speak up, saying to him, "That was not OK for you to say."

Emma felt that the most challenging thing for her was to know when to rock the boat and when to keep quiet during uncomfortable conversations about race and racisms within her own family. Sometimes she encountered a microaggression, and sometimes she experienced discrimination that deeply hurt her. She did not want everything to build up to breaking point and then explode at her family members—that would never be a learning moment. She had to stay calm and choose her battles, as the fight would be endless.

Despite all the challenges that she faced, Emma still loved her adoptive father and treated her in-laws as family members. She thought that there was good and bad in people, and while everyone was capable of doing good things, those things might not be for her—therefore, she had to set boundaries. She also felt that the pandemic made her father aware of how crazy and chaotic life could be. One day she went back home to say hello and pick up some things. Her father was canoeing and said, "This is for when the world ends. So, you can come over to our house when the world ends." It was hard for Emma to see how anxious and scared her father had become, and she now saw her father more as an adult friend than as a parent. Ultimately, she was grateful that she had a house, that both she and her husband were employed, and that they had food on the table and a roof over their heads. Life is hard, and it is complicated to be a Chinese adoptee in a White American family. Emma valued her own roots and thought that becoming Chinese American was whatever one made it to be.

Although White adoptive parents may have previously undermined their children's racial experiences, some contributors tried to foster their White parents' empathy by sharing personal incidents of racisms. My contributors also discussed the challenge of educating their White parents and family members about racial issues by initiating racial dialogues. They recognized that constant exposure to racial denial can lead to feelings of isolation and even a sense of being unsafe, ultimately resulting in racial battle fatigue (Smith 2008). Some adoptees chose to become disconnected from their families, some felt burdened by the emotional labor involved in education about race and racisms, and some worried about appearing ungrateful for being adopted (Wing and Park-Taylor 2024).

COMPLICATED AGENCIES OF CHINESE ADOPTEES AND IDENTITY CRISIS

The agencies of Chinese adoptees are very complicated, nuanced, and situational. Some adoptees articulated that they felt they were deprived of agency for their adoption and life experiences. For instance, Ni Zhuhua has faced racisms since she was young, and she strived to be as Chinese as she could. She liked that America had freedom, but she would go back to China if she could. She expressed her feelings of lack of "choice" and agency this way:

> I don't know if I can ever become Chinese, like culturally where I grew up in China. I don't think I could because I can't go back in time and be like, "OK, I'm just going to stay in China and not move to America." I didn't really have a choice. I was too young, and they didn't ask me, "Do you want to live in America with this family?" They kind of forced me. Part of me wishes I could have just grown up in China with a Chinese family. But I also know that if I

did, I wouldn't have the opportunities I have in America. Sometimes it's like a give and take [situation]. You have to just find out what's worth sacrificing for. (Interview on February 21, 2021)

As Zhuhua was adopted by a White Christian family, she thought being American meant just "believing in God." The intersection of racial privilege and religious privilege is very obvious to her and many other Chinese adoptees. Most Chinese adoptees were adopted by White Christian families, and Christianity is the most prevalent religion in the US (PRRI Staff 2021). As Zhuhua said, she did not have a choice to decide where she wanted to live. She also could not choose her own religions and beliefs. Lack of religious choice is also forced on Chinese adoptees by systemic racisms and White supremacy.

Chinese adoptees often had no control over their adoption and their immigration to the US. They had limited or no control over their experiences and relationships after they were adopted by their American parents. They often experience a sense of loss and face difficulties in navigating their sense of belonging. Some key factors that contribute to their lack of agency include (but are not limited to) the power dynamics embedded in the adoption process and the systemic racisms they face in American society. Chinese adoptees were often adopted when they were infants or toddlers, and international adoption programs had significant power to decide on their adoption paths. After adoptees were placed with their adoptive parents, those parents often had the authority to decide what foods they ate, what schools they attended, and which communities they lived in. As many Chinese adoptees were adopted by White American parents in the US, it was very difficult for them to be immersed in their own cultural roots and heritage. Moreover, they often faced marginalization, exclusion, and discrimination based on their race and ethnicity, which made it challenging for them to adapt to their lives in America. It was even harder for them to combine and balance the two different cultures, value systems, and identities in their everyday lives. No matter what they chose to do, they had gains and losses at the same time. As another Chinese adoptee, Sarah, said, they would work through these issues until the day they died.

Living in predominantly White environments, many Chinese adoptees experienced a sense of "in-betweenness" as they were not perceived as White enough by their White peers or Asian enough by their Asian peers. Zoe summarized these ambiguous feelings in this manner: "You have all of these 'basic White people things' like you go to Starbucks and have Apple products and scrunchies, etc., but then you don't look like them and you don't fit in properly. And then with Asian people who have Asian parents, you don't face the same pressure that they do, and you don't follow the same rules that they do. So, there's always this place where you're stuck, and you just have to be your own person" (interview on May 23, 2021). This "in-betweenness" is forced on Chinese adoptees by America's racist systems from the beginning. Systemic racisms have made it very difficult for Chinese adoptees to develop a personal or group identity substantially by and for themselves. Before COVID-19, transracial adoptees had to navigate or reconcile their sense of in-betweenness—being caught between their adoptive and birth countries, adoptive and birth families, and American and birth cultures. This duality is known as the *transracial adoption paradox* (E. Lee 2003) and is further intensified by the perception that transracial adoptees are not legitimate members of their adoptive families due to racial appearance incongruence (Goss 2017). While Chinese transracial adoptees may have previously felt self-conscious about this, the pandemic has exaggerated their sense of in-betweenness and complicated their identity formation. This is especially true for those in emerging adulthood, a stage where identity is notably unstable (Wing and Park-Taylor 2022, 2024). Sarah further expanded this ambiguous "in-betweenness," noting:

> Your origins at some point were from China, and now you live in America, right? So that I would say [being Chinese American] is kind of like the mixing of cultures and kind of being in two worlds at one time . . . obviously, there's a positive that you can go in between two different places, right? And still kind of feel some sort of belonging, right? And then at the same time, it's like you're kind of not really either one. So, I feel like . . . people's identity issues are probably one of the most defining things about being Asian American, especially for people our age who kind of grew up in America and then feeling the pressure to become Asian but then at the same time, knowing that you were something completely different just like fifteen years ago, right? (Interview on August 11, 2021)

Sarah thought that being Chinese and American were both very complex, and citizenship simply could not label one's identity. She continued:

> For the cultural criteria, I definitely feel like we as a group, with Asian Americans, don't really feel fully American in part because we have different cultures, but then also we look different. And that's something we can never escape. And I feel like adoptees feel that the most because we are fully American almost from birth, it's all we know, right? So then when we get older, we have a choice, right? We can be who we want to be. But we can never shed the fact that we look Chinese. People are always going to judge us for that. No matter where you are, Chinese or Western, people just see that. So, I feel like that kind of wakes a lot of people up per se. It is that no matter how much you have internalized hatred or anger about that, that will just always be with you. So, I think that for

adoptees especially, it's hard for us to embrace that, but it is something that we struggle with our whole lives.

Identity struggles and searching for belonging are a lifetime process for many Chinese adoptees, but they experience these identity crises differently at different moments in their lives. Emma struggled not only with her own racial identity, but also with other identity issues after she married her White husband. She changed her legal name from her maiden name to her married name and saw it more and more on credit card bills and her license. She had a hard time identifying not only as Chinese but also as White because she knew that she was not White. Grace also did not know how she should identify herself. As a Chinese adoptee who grew up with a White American mother, Grace often had hard conversations with herself about her identities. She tried to have some of these conversations with other people, but it was challenging. During the pandemic, being isolated from everyone else was even more difficult for her as she could not get the interactions she wanted on Zoom and Facetime.

For Chinese adoptees raised in White American families, some have difficulty identifying themselves as Chinese because they do not speak Chinese languages and eat Chinese foods and are not immersed in Chinese cultures. On the other hand, some confidently identify themselves as Chinese simply because they were born in China, and their genetics are almost 100 percent Chinese. For Sydney, genetics is very affirming to her because it has been hard for her to connect with her Chinese identity and heritage as she has been raised in a White family and lived in a White community. Seeing her DNA test in front of her and having the literal proof that she is Chinese has helped her identify as Chinese.

Jiang Liang-Liang indicated that she experienced identity crises before the pandemic. She was born in 2000 and adopted by a mixed single mother who was part Taiwanese. Her mother was also an adoptee, and Liang-Liang had an older sister who was five years older than her. Her sister was also adopted from China but from a different province. When growing up, Liang-Liang and her older sister went to a Jewish school, and her family was the only Asian family in the neighborhood. As an adoptee, Liang-Liang did not have a strong sense of being Chinese. She knew that she was Chinese, but she did not feel Chinese. She identified herself as a Chinese American and felt isolated from the Chinese part of her identity. She wanted to actively seek it out and explore her Chinese identity.

Liang-Liang felt lost when she went to China for a high school trip in the summer of 2017. She had an identity crisis and did not feel that she was Chinese at all. She felt like an American, but people did not treat her like an

American. In China, her White friends got a lot of attention, and some Chinese people took pictures with them. But nobody paid attention to her, and she was treated like "a random girl." Liang-Liang learned Mandarin Chinese at school, but her Chinese language skills did not help her as much as she had hoped. One day, she tried to ask for chopsticks in a restaurant in Shanghai; however, she suddenly forgot the word, and the situation went badly for her. After she came back to the US, she decided to continue learning Chinese. She went to CoW in the fall of 2018 and chose to take Chinese language courses and major in Chinese studies. She made the choice partially because she did not feel like she was Chinese enough and that studying Chinese would make her closer to that part of her identity.

Despite feelings of loss and lack of agency, many Chinese adoptees have exerted their creative agencies in a variety of ways. The identity crisis—viewing herself as "ethnically Chinese" and "culturally American"—made Liang-Liang suffer tremendous pain, but it also motivated her to advocate for her communities. For her senior independent study, she interviewed fifteen Asian and Asian American students at her college, recorded their lived experiences during the pandemic, and created a digital archive for it (Jiang 2022). Her goal was to examine how racisms and stigma during the pandemic had impacted Asian and Asian American students and to create visibility for their lived experiences and narratives. Liang-Liang brought visibility to Asian and Asian American college students' experiences and proposed proactive steps to mitigate anti-Asian hate nationally and locally.

Some Chinese adoptees have exerted their active agencies in defining their identities and personalities when sharing their adoption stories. Nina, adopted by her White parents in 1998 when she was eight months old, loved to tell people she was from China. However, as time went by, she wanted to be the same as everyone else, and during middle and high school, she did not want to be or be seen as different. When people asked where she came from, she simply answered: "I'm American." For one week when she attended an all-Asian cultural camp, she said, "I am Chinese American." When she became a young adult, she realized being different was fine. Sometimes she had fun with her own identity. When she was eighteen years old, she went to have lunch with her White father. In the restaurant, she got many weird looks, and she felt that people wondered who the White guy was with this young Chinese woman. Rather than confront them or remove herself from the situation, she just let those onlookers be uncomfortable and found humor in their reactions.

Chinese adoptees' identity struggles were exacerbated by the pandemic, but those struggles also created spaces for them to explore their own identities and fight for social justice. When the pandemic started, Zoe realized for the first time that some Americans did not like the fact that she was Chinese, although she had always enjoyed being Chinese and loved to share that part of her identity with her friends. She also felt ashamed of being American because some Americans were the ones hurting Chinese people. She asked herself: "If I can't be Chinese and I can't be American, where can I go?" The Atlanta spa shootings made her feel even more ashamed of her American identity, and she did not know where to identify because someone who looked like her White adoptive family killed people who looked like her. In response to this uncomfortable truth, she stood up for people who looked like her and coled the March for Asian Lives in March 2021.

ANTIRACIST SOLIDARITIES, COMMUNITIES OF SUPPORT, AND AAAPI FESTIVALS

Chinese adoptees build antiracist solidarities and craft diverse communities of support through their shared experiences of adoption and racist encounters. They build diverse relationships with other adoptees, AAAPI young adults, and activists and form or strengthen various nonprofit civil rights groups and organizations. With the surging anti-Asian racisms during the pandemic, there has been an increase in political activisms within AAAPI communities. For instance, Grace joined Asian American Justice + Innovation Lab (AAJIL, pronounced "agile"), which was founded in 2019 by Dr. Sandra So Hee Chi Kim. AAJIL grew out of a need Dr. Kim had observed in the diversity, equity, and inclusion world, where the majority of trainings tended to revolve around a Black/White binary. Although the Black/White binary construct and anti-Black racisms are very important to dismantle, the focus on this binary has left out the histories and experiences of other racialized groups, including AAAPI communities. All racializations are co-constitutive and interlocking within systemic racisms and White supremacy. AAAPIs have faced the harms of both the "yellow perils" and "model minority" stereotypes, and AAAPI histories have often been erased from textbooks and course requirements as well as in society at large. Dr. Kim started AAJIL to offer a different kind of racial justice education, free to anyone who is interested. Using a decolonial framework that emphasized the interlocking racializations in the US with a deliberate integration of AAAPI histories and experiences, AAJIL's racial justice trainings revolve around the practice of mutual care and aid through community-building, and participants are expected to make important social changes in the long term.

Grace connected with AAJIL after she heard Dr. Kim's talk on a panel about COVID-19 and anti-Asian racisms. Grace was inspired by what was said in that talk as she was starting to learn about the myth of the "model minority" and its history. Grace connected with the group and joined one of their book clubs, reading *Minor Feelings* by Cathy Park Hong. She also attended some workshops that they hosted on "Telling Your Story." Grace felt that connecting with that intelligent and diverse community over the summer of 2020 was very liberating because they validated the way she had been feeling. It reminded her that she was not alone and that other people were thinking about the same things.

In addition, Grace connected with a group formed by some professors and students to talk about antiracism at their university. When setting up the group, they tried to tear down the typical boundaries that existed between professors and students because they wanted it to be a more casual group. Grace felt hopeful when she was able to be more upfront and honest with a group of professors who were passionate about antiracist efforts and helping the Black, Indigenous, and people of color (BIPOC) students. It was very helpful for Grace to know that there were allies and sources to help her as they continued the fight and made their campus a better and more inclusive place for BIPOC students. Grace summarized her personal experiences of becoming an activist during the pandemic as follows:

> It was a time for me to think about what it meant to be Chinese American in America. And it was a time to think about how my identity—adoptee Asian American—fit into America's history of racist violence and how I could become proactive and deliberately antiracist and actually become a force for change. I think that's one thing that did happen was I became more active, like socially active, more outspoken about what I think. One lesson that really hit me from Cathy Park Hong's book, which was *Minor Feelings*, was she had written about her experiences entering a college classroom and, in this classroom, all the Asian Americans, she was so annoyed because they wouldn't speak and she wrote, "Don't you know if you don't speak, they'll walk all over you." And that's what's kind of going through my mind and classes and actually being willing to step on toes in order to make it clear that some things are not OK. Racism is not OK. But it was also a time to be in a new type of community. Rethinking community. I think [that] is really important in order to stay sane and not feel totally alone. (Interview on March 12, 2021)

Grace understood the importance of speaking up and building communities when facing anti-Asian racisms. She also learned how to discern who is truly an ally and to understand the difference between "performative activism" and true activism when people were actually taking steps to make change. She was very angry to find that those distinctions existed, but she felt happy about the communities that had been strengthened through activism. These action-oriented attitudes are widely shared by many Chinese adoptees. For instance, Helen told me that she had been invested in racial justice since the COVID-19 outbreak:

> I really am invested in social justice. So, justice for many communities, but especially issues that deal with race and racism. And during May [or] June of last year [2020] with the Black Lives Matter protest, I was very angry then. Still am pretty charged whenever there's a news article that talks about racism and people getting hurt. . . . And I do a lot of advocacy work from home, from my phone, from the words that I have, and I think whether we're donating money to go to justice organizations or for speaking up, I think using our platforms—because at this point [with] technology, everyone has their own social media [platform]—[gives us] all a space to speak our mind and to take a stance on something. Sometimes people feel like, "Oh, that's just talking, it's not doing anything," but I think it is doing things because we can have discussions with the public, but also, I think it's actually more important, to have discussions with friends and family. For adoptees very specifically, if we're growing up in families that aren't the same race as us, it's our time [and] it's our job to have difficult discussions about race and racism within our own families, and that's the work that we have to do. But it gives me energy. Here's the thing: it's a two-sided coin, it's angry and happy. Because even though me taking being very involved in social justice, there's—I don't know if you've heard this expression—fire to the butt, like a flame, kind of like the anger from the racism gives me power and energy and inspiration to make changes and do better things, which is also happy as well. (Interview on March 10, 2021)

As Helen said, anti-Asian racisms made her very angry but connected her with broader communities of support to fight for racial justice. Despite various challenges, many Chinese adoptees have formed diverse communities of support to combat racisms. Both Black Lives Matter protests and March for Asian Lives protests have made Chinese adoptees see systemic racisms and violence clearly and empowered them to make important social changes.

The Atlanta spa shootings were a turning point for many Chinese adoptees. Lilly, a student in my Anti-Asian Racism class, thought that the shootings made her realize she was indeed Asian in a world filled with hate. It also made her realize how the victims of these crimes could be her or someone like her. Since the Atlanta spa shootings, she was a lot more aware of her existence in society as an Asian American woman. It was very difficult for her because her White adoptive parents and siblings could not directly relate to her feelings. However, during the height of the pandemic, her adoptive family became aware of what was happening and were very understanding of what she was feeling and experiencing. She also met people who had similar feelings at her college and talked with them. She thought that AAAPIs had often been seen as a threat to the primarily White society in the US, a view that had led to many legislative and institutional efforts to segregate them by enacting immigration quotas, restrictions on citizenship and property ownership, and limits on employment—all violations of Asian Americans' civil rights. She knew that AAAPIs experienced exclusions and limitations to immigration by US law for almost a century because of legislation such as the Chinese Exclusion Act of 1882 and the Immigration Act of 1924, and they were largely prohibited from naturalization until the 1940s; it was only through changes in the immigration laws and the activism of the 1960s that AAAPIs were able to gain some acceptance and recognition in the US. Few Americans realize that the lives of AAAPIs are constantly stressed by racisms. In light of the COVID-19 pandemic and all the racisms that AAAPIs have faced, Lilly invited her classmates and friends to help fold one thousand paper cranes to promote peace, love, hope, and healing within the AAAPI communities at her college. Her project was inspired by the classic Japanese story *Sadako and the Thousand Paper Cranes*, a work of historical fiction based on the life of Sadako Sasaki, a young girl who was exposed to radiation during the 1945 atomic bombing of Hiroshima. After being diagnosed with leukemia, she began to fold one thousand paper cranes, inspired by the Japanese legend that said she would be granted a wish upon completion. Although folding one thousand paper cranes could not stop AAAPI hate, Lilly's wish was to spread positivity within the community during such a difficult time. After the completion of her project, all the paper cranes were exhibited near the entrance to her college library, a beautiful representation of AAAPI students' determination for action and hope for a better future.

Similarly, Zoe used a creative outlet to speak up about anti-Asian racisms in the US. She composed a dance to explore the impacts of anti-Asian racisms on an Asian American adoptee like her who grew up in the US in a White family and a predominantly White community. Through her choreography, she explored her intersectional identity of being a transracial and transnational adoptee from China and illustrated how her own identity and mental health had been impacted throughout her life and especially during the pandemic with the rise in anti-Asian hate. She made a video of her dance and posted it on YouTube on May 4, 2022 (Seymore 2022). In the video, she chose to wear a shirt bearing the name of a Facebook group called Subtle Asian Adoptee Traits, which consists of over five thousand adoptees who live all over the world and were adopted from different Asian countries. This group helped Zoe a lot during the early lockdowns and has been a good support system throughout the pandemic, and it has also helped Zoe navigate the hardships of being a Chinese adoptee in the US. For her dance, Zoe chose

Fig. 4.1. *More Than a Hashtag*, 2021, drawn by Maya BingLi Seymore.

the Chinese song "Selfless" by G.E.M. because she believed that the only way we could beat the COVID-19 pandemic was by being selfless.

Throughout the pandemic, Zoe went through many emotions—sadness, anger, frustration—that were portrayed in her dance. At the end of the video, Zoe added an image drawn by her adoptive sister after the Atlanta spa shootings depicting the difficulties of being an Asian American woman in the US; it was an image that spoke to her personally (seen in fig. 4.1). By composing her dance, Zoe hoped to raise awareness of the mental health struggles of AAAPIs in the US due to the perpetuating racisms against them. She also hoped that AAAPI communities would continue to work together to make this world a better place for all.

In February 2023, Zoe completed her independent study thesis to examine the effects of perceived discrimination during the COVID-19 pandemic

Coming Out of "the Fog"   133

and ethnic identity on the psychological well-being of Chinese transracial adoptees in the US. Her research indicates that adoptee identity, ethnic identity, and prejudice were not significant predictors for psychological well-being, although ethnic identity was found to be a significant predictor of collective self-esteem (Seymore 2023). Zoe created a website to share her research with the broader public (https://www.overlookedadoptees.org). Moreover, Zoe cofounded Wooster Adoptee Student Union (WASU) with another Chinese adoptee in her college on October 26, 2022. WASU aims to serve as both an advocate and support group for adoptees, and an educational group for the broader community. Adoptee advocacy, activism, and education are important to Zoe and her friends, and they support each other to succeed and thrive despite various challenges and hardships they face.

In addition to personal narratives, arts, music, and dance, Chinese adoptees also use festivals to build diverse communities of support to combat racisms. In the spring of 2022, four students in my Anti-Asian Racism class organized the first annual AAAPI Arts Festival as their final project. Japanese American student Mochi led Chinese adoptees, AAAPI students, and Native American students to work together to make it a great success. Numerous AAAPI student groups were invited to participate, and the festival provided significant opportunities for them to come together, collaborate, showcase their artistic talents, and celebrate their cultural traditions and accomplishments. The festival featured a rich tapestry of traditional and contemporary performances, art exhibitions, foods, workshops, and interactive activities that engaged participants in a journey through the diverse landscapes of AAAPI cultures. The success of the festival was a testament to the dedication and passion of AAAPI students, who worked tirelessly to create safe and welcoming spaces for all members of the campus community.

Lunar New Year is another important festival for Chinese adoptees to celebrate their cultural traditions and craft diverse communities of support. On January 21, 2023, Zoe worked with several organizations to organize the Lunar New Year celebration, which featured Chinese foodways, games, arts, and creative activities. Nearly three hundred individuals participated, and I attended the celebration and met many colleagues and students from diverse backgrounds. One colleague said that it was great that we could finally celebrate the Lunar New Year on campus together, while another noted the desire to be together like this more often after the pandemic. The celebration not only fostered a deeper understanding of AAAPI cultures, but it also strengthened connections among participants, promoting mutual appreciation and respect.

Festivals, bounded in time and space, often amalgamate various folkloric genres such as songs, dance, arts, foodways, costumes, and narratives to create synergistic experiences that surpass the sum of their individual parts, construct alternative worlds to transform reality, and help create communities (Gabbert 2011, 2018). Dorothy Noyes (2003, 4) writes, "It [festival] dramatizes actual or proposed social arrangements, especially collective identities and hierarchies, in order to win consent, force acquiescence, or destabilize other such representations." It is crucial for scholars to examine what values, relationships, ideas, and identities are showcased through cultural performances and enactments in festivals as well as whose ideas and values these representations embody. It is also important to explore how those values and ideas are contested and by whom (Gabbert 2018; Magliocco 1993).

The AAAPI Arts Festival and Lunar New Year celebration cocreated by Chinese adoptees and their AAAPI communities have served as platforms for fostering inclusivity, promoting cultural exchanges, and celebrating diverse AAAPI arts and cultures in White dominant society. As identities are constructed and remade, the festival plays a transformative role, providing individuals with opportunities to engage and participate actively in the festivities in meaningful ways. The structures of participation are diverse, offering avenues for people from different backgrounds to engage in various ways, fostering a sense of belonging in times of crisis. By showcasing cultural values and traditions, the festival has become a medium to affirm and reaffirm presences and achievements of AAAPI communities. It contributes to the creation of communities of support that transcend individual identities; fosters a sense of belonging and recognition, catalyzing collective support and solidarity; and represents not only cultural displays but also powerful expressions of resilience, coalitions, and the crafting of inclusive and vibrant communities of support that thrive on their shared cultural traditions.

BECOMING CHINESE, CHINESE/ASIAN AMERICAN, AND DISIDENTIFICATIONS

Searching for belonging and identities is an ongoing process for many Chinese adoptees. In our interviews, eight contributors emphasized that the pandemic made them assert their identities as Chinese or Asian and as an adoptee. Eva knew that nothing would change the fact that she was Asian, and she recognized her power and authority in being who she was. Madelyn—born in 2001, adopted in 2002, and double majoring in psychology and music at her university—articulated her feelings in a nuanced way:

> During COVID I started thinking more about my identity as an Asian American, I think partly because of the discrimination and violence that Asian Americans started, or not started, but the rise in violence on the news and things; it was more publicized. That was always in the back of my mind I think when I

was going out, or just knowing how I was perceived in public. And I think at the same time with the Black Lives Matter movement, that also made me question my background and my identity because as an adoptee, I was raised in a White family, which is typical, so I wasn't Black and I wasn't White and I was Asian, but I wasn't culturally Asian. So, it sort of was a catalyst for my exploration and identity search. So, I did a lot of thinking over the summer [in 2020]. (Interview on May 18, 2021)

Madelyn primarily identified herself as "a Chinese adoptee" and said, "I think that's how I most connect with my Chinese heritage, where I came from, and I like to connect with the other adoptees too." She also identified herself as "Chinese American" because that was how she was "perceived" and how she "experienced the world." She knew that being Chinese means different things to different people, and it is not solely based on culture or appearance. Some Chinese adoptees often make efforts to learn Chinese languages and explore their cultural heritage, but she did not do that extensively. She asserted herself as a Chinese American adoptee and emphasized that being American was "a very varied and diverse experience." For her, ideally, being or becoming a Chinese American is a combination and mixture of both Chinese and American identities and is being as connected as one wants to be to both cultures.

Many Chinese adoptees think that they could be anyone they want to be, but the realities are much more complicated than what they have imagined. Being American is racialized. The stereotypes of "yellow perils" and "model minority" are imposed on AAAPIs by systemic racisms, and Chinese adoptees have been further marginalized in the racialized hierarchy. Because of their limited exposure to Chinese languages, foods, and cultures, some Chinese adoptees have deep-seated insecurity about their adoption and their racial identities. The pandemic has made them aware that being Chinese is in their blood—it is a part of who they are, no matter what. They have found groups online and built broader communities of support. Some have attempted to learn Chinese, cook Chinese dishes, and learn Chinese culture. Some have become proud of being both Chinese and American, "blending the two," even though they acknowledge the mistakes and shortcomings of America and recognize the issues that America needs to work on. They recognize where these two cultures have crossed over and the contributions that Asian Americans have made to America and the unique challenges that Asian Americans face.

For Chinese adoptees, being Chinese American is complicated; it means different things for different individuals, with many nuances and struggles related to any given meaning. Building broader coalitions with other people of color is important for them. Emma understood that other people of color faced different kinds of discrimination and problems, and she appreciated hearing about how they faced racisms and what they did to navigate their spaces. Emma had trouble connecting to her own Chinese culture and identity, and she liked to learn about the stories and experiences of BIPOC who had similar struggles.

As a social construct, race has impacted Chinese adoptees in complicated ways. When responding to my questions about what it means to be/become Chinese, American, and Chinese American or Asian American, Helen expressed her feelings about these identities:

> What it means to be Chinese is a combination of . . . it's very complicated . . . being Chinese is a bit of having pride, I think just having pride or identifying with the Chinese nation, the Chinese culture, whether [it] is taught to you and you're raised in it or if it's part of something . . . It's like how much I identify with being Chinese and I would say there are points in my life where I think growing up, I didn't want to identify as Chinese or didn't even want to think of myself as an Asian person. But I think especially for adoptees, international adoptees, whatever our home mother country is, whichever country we are adopted from, we have a hard relationship with that because we're a bit angry, I think. Especially for Chinese adoptees, it's like our country didn't want us so why should we have pride in the situation that we were born into? But it's still part of our story. I don't have to say that I love absolutely everything about China. I think there are things about China that I will like and enjoy: some of the music, the food, the people. But there are also critiques of the country in politics and all those things, and that's OK that I can like some things about China and dislike other things about China. I think for every citizen of whatever country you belong to, there are things that you're going to like about your own country and things that you dislike about it.
>
> I guess now I'll transfer to what it means to be American. That's if you identify with the history and culture of America, whether you're raised in it here . . . to have that pride in what it is to be American; the values in the history that this country has. My relationship with being American is also I like it sometimes and I don't like it other times. One is that there are certain privileges that come with being American, like I have an American passport. If I have an American passport, it's easier for me to get around the world, whereas if I have citizenship in other countries[, it is not as easy] . . . But then, I think especially being in my sector of who I surround myself politically with like what kind of community, I'm right on the edge of liberal and leftist, I kind of bounce back between the two. But I think all of us, if I would call myself and consider myself in those political communities, we do so much critique, so much hate of our own . . . we're guilty of our own country. We hate the things that this country has done. . . . I think you still can't be fully so blind to your way only and you need to balance both. Because I would say there are some positive things I do like about America and the USA. (Interview on March 10, 2021)

Coming Out of "the Fog"   137

Helen has thought carefully about the complicated intersections of her adoptee, Chinese, and American identities, and she recognizes the challenges and mixed emotions associated with being an international adoptee and her complex relationships with both the US and China. She has navigated the balance between appreciating and critiquing both Chinese and American cultures and politics. By examining the complexities of identity formation, the interplay between pride and critique, and the influence of personal experiences and political alignment on her perception of Chinese and American identities, Helen has developed a very nuanced view of her identities.

In the interview, Helen also discussed what it means to be Asian American. She thought that being Asian American meant having Asian heritage from a country in Asia and acknowledging the diversity of Asian countries. She emphasized that Asian adoptees, including Chinese adoptees, did not choose to become Asian American but rather ended up in the US due to adoption. She mentioned the possibility of being Asian with another cultural identity if they were adopted by families from different countries. She contrasted Asian adoptees with immigrant families who intentionally chose to move to the US and embrace an Asian American identity. She recognized the sacrifices made by immigrant families in leaving their homeland and intentionally choosing to experience life in America and acknowledged the unique challenges faced by immigrant groups in terms of acceptance and belonging.

Being Asian American, according to Helen, involves finding a balance between embracing American values and holding pride in one's Asian heritage. She emphasized the importance of both cultural backgrounds and the ability to incorporate beliefs and behaviors from both American and Asian values: "Being Asian American is having that balance between knowing that you act and behave and believe things that are both of American values and of your Chinese values, of your whatever homeland you're from in Asia. . . . Both holding pride in your mother country, your ancestry, and in whichever country, in the new country, that you decide to invest in its history."

Grace articulated similar understandings and defined being Chinese American as being able to accept or not accept, to proclaim and be proud of, one's ethnic heritage. Although she acknowledged that she was from China, she was not entirely resonant with the Chinese culture and dominant values as well as American ones. For her, "the synchronistic synthesis of cultures" is a very challenging process. Grace emphasized that being Chinese was being accepted by the Chinese community, and one of her biggest fears was being rejected by them as an adoptee. Even though Grace enjoyed studying the Chinese language, she learned it partially because she did not want to be rejected by the Chinese community. She believed that being connected with her heritage and culture was part of being Chinese and having that cultural identity. Grace struggled with her definition of being American, as she did not want to essentialize it and reinforce any stereotypes. She knew that America was made up of a diverse number of races and cultures. For her, being American was a "plethora of experiences," though she admitted that Americans struggled to accept others fully despite their diversity.

Jade, raised by her Latinx American mother and White Canadian father, felt comfortable identifying herself as "Asian American" instead of "Chinese American." Because she did not grow up with Chinese culture in the home, she did not feel "Chinese enough" to label herself as "Chinese American," and she hated it when other Chinese people thought she was not Chinese. As an American citizen, the broader term "Asian American" was more comfortable to her as an identity marker. In comparison, Katara felt more flexible about being Chinese American and Asian American. She discussed her definitions this way:

> I think being a Chinese American, bridging the gap between two cultures is important [and] being a role model for younger Asian Americans is also important. And there's such a spectrum that I think just being open to learning and accepting other Asian Americans of different backgrounds is important because maybe your parents are first-generation immigrants or maybe you were adopted. And I've definitely seen [that] this can get really cliquey. Just "Oh, I'm more Asian than you are" or "I'm a different Asian than you are," so I think just trying to be accepting [of] anyone who identifies in the realm. (Interview on March 3, 2021)

Katara opposed having "oppression Olympics" among Asian Americans and advocated for an inclusive view of Asian American identities. Sarah had similar ideas, but she realized the restricted agency that Chinese adoptees had in deciding who they wanted to be and how they wanted to live as well as the dilemma that Chinese adoptees faced in their daily lives:

> I think for adoptees like it's always framed as we're Chinese because we're born there, but like once we're adopted, we're the fake Chinese now. We feel even more fake than the American Born Chinese [ABC] do. And I think it's kind of sad because like we were born there, that's literally our motherland. And I feel like while all Asian Americans and all diaspora really in the US feel the pressure to either assimilate or to like completely reject it. I feel like adoptees, in particular, experience that from like day one and we feel like we don't really have any agency over it because our choice was already decided when we were shipped off here, right? So that's definitely something harder for us to work through because when we consider what it means to be Chinese, it's always

stuff that we never did growing up. So, for us, it's like a condemnation saying you aren't real, right? But again, I just feel like it's not so much real versus fake, it's just different experiences that are all real in their own way, right? So, all diaspora, whether we're assimilated or not, experience that and that's our reality. So, I feel like to be Chinese usually means learning language and culture first and foremost, because that's the initial thing that we lost. But then a lot of us feel that being Chinese means identifying with that more than White American society, which is making a choice to separate yourself from what you have experienced the majority of your life. (Interview on August 11, 2021)

Sarah articulated the complicated agencies of Chinese adoptees in making and representing their Chinese and Chinese American identifications. Being born in China and growing up in the US, Chinese adoptees often feel both connection and disconnection to Chinese and American societies and cultures. Different from ABC, who feel the pressure to either assimilate into or reject mainstream American culture, Chinese adoptees often feel that they do not have any agency in decisions around identity because this important choice was made by others when they were "shipped off" to the US at a very young age. Although many Chinese adoptees want to learn more about their cultural roots and heritage through languages, foods, and cultural traditions, some do not have enough resources to support them to do so. In addition, racisms in the US make it hard for them to identify strongly as Americans. They often have difficulties in feeling a sense of fully belonging to either Chinese or American communities. Sarah further articulated this dilemma: "It's always a hard decision, no matter which side you're going to pick for an adoptee. It's like you can never win, right? You're always going to be losing something that you experience. So I think for us, what it means to be Chinese will always be something that we're internally working through until we die really."

Some Chinese adoptees use "disidentifications"—different levels of disconnection from both Chinese and American identities—as a strategy to express their creative agencies in articulating their complicated feelings and fighting against racisms. José Esteban Muñoz (1999, 11) defines "disidentification" as a mode of dealing with dominant ideology that "neither opts to assimilate within such a narrative nor strictly opposes it" and that "works on and against dominant ideology." He writes, "Instead of buckling under the pressures of dominant ideology (identification, assimilation) or attempting to break free of its inescapable sphere (counteridentification, utopianism), this 'working on and against' is a strategy that tries to transform a cultural logic from within, always labouring to enact permanent structural change while at the same time valuing the importance of local or everyday struggles of resistance" (11–12). According to Muñoz, disidentifications are a way of negotiating one's identity in relation to the dominant culture, without fully conforming to or rejecting it. They are especially relevant for marginalized groups, such as queer people of color, who face multiple forms of oppression and discrimination. Muñoz argues that disidentification is a creative and performative act that allows these marginalized groups to create alternative spaces and modes of expression that challenge the normative structures of society. As discussed, Chinese adoptees draw on disidentifications as a strategy to combat racisms and build social justice by producing creative arts, music, dance, narratives, and festivals. They work "on and against" prevailing cultural norms, seeking to effect permanent structural transformation while recognizing the significance of everyday acts of resistance. Through their creative expressions, Chinese adoptees not only challenge existing cultural logics but also strive to enact lasting social change, forging a path toward a more inclusive and equitable future.

CONCLUSION

The pandemic has been a crucial time for many Chinese adoptees to come out of "the fog," understand the impacts of adoption and racisms on their lives, explore their cultural "origins" and "roots," reevaluate their friendships and family relationships, fight for social justice, and remake their (dis)identifications. The surging anti-Asian racisms caused tremendous pain and trauma for Chinese adoptees but also pushed them to take important actions to change the unjust social systems. They have formed their communities of support and crafted antiracist solidarities during the pandemic, not only because they wanted to, but because they had to. They have come together to face discrimination and racisms and fight for a just world, which has made them stronger and more united. Many Chinese adoptees have reconnected with their Chinese or Asian and adoptee identities and grown closer to their Chinese American or Asian American peers during the pandemic. When they help each other to go through crises, they become stronger and more hopeful.

When teaching my Anti-Asian Racism class in the spring of 2022, I asked my students to reflect on what it meant to be or become Asian American. One of the favorite responses was from a first-year female Native American student: "I think it means to accept who you are; to look forward to the future; to be determined; to be strong and resilient; to fight for what's right; to stand up for who you are and what you believe in, all the while not losing sight of either of those." Another popular response came from an Asian American queer student: "To me being Asian American means having hope, resilience, love, and beauty flowing through our veins. The stories of the traumas inflicted on the past generations who immigrated seeking new opportunities for their families resonate in our collective identity. Overcoming adversities and building cultural bridges while establishing new intersectional identities revolutionized our modern understanding of race as a social construct and creating new conversations around nationality, culture, and ethnicity." These two responses presented my students' solid understanding of becoming Asian American. As members of AAAPI and BIPOC communities, we are determined not to forget our history and the lessons it teaches us. We strive to create a better life and a better world by actively finding, forming, and fostering our communities of support and advocating for social justice for all.

Chinese adoptees in the US face unique challenges and opportunities as they navigate their (dis)identifications. According to International Adoption (Black 2018), from 1999 to 2016, 78,257 Chinese children were adopted by Americans, accounting for almost one-third of all Chinese children adopted internationally. Originally, healthy baby girls were readily available for adoption, attracting many American families. However, recent changes in governmental policy have led to a decrease in healthy girls available for adoption. Currently, the majority of adoptions from China are of children with special needs (ibid.).

Chinese adoptees in the US need support to overcome challenges and thrive. Addressing systemic racisms involves tackling underlying factors such as disparities in housing, education, and healthcare. Governments can help by funding mental health services for adoptees and their families and supporting Asian American and Pacific Islander (AAPI) studies in education. Respecting adoptees' self-identifications, building diverse communities, supporting their political activisms, and providing mentorship are also important. Supporting Chinese adoptees requires a continuous commitment to listening, learning, and taking action from everyone.

First, addressing interpersonal hate-fueled violence alone is insufficient to combat systemic racisms. Our efforts must address the underlying factors contributing to systemic racisms and promote the well-being of individuals and communities. These factors encompass unjust disparities in housing, education, employment, healthcare, transportation, and immigration status experienced by marginalized groups such as AAAPI communities. These inequities make certain groups—including the elderly, disabled, LGBTQIA+, youth, and women—more susceptible to interpersonal and systemic racisms. It is crucial to improve conditions for AAAPIs, particularly women, by ensuring access to economic assistance, childcare, and healthcare. We need to dismantle the White racist logics and systems that unjustly marginalize and exclude AAAPI communities and other communities of color.

Second, governments need to provide funding for mental health services for Chinese adoptees and their families, including fully funding services and training programs for mental health professionals serving AAAPIs. Special fellowships could be created to support young adult adoptees in becoming mental health providers who can act as first responders in AAAPI mental health crises. Moreover, governments should assist Chinese adoptees and their families in accessing adoption-specific resources such as support groups, counseling services, educational programs, and online materials related to Chinese languages, literature, cultures, and history.

Third, governments should support AAPI studies in both K–12 and higher education, a change that will benefit all students across diverse racial and gender identifications. By recognizing and valuing AAPI voices, stories, and experiences, AAPI studies foster a deeper understanding of systemic racisms, confront the root causes of racist beliefs that lead to hate crimes and violence, and encourage students to create action-based, future-oriented solutions to our long-existing problems of racisms.

Fourth, we should respect Chinese adoptees' choices and preferences regarding their (dis)identifications. Some adoptees prefer to self-identify as Chinese, Asian American, or both, while others do not feel a strong connection to either. Some want to search for their birth families, while others may not. We should not impose our expectations or assumptions on them but rather listen to their voices and support them in doing whatever they want to do.

Fifth, we need to continue to build diverse communities of support to engage Chinese adoptees and their families. AAAPI families may collaborate with Chinese adoptees and their families to celebrate Chinese festivals, cook traditional meals, and participate in cultural events that create spaces for open dialogues and cultural exchanges. These communities could facilitate opportunities for Chinese adoptees to connect with China, such as returning tourism, cultural ambassador programs, or internship opportunities in China. They could also support organizations and initiatives that advocate for the rights and well-being of Chinese adoptees.

Last but not least, we should support Chinese adoptees in their political activisms as best we can. It is important to provide platforms and opportunities for Chinese adoptees to share their perspectives and experiences and to speak out. We need to understand and validate their unique experiences and challenges and learn about the historical and systemic factors that influence their lives, such as transracial adoption, racisms, and the intersectionality of their identifications. Policymakers need to engage in collaborative efforts and allyship with Chinese adoptees; actively seek partnerships with adoptee-led organizations, groups, and communities; and support their initiatives and campaigns. Schools, colleges, and universities should offer mentorship and guidance to Chinese adoptees, connect them with supportive networks, provide educational resources, and help them grow personally and professionally. Legislators should support legislative initiatives and policies that promote equality, inclusivity, and the rights of Chinese adoptees and AAAPIs and stand in solidarity with them. Supporting Chinese adoptees is an ongoing process and commitment to listening, learning, and taking action from everyone. It is important to follow their lead, respect their autonomy, and provide the necessary support and resources to empower them to pursue their political agendas and advocacy efforts.

5

"GOING HOME"

Chinese Lay Buddhist Women, Diverse Agencies, and Hybrid Communities

BEFORE THE PANDEMIC STARTED, I worked on a collaborative project about the transmission of Buddhism among lay women in rural northern China. I conducted my fieldwork at Z Temple in southern Shanxi and Longquan Monastery in suburban Beijing in the summer of 2019. I interviewed about twenty lay women from all social classes about their situations and experiences of becoming Buddhists in contemporary China. I expected to go back to do follow-up fieldwork; however, the COVID-19 pandemic broke out in late 2019, and strict travel restrictions prevented me from traveling to China in 2020. I consequently conducted virtual ethnography by participating in two WeChat sutra study groups in 2020.

Due to lockdowns, my whole family was stuck in Florida from early March to late July 2020. In early 2020, I collaborated with a group of interdisciplinary scholars in China to conduct interviews about ordinary Chinese people's experiences of and reflections on the pandemic, and I soon also focused on the lived experiences of Chinese and Chinese Americans (CCA) in the US after the pandemic became global. In the beginning as people dealt with the health crisis and its effects, I had difficulty recruiting participants. Fortunately, Andy Dai, the president of the Huagen Chinese School, which my son attended, kindly offered his help and recruited about twenty contributors for me; I used snowball sampling to recruit more contributors. I then met Jingshu (born 1962), a lay Buddhist woman, and she introduced me to her Chinese Buddhist reading group. All group members were CCA women and first-generation immigrants.[1] They met every Sunday afternoon for Dharma study in the Chinese language. The host, Shuilian (born 1966), along with several of the women, was associated with a nearby Tibetan Buddhist meditation and practice center (TBC). Led by Lama L, a White male American lama and resident teacher, the center was supervised by the national TBC organization. The center is affiliated with one of the four main schools of Tibetan Buddhism, and their tradition emphasizes practice. This entails not only studying Buddhist concepts but also actively applying these teachings, both during meditation sessions and in daily life. Their teachings encompass the three vehicles, or *yanas*, of the Buddhist path as taught in Tibet: the smaller vehicle of Hinayana, the greater vehicle of Mahayana, and the Vajrayana, a form of Mahayana that upholds the bodhisattva ideal and offers potent techniques leading to enlightenment within a single lifetime. This continuous lineage of teachings prioritizes the practice of compassion and meditation.

Shuilian founded the reading group in the spring of 2016, and when COVID-19 emerged, the group transitioned to online meetings, utilizing WeChat as their meeting platform. However, in September 2020, the Trump administration issued an executive order prohibiting the operations of TikTok and WeChat, the popular messaging service owned by the Chinese company Tencent (Rogers and Kang 2021). Faced with uncertainties, the group swiftly shifted to using Zoom while continuing to use WeChat for group chats. In June 2021, President Biden revoked Trump's executive order attempting to ban TikTok and WeChat (ibid.). Nevertheless, the group continued to meet on Zoom until the time of writing this chapter in 2023.

Starting from June 21, 2020, I became a regular attendee of the virtual reading group's Sunday afternoon meetings. The group was diverse in terms of age, experiences, and family backgrounds. Most members held MA or PhD degrees earned in the US, and a few were tenured professors at prestigious research universities. In 2020, our focus was on reading the Chinese edition of *In Love with the World: A Monk's Journey Through the Bardos of Living and Dying*, authored by Yongey Mingyur Rinpoche (2019). During our meetings, we took turns reading the text aloud and engaged in profound discussions. I found great delight in these open conversations, as group members shared their personal experiences and practices openly. One of our youngest members was Fanghua (born 1990), a graduate student at a renowned research university; unfortunately, she left the group upon graduating. Soon after, Lan, a newly tenured professor at the same university, joined us. At one meeting, Lan recounted a challenging episode of illness when she found herself alone in bed with a high fever, without anyone to assist her. Other group members immediately offered help and asked her to call them for anything

146   Impacts of the COVID-19 Pandemic on Chinese and Chinese American Women

she might need if she got sick again. Some of the members were single professional women, and some lived alone when their spouses and children were working or studying in other places. The pandemic exaggerated their sense of loneliness, and through the reading group, they crafted hybrid communities and supported each other to go through the pandemic together.

This chapter focuses on the impacts of the COVID-19 pandemic on Chinese lay Buddhist women in the US, and how they responded to the pandemic and anti-Asian racisms. Here Chinese lay Buddhist women in the US refer to Chinese women who practice Buddhism but are not ordained as nuns and who have settled permanently or temporarily in the US. They live a secular life, engaging in daily activities like work and family responsibilities while integrating Buddhist practices and teachings into their lives. In contrast, Buddhist American women refer to more diverse individuals and groups. This category may include American women from various racial and ethnic backgrounds, including those who are not of Asian descent. They might have converted to Buddhism or been born into Buddhist families. Their practices, traditions, and cultural integration of Buddhism can differ significantly based on their individual backgrounds, schools of Buddhism they follow, and personal interpretations of the teachings. Chinese lay Buddhist women in the US have specific cultural traditions that influence their practices and understandings of Buddhism, whereas Buddhist American women may come from a variety of cultural backgrounds and thus have a more diverse range of practices and interpretations of Buddhism.

Throughout history and in the contemporary world, Buddhist ideas and practices both empower and limit women in pursuing their personal and spiritual interests and agendas (DeVido 2010; Y. Li 2020; Tsomo 1999, 2004, 2006). Women have played significant roles in Buddhist societies since the time of the Buddha, but their contributions have largely gone unrecognized until recently. In the past several decades, Buddhist women have "come out of the shadows" and begun to take active roles in both the spheres of religion and social transformation (Tsomo 2006). Current scholarship on Buddhist women primarily centers on the lives and experiences of nuns or lay Buddhist women in Asia (Cheng 2007; DeVido 2010; Y. Li 2020; Yü 2013). This focus has led to a significant gap in scholarship, particularly in the study of Asian lay Buddhist women in the global contexts. My research aims to bridge this gap by exploring the unique experiences, practices, challenges, and opportunities faced by Chinese lay Buddhist women in the US. By shifting the lens to include this specific group, my study not only broadens the scope of understanding in Buddhist studies but also contributes to a more inclusive view of the diverse Buddhist communities in global contexts.

The data for this study were gathered through virtual ethnography conducted with the Buddhist reading group and three other Buddhist WeChat groups (368 members) from 2020 to 2023, supplemented by seven in-depth interviews. Among the seven interviewees, Jingshu, Shuilian, and Fanghua were in the reading group; Ning (born 1971) and Xianhong (born 1968) came to visit their family members in the US; Sarah (born 2001) was a Chinese adoptee; and the last one was Lama Kate, a White American Buddhist woman. Particularly, Xianhong was affiliated with Longquan Monastery in China, and she was my research guide when I conducted my fieldwork there in 2019. She visited her son in the US from November 22, 2021, to July 20, 2022, and I interviewed her officially on December 26, 2021. Sarah, a college student, was interviewed on Zoom on August 11, 2021. Lama Kate, a colleague of Lama L, is the resident teacher of a TBC in central Ohio, and I invited her to share her stories with my students in the fall of 2021. I also integrate the twenty interviews that I conducted in China in 2019 into my analysis.

When Buddhist practitioners practice taking refuge, with Sangha or spiritual community surrounded, they join their palms and say: "I take refuge in the Buddha. I take refuge in the Dharma. I take refuge in the Sangha." This is viewed as the practice of "going home" or "coming home," an important metaphor in Buddhism (Hanh 2000, 2016; Robyn 2019). As Satya Robyn (2019, 33–34) writes, "When we practice taking refuge, sometimes we feel a result, and sometimes we don't. Over time, however, we begin to notice a firmer kind of ground under our feet. We get a glimpse of how it might be to live with the freedom of faith. We begin to find our way home."

For my contributors, "going home" or "coming home" means understanding the Four Noble Truths and achieving nirvana. The Four Noble Truths comprise the essence of Buddha's teachings, and they include the truth of suffering, the truth of the cause of suffering, the truth of the end of suffering, and the truth of the path that leads to the end of suffering. They believe that when one achieves nirvana, a transcendent state free from sufferings and the cycles of birth and rebirth, spiritual enlightenment would be obtained. According to Shuilian, everyone has the Buddha nature, and "going home" is to realize one's Buddha nature and achieve enlightenment.

Chinese lay Buddhist women are active agents of their diverse religious lives, but their stories and voices are often overlooked in Asian studies, Asian American studies, religious studies, and women's, gender, and sexuality studies. My goal is to examine how Chinese lay Buddhist women articulate, cultivate, and exercise their creative agencies in constructing their identities, crafting hybrid communities, empowering themselves to go through their life crises and the pandemic, and fighting against racisms.

In this chapter, I present the following themes that illuminate the experiences and agencies of Chinese lay Buddhist women in the US: (1) a brief introduction to Buddhism in the US and racisms against Asians; (2) agencies of Chinese lay Buddhist women; (3) self-identifications of Chinese lay Buddhist women; (4) crafting hybrid communities; (5) the role of Buddhism in coping with the pandemic; and (6) combating anti-Asian racisms and facing death.

Buddhism in the US and Racisms against Asians

Buddhism has been practiced in Asian countries and regions for more than 2,500 years (Cantwell 2009). It primarily has two major traditions: Mahayana Buddhism, prevalent in China and Japan, and Theravada Buddhism, prevalent in Southeast Asia. Theravada Buddhism, the older tradition, still adheres to the early Buddhist canon written in a classical Indian language, Pāli. Mahayana Buddhism was developed in India around the first century BCE and integrates the main sutras of early Buddhism and various newer sutras (Burton 2017; Cantwell 2009). Buddhism was first introduced to China during the Han Dynasty (202 BCE–220 CE), and it is the most influential religion among the five officially legitimatized religions (Buddhism, Daoism, Catholicism, Protestantism, and Islam) in contemporary China (Ji 2012; Ji, Fisher, and Laliberté 2019).

Buddhism is the largest institutionalized religion in China and also a major religion among Chinese communities worldwide. Buddhism was introduced into the US by Asian immigrants in the nineteenth century, and since then the US has been the home to diverse groups of Asian Buddhists, including Chinese, Japanese, Korean, Sri Lankan, Thai, Cambodian, and Vietnamese Buddhists, along with Buddhists with family backgrounds in most Buddhist countries and regions (Prebish 1999; Seager 2012). The Immigration and Nationality Act of 1965 increased the number of immigrants—and thus Buddhists—arriving from China, Vietnam, and the Theravada-practicing countries of Southeast Asia (Seager 2012). But this law privileged highly educated and professional immigrants from Asia and excluded immigrants with lower levels of education and those lacking professional skills.

The first Buddhist temple in America was built in 1853 in San Francisco by the Sze Yap Company, a Chinese Buddhist fraternal society, followed by a second Buddhist temple built in 1854 by another Chinese American fraternal society (ARDA, n.d.; Seager 2012). By 1875 there were eight Buddhist temples, and by 1900 about four hundred Chinese Buddhist temples could be found on the West Coast of the US (ibid.). Unfortunately, these Chinese

"Going Home" 149

Buddhist temples became targets of racisms and were viewed negatively by some Americans (Ford 2006).

From 1878 to 1952, a series of court decisions and laws barred Asian immigrants from becoming US citizens, and immigration itself was restricted in various ways from 1858 to 1965. There were countless acts of terrorism and violence against Asian immigrants, from the ghettoization and lynching of Chinese during and after the California gold rush, to the World War II internment of Japanese and Japanese Americans (Takaki 2008). In response to racisms enforced by law, propaganda, and violence, Asian immigrants and their descendants developed various Buddhist communities on the ground to cope with their life struggles and living situations (Hickey 2010).

It is difficult to know the accurate number of Buddhists in the US today. According to *The 2020 Census of American Religion* (PRRI Staff 2021), Buddhist Americans make up 1 percent of the US population as of 2020 (about three million people); Buddhist Americans are primarily concentrated in Hawai'i and the West Coast, particularly in the San Francisco Bay Area. In addition, 9 percent of Asian Americans and Pacific Islanders (AAPIs) are Buddhists, and the median age of Buddhist American adults is thirty-six, significantly lower than the median age for all Americans (forty-seven) and among the youngest of all religious groups (ibid.). However, the self-identification of religious affiliation is complicated in the US. Many individuals who are deeply devoted to the Dharma and Buddhist practices do not openly identify themselves as Buddhists.

This census and other similar surveys reveal racisms and White supremacy in at least three ways. First, who has the authority to define "Buddhist Americans"? In the US, it is mainly White Buddhists who are busy creating that definition and defining it on their terms (Hickey 2010). This sense of entitlement is often a form of racism. Second, the surveys were often conducted in English, and thus the results exclude Buddhists (and others) who speak diverse Asian languages. In other words, the linguistic parameters of the census exclude Asian, Asian American, and Pacific Islander (AAAPI) Buddhists (and others). Third, these surveys often pay no attention to Asian international students and other Asian individuals who lived in the US temporarily and are not American citizens—the reports simply exclude them from the American religious landscape.

Over the past several decades, scholars who study Buddhism in America have created numerous typologies to describe different categories of Buddhists in the US, including styles of practice, degrees of institutional stability, modes of transmission to the US, race, ethnicities, and so on (Layman 1976; Numrich 1996, 2000, 2003; Prebish 1999; Seager 2012). Most taxonomies include a divide between convert Buddhists, characterized as predominantly White, and "heritage" or "ethnic" Buddhists, characterized as AAAPI immigrants and refugees and their descendants. Wakoh Shannon Hickey (2010) critically reviews these taxonomies and considers two dynamics: the impacts of racism and White supremacy on the development of American Buddhist communities and the impacts of unconscious White privilege in scholarly discourses and debates about these communities. Hickey criticizes the "ethnic" category and proposes other ways to conceptualize the diverse, dynamic, and fluid forms of Buddhism in the US.

While race and ethnicity as social constructs are important, any academic typology of Buddhist communities that bases categories on race and ethnicity must be viewed with caution. The category of "ethnic Buddhists" has reified identities that are multiple, fluid, and dynamic. It is also problematic to objectify diverse AAAPI communities, groups, and individuals as if they were homogenous. Taxonomies that reify "ethnic Buddhists" apply the term *ethnic* only to people who are not White. To assume that Whiteness is the norm against which "ethnic" is defined is another example of racism and White supremacy (Hickey 2010).

To dismantle racisms and White supremacy and to decolonize the field of religious studies, the key step is to recenter those marginalized and peripheral individuals and communities and to make them visible. The decolonizing approach "challenges mainstream, hegemonic, dominant theories of knowledge, language, power, and politics . . . it is an active, ongoing struggle for social justice in every sense—economic, political, cultural, racial, gender, and so forth—at every level in every arena" (McLaren 2017, 10). Employing a decolonizing approach, I intend to explore the self-identifications of Chinese lay Buddhist women on their own terms and delve into their endeavors of self-empowerment, community building, and social engagement with their creative agencies before and during the pandemic.

Agencies of Chinese Lay Buddhist Women

Scholars from various disciplines have been actively exploring the complicated relationships between individuals and structures. The development of agency theories emerges out of the sense that many power theories overlook the role of agency exercised by individuals, groups, and communities. Both Pierre Bourdieu (1977) and Anthony Giddens (1976, 1979) have shown that structures exist in their instantiation through performances and actions of hybrid social agents in a given situation, historical time, and sociopolitical contexts, and agency always has relative independence and contingency.

Religion has proved to be a fertile site to interrogate, develop, complicate, and export gender theories of agency and to articulate the concept's limitations and enduring biases (Avishai 2016). Orit Avishai (2016, 266) writes, "Religion emerged as a double-edged sword that reproduced gendered power dynamics but also empowered women—thus, an ideal site to develop and refine feminist notions of agency in the context of ostensibly oppressive social structures." The work of anthropologist Saba Mahmood (2005) created spaces for alternative theories that represented a nonliberal agentic subject and located agency, docility, compliance, and piety in conforming with religious ideals in the way that individuals comply, produce, and transform selves into virtuous religious subjects. She suggests that women's agency could not be defined only in terms of resistance, counterdiscourse, subversion, and dislocation of dominant structures, but must also consider humility, modesty, self-effacement, and self-sacrificing morals of pious, submissive, and socially conservative women.

Mahmood's postcolonial approach to women's agency has been applied to Chinese religious studies. Mayfair Yang (2020, 227) tackles the question of "how female agency works historically to reproduce, as well as to reconfigure or derail, patriarchal structures." By examining five different modes of women's religious agency in Wenzhou—self-sacrifice, self-cultivation, religious sisterhoods, divine social actions, grassroots initiatives, and leadership—Yang illustrates diverse ways that women "contributed to strengthening, adjusting or transforming patriarchal structures" (253).

Recent scholarship shows that Buddhism often provides Chinese women with a means of more personal self-fashioning and self-expression (Y. Li 2020; Yü 2013). Chün-fang Yü (2013) studies the Incense Light (Xiangguang) community of Buddhist nuns formed in Taiwan in 1974 and illustrates how the nuns have fashioned their own approaches to Buddhism and the promotion of Buddhism by college Buddhist studies societies, Xiangguang's seminary, and its curriculum for adult laypeople. In particular, she describes the contradictory ideas of nuns about their femininity. For example, some nuns conceal their feminity to transcend the idea of gender. Meanwhile, they see this feminity as an essence that is, according to the nun Wuyin, very similar to the essence of Buddhism. Wuyin might not be a feminist in the eyes of Western feminist scholars, but she has problematized unequal gender relations in both societies and Buddhist institutions and found her own way to empower herself and other nuns. Yuhang Li (2020) examines how lay Buddhist women in late imperial China used their bodies to creatively express devotion to the bodhisattva Guanyin, whose fluid gender identity had become largely feminized by the late imperial period. These lay women identified with Guanyin through their own artistic and aesthetic skills in different "modes" to build connections with Guanyin that were uniquely and intimately their own, and these "modes" included dance performance, painting, embroidery with hair, and jewelry making.

Here I intend to illustrate how Chinese lay Buddhist women in the US have reproduced and negotiated their diverse agencies across various contexts. Traditionally, a Chinese woman's role was defined by her submission to three men: her father, her husband, and her son during different stages of their lives. The neo-Confucian cults of feminine chastity and virtue to constrain women's sexuality were especially strong in the Ming (1368–1644) and Qing (1636/1644–1912) Dynasties (Carlitz 1994; Johnson 1983). These Confucian moral values known as the "three obediences" met fundamental challenges beginning in the early twentieth century in China and no longer have a significant impact on Chinese women today. However, Chinese women continue to face unequal gender relations and patriarchies in both public and private spheres despite rapid social, cultural, political, and economic changes (Fincher 2014; Sung 2023). As China began to reform in the late 1970s, promises of equality bolstered in the Mao era became intertwined with reemerging elements of the Confucian patriarchal system (Hershatter 2007; Rofel 2007; Zarafonetis 2017). As such, Chinese women continue to encounter difficulties in their lives such as discrimination, illness, poverty, family woes, domestic violence, human trafficking, disproportionate impact from crime, and others. When some Chinese women immigrated to the US, they could pursue roles that were not available to them in their home societies (C. Chen 2005; Di 2021). As gender norms shift in transnational contexts, Chinese lay Buddhist women have created their own spaces to exert their creative agencies in their everyday lives.

Sarah was born in 2001 in Jiangsu Province, China, and adopted in 2002 by her White Christian parents in New York state. She was raised in a predominantly White environment and did not have much exposure to Asian culture. Most Asian people she knew growing up were also adoptees, and they knew each other because they came from the same adoption agency or through adoption networks. Sarah did not know a lot about her cultural roots and heritage, and she felt "stuck" within the adoptee community as a result. Sarah explained how and when she became a Buddhist and how Buddhism helped her cope with life crises:

SARAH: I was raised by very, very evangelical Christians. So that's like a complete 360. So that's really all I was exposed to when I was younger and that's obviously very American, too. But then when I got older, I obviously left that for a number of reasons like personal and political motivations. But I started learning more about Eastern philosophy and that's how I got exposed to Buddhism and, yeah, that's how I started practicing.

INTERVIEWER: When did you start practicing Buddhism?

SARAH: I would say probably in high school because, in my senior year, I went through a really bad period of depression. So that's kind of what motivated me to start practicing more.

INTERVIEWER: Did you find any masters or Buddhist groups?

SARAH: I listen to a lot of those online because there's a various amount of good resources and stuff both in English and Chinese to talk about different teachings. I don't live in an area that has any Chinese Buddhist temples and groups. Obviously like it's . . . there aren't very many Chinese people at home. But I am hoping after I graduate, I am hoping to move back to China and then get involved with the community then.

INTERVIEWER: How do you think that Buddhism helps you cope with a crisis like depression and also the COVID-19 pandemic?

SARAH: I think, honestly, it kind of helped me cope with adoption in the beginning, because like I started seeing someone to talk about the adoption stuff, because like it got really bad, and obviously I didn't really know anyone else that was experienced in the field of adoption. So, I ended up seeing counselors later when I was in high school. And honestly, just a lot of like the teachings and stuff help[ed] me like work through a lot of like the aspects of adoption. So basically, the first thing that all adoptees experience in life is loss. From the very beginning, we lost pretty much everything we knew, right? We had that replaced by whatever it is when we were adopted. So, the idea of impermanence and suffering and stuff is just very applicable to us. But in the same way, Buddhism is very transformative, it teaches you to basically transform all of that into wisdom and compassion and just all that stuff is just like really moving. (Interview on August 11, 2021)

As an adoptee, Sarah experienced loss, pain, and suffering, and she turned to Buddhism to cope—it helped her transform her sense of loss and suffering into "wisdom and compassion," and it changed how she perceived herself, her adoption, and the world around her. She learned how to move beyond her feelings of loss, recover from the trauma of adoption, and live her own meaningful life. During the pandemic, Sarah continued to practice meditation and study the Dharma, and her peaceful mindfulness helped her get through this difficult and frightening time.

Buddhism seeks to address various social challenges, such as psychological stress, emotional imbalance, and the strains of modern life. It promotes self-control, respect for others and the environment, frugality, temperance, reflexivity, and altruism. These principles are seen as potential remedies to current ecological, climatic, economic, or spiritual crises (Obadia 2020). Buddhist traditions and practices are very diverse and are not exclusive to the context of the pandemic, but they are significant parts of Buddhism's global spread. Many lay Buddhist women whom I interviewed in both China and the US drew on Buddhism to get through crises in their lives. In China, Lian lost six children and many other family members. She also went through the painful experience of divorce. Her soul was relentlessly tortured with loss and separation. Eventually she found peace when she first became a lay Buddhist and then a nun. Di also experienced betrayal and divorce in her marriage; she was ordained as a nun in July 2019. Hao was diagnosed with uterine fibroids and had several surgeries before she became a Buddhist. Thirty-year-old lay Buddhist Miaoru was fired by her company without legitimate reason, causing her to lose her desire and motivation to find new work. Wang felt trapped in her real estate business by her peers and lost a great fortune before practicing Buddhism. At Z Temple I met three women in their late seventies and early eighties who knew that death was right around the corner and wished to achieve nirvana. Hao said that women, particularly those who suffer tremendously in their lives, made up most of the participants in all the Buddhist temples she visited and that they made a "merit field" (*futian*)—a conceptual space or field of positive energy created by the virtuous actions of enlightened beings, which serves as a source for accumulating merit and generating good karma—for their entire families after taking refuge in the Three Treasures. Many lay Buddhist women emphasized that Buddhism helped them find meaning in life and empowered them to transcend life and death.

Both Jingshu and Fanghua told me that they encountered some life crises before joining the reading group in Florida. As Jingshu summarized, "I think what Buddhism has inspired me the most is that the Buddha teaches us to let go of our attachment. If we let go of our attachment, we will face fewer problems, relatively we will become more flexible, and we will have more and broader choices. Of course, this is related to the idea that I could only transform myself, and I could not transform the environment or anyone. So it is this idea that makes me live a free and happy life" (interview on July 3, 2020).

Living a peaceful, "free and happy" life is what many Chinese women desired before and during the pandemic, although they experience and practice Buddhism in different ways. They cultivate and exercise agencies in their lives by seeking a peaceful mindset, joy, a sense of meaning and belonging, and self-empowerment. Within transnational contexts, Chinese women have navigated through different gender norms, cultures, and systems and created space to transform themselves and their communities.

Self-Identifications of Chinese Lay Buddhist Women

On October 17, 2021, the study group read and discussed the final chapters of the Chinese edition of *Almost Buddhist* (正见), written by Dzongsar Jamyang Khyentse Rinpoche (2018). In our discussion, the main questions included the following: Who are Buddhists? How do we define our own identities? Is Buddhism religion? What is religion? Reading group members' definitions of Buddhist varied, but their main ideas could be summarized into three categories: (1) Buddhists are people who take refuge in the Three Treasures (the Buddha, the Dharma, and the Sangha), including lay Buddhists and monastics; (2) Buddhists are people who believe in Buddhism or are willing to believe in Buddhism; and (3) true Buddhists are those who accept and practice the Four Noble Truths. The first definition is a popular response among group members, the second one is very inclusive, and the third one is from *Almost Buddhist*.

Despite different definitions, "Buddhist" is not a term used by all group members. Wenxin preferred to call herself and her fellows "the followers of the Buddha." Wenxin was a scientist and a retired professor who earned her BA degree at a top university in China and then came to the US to pursue her PhD in physics. After graduation, she became a university professor and had a successful career. She was one of those intellectuals who opposed situating Buddhism in both religious and organizational frameworks. She knew it was normal to have religious leaders and hierarchical organizations in many religious traditions, and religious leaders often had the power and authority to make important decisions and judgments. But Wenxin believed that there were no such leaders and systems in Buddhism, and there were no authoritative figures who had the power to decide who was or was not a true Buddhist. This lack of organization and centralization might seem confusing to some people, but Wenxin thought that it was a blessing because every system and every source of power in the human world might be corrupt.

Wenxin called herself "the follower of the Buddha" and believed that she was her own master. She also knew that it was important for her and other "followers of the Buddha" to find qualified gurus (spiritual teachers) to take efforts to teach them. According to her, one's guru was respected more than the Buddha, because it was this guru who brought the truth to one's door— looking for a guru was like looking for one's adviser in graduate school, and one must choose cautiously because once one chose a guru, one must fully value, respect, and accept this guide.

The group members had different opinions about whether Buddhism was a religion and how to define religion. Shuilian thought that Buddhism was a body of teachings, not religion. Wenxin recalled how she once debated the definition of religion with a Christian, a Daoist, and an atheist. She articulated how Buddhism was different from other religions, highlighting that there was no creator in Buddhism and that Buddhism stressed the central role of the mind in knowing and experiencing the truth. Although Wenxin and her friends disagreed with each other about the definition of religion, they understood and respected the significant role of religion in people's lives.

The definition of religion is further complicated if we situate the concept in translingual and transnational contexts. In Chinese language, there is no word and concept exactly equivalent to the English word and concept of "religion." The Chinese word frequently translated as "religion," *zongjiao*, means organized bodies of spiritual teachings. In Chinese culture, the sharp opposition and separation of sacred and secular that occurs in the West does not exist. This distinction was made part of Emile Durkheim's ([1912] 1995) widely used definition of religion, but it is problematic in Chinese contexts.

No matter whether they viewed Buddhism as religion or as being close to "a philosophy of life" and "a science of mind," group members agreed that Buddhism was straightforward and down-to-earth in practice. By studying and practicing together, they have helped each other pursue Buddhism's knowledge of the mind, use that wisdom to empower their lives, and achieve enlightenment. It is this sense of belonging that matters the most to these women.

The discussion among group members is always ongoing in WeChat, which strengthens their sense of belonging. On October 19, 2021, Lan cited one paragraph from *Emotional Rescue* to summarize our discussion about Buddhism and Buddhists: "To be a Buddhist means you are willing to actually work with your mind to develop your inherent potential to manifest wisdom and compassion" (Ponlop 2016, 191). In response to Lan's citations, Shuilian emphasized that everyone possessed the Buddha nature, and everyone had the inherent potential to attain Buddhahood, a state of enlightenment filled with compassion and wisdom. According to her, ultimately, the Buddha path was about who we were, and how we worked with our mind and our Buddha nature. The path was not something "out there" that we need to go find; instead, it was about dealing with who we were, what we were, and how we could let our Buddha nature shine.

CRAFTING HYBRID COMMUNITIES

By integrating Gareth Fisher's (2016) "textual-community approach" with Cristina Rocha's (2006) concepts of "hybrid" and "creolization," I use "hybrid communities" to refer to the integration of teaching-centered, master-centered, and free-distribution textual communities that exist both on- and off-line with the diverse individuals and groups in Buddhism. The Buddhist communities that I study are hybrid communities in myriad ways.

Fisher proposes "a textual-community approach" to studying religious beliefs and practices of lay Buddhists in post-Mao China. He defines "the model of textual community" as "a type of discursive community where people belong to particular social (and, in this case, religious) units based on whether they share the reading and discussion of a particular set of texts" (2016, 260). He uses the term *text* broadly to refer to various printed and multimedia materials and further delineates three broad types of Buddhist textual communities in post-Mao China: "(1) teaching-centered communities based largely on particular schools of Buddhist thought, such as Chan; (2) master-centered communities, sectarian-type Buddhist movements centering on the spiritual instruction of a particular monastic or lay teacher who usually produces their own closed sets of texts and multimedia materials; and (3) a free-distribution textual community centered on the writing, printing, and distribution of a wide variety of Buddhist texts and multimedia materials on different Buddhist topics that are exchanged and discussed at state-recognized Buddhist temple sites" (261). Fisher examines these groups as "largely nonoverlapping textual communities" and argues that "individual religious groups are often more socially homogeneous than they might first appear" (261–62). I find that these "textual communities" are not separated in transnational contexts. Furthermore, Buddhist groups and communities are not socially or culturally homogeneous on the ground. Participants in Buddhist communities vary widely in age, class, education level, occupation, and individual agenda, although they might study the same sutras with the same Dharma masters. Such communities are not stable but rather fluid and constantly changing.

The Buddhist communities that I study are simultaneously teaching-centered, master-centered, and text-centered. The participants in the reading group share knowledge of a collection of Buddhist scriptures, especially *A Lamp for the Path to Enlightenment*, interpretations of Buddhist teachings by contemporary masters, and various printed and multimedia materials centered on the sutras. Moreover, these communities have been bonded both in person and online. Before the pandemic, masters at TBCs offered both in-person and online classes, but all the activities went online during the early lockdowns. Jingshu explained why the reading group decided to meet virtually: "our Lama is an American; he is more than seventy years old. At the beginning of 2019, he had his second or third stroke. Later, when he had recovered, we said that because of the pandemic we did not want to go to the Buddha Hall [*fotang*] again. Therefore, for the sake of Lama, we basically study Buddhism online.... We learned about meditation online, and masters also taught us how to coexist with COVID-19 during the pandemic, and how to reduce our anxiety" (interview on July 3, 2020).

Shuilian also discussed the transition of Buddhist classes and retreats to online platforms during the pandemic, highlighting both positive and negative outcomes of this shift. On the positive side, she noted that the accessibility of online classes and retreats made it convenient for individuals to engage in Buddhism without the need for travel, air tickets, and hotel accommodations. But she expressed concerns that the ease of access might diminish the value of these learning opportunities for some participants, leading to a lack of appreciation. In addition, distractions in their surroundings could hinder their ability to fully concentrate on their learning. Shuilian also observed a trend where more people sought classes with influential masters, leaving lesser-known and upcoming masters with inadequate attention and recognition. This disparity in attention might have adverse effects on the prospects of young and rising masters. Moreover, the shift to online formats resulted in declining donations to Dharma centers, leading to financial crises in some Buddhist centers.

In *Zen in Brazil*, Cristina Rocha (2006) provides an insightful interpretation of the concepts "hybrid" and "creolization," both of which she uses to describe processes of cultural mixing and globalization as Zen develops in Brazil. The term *hybrid* refers to "the meeting of two or more cultures, practices, and beliefs" (19). The trope of creolization shows "how the process of hybridity takes place" (16). It is "not a product but a process of interaction and change" (18). Although Rocha understands that the term *creole* is embedded in a history of racism and colonialism, she believes the trope of creolization has some advantages over the term hybridity in her study. Chee-Beng Tan (2018) also prefers to use *creolization* to refer to creative processes of cultural formation and localization in transcultural contexts.

From a feminist decolonizing approach, I prefer to use *hybrid* or *hybridizations* in my research. Here being or becoming hybrid or hybridizations means "to create a home where one is not at home" (Stoddard and Cornwell 1999, 349) and carries "notions of creativity, agency, and innovation" (Rocha 2006, 19). It reveals a dynamic process of identity construction and negotiation; it is an "energy field of different forces" (Papastergiadis 1997, 258). It reflects both relations of dominance and resistance to domination.

Lama Kate's story reveals how hybridizations make the arbitrary boundaries between "ethnic" and "convert" practices ambiguous on the ground, and how identity is an ongoing process of construction through encounter, contact, interaction, exchange, and negotiation. Lama Kate's journey to

"Going Home"   159

Buddhism began in her early adulthood. As a White American woman, she grew up in a Christian church and attended Catholic school for twelve years. However, as she entered college, the demands of her new life left her feeling overwhelmed, and she gradually stopped attending church. In her senior year of college, she began experiencing significant stress, prompting her to seek ways to alleviate it. She decided to take up yoga and meditation, finding that meditation helped her let go of her thoughts and provided relief. This newfound interest in meditation became a turning point for her. After graduation, Lama Kate got married and secured her first job as a newspaper writer. She returned to her hometown in Ohio with her husband and continued her yoga practice at The Yoga Place. One day, she had the opportunity to attend a lecture by a Tibetan Buddhist monk at the yoga center. Intrigued by the talk and deeply impressed by his compassion and wisdom, she interviewed the monk for her newspaper, and they connected well. The monk graciously offered to assist her with her meditation practice. This encounter marked a significant shift in her life, and with the guidance and support of the monk, she embraced Buddhism and began her path as Lama Kate.

Lama Kate joined the monk's Buddhist center in Columbus, Ohio, which was originally cofounded by two White American couples who had been part of the 1960s hippie movement, advocating for freedom, peace, and love. Lama Kate found great joy in becoming a member of this center and studying Buddhism there. The monk she met had a fascinating background, having grown up in Tibet and later leaving China in 1959. He settled in India before traveling to the US in 1976, where he founded the Columbus TBC in 1977. This center has been a "lamp" of Tibetan Buddhism in central Ohio ever since. In 1988 the monk visited Florida where a study group was formed; this group eventually evolved into a local TBC. Lama L, a fully ordained monk, became the resident teacher there, leading weekly Dharma studies and practices. Lama L completed a three-year retreat in 2004, a significant accomplishment within the Buddhist traditions. Lama Kate also completed a three-year retreat, but she chose to maintain her family ties, showing a unique approach to balancing her spiritual practice with her familial responsibilities.

The mission of the Columbus TBC is to provide a respectful and open community for the study, practice, and engagement in Tibetan Buddhism at all levels, under the guidance of experienced masters in the specific tradition. This center has successfully drawn a diverse group of practitioners, including CCA, African Americans, and White Americans. To support the practitioners on their path to enlightenment, the center hosts a variety of free lectures and events. Moreover, resident teachers and masters regularly teach online and in-person classes to provide valuable instructions.

After an arson fire destroyed the Columbus TBC building on Sunday, January 31, 2016, local Buddhists embraced the teachings on impermanence to overcome the tragedy and focus on rebuilding. Tifereth Israel (TI) synagogue leaders then invited the group to use the synagogue's Lower Social Hall for the TBC's weekly meditation sessions. Thus, from the spring of 2016 to the spring of 2020, the TBC conducted its Sunday-morning dharma programs and Tuesday-night Chenrezig pujas at TI. Local Buddhists were reminded of impermanence by the master. Lama Kate said that after hearing of the fire, the master advised them, "Don't be sad, rebuild." He further said, "Make it bigger than the last one." The group raised more than $1 million to rebuild the temple, and finally, the new temple was opened in late 2021. Despite the hardships, the communities have continued to uphold their principles, offering prayers for all sentient beings and remaining committed to their teachings on the importance of compassion and wisdom.

The reading group that I participated in was started by Shuilian in the spring of 2016, and her engagement within hybrid communities was a long process. Shuilian was born in mainland China in 1966, and she attended a medical school from 1983 to 1988. Her husband went to pursue his PhD at the Massachusetts Institute of Technology (MIT), and she then joined him in Boston in February 1989. She found a job as a technician in a medical laboratory and lived a comfortable life. Her husband graduated and then worked as an assistant professor at a state university from 1991 to 1994. Shuilian moved with her husband and worked at the same university. She gave birth to her daughter in 1992. In 1994 her husband changed jobs, and the whole family moved to Florida. In 1997 she gave birth to her son. During her pregnancy, she finished her master's degree in pathology. After graduation, she worked as a senior bioscientist and lab manager for about ten years, and in 2008, she quit her job due to illness and also to devote more time to taking care of her household and family.

As soon as she arrived in the US in 1989, Shuilian was invited to go to Christian churches in Boston. She wanted to practice her English, so she went to church every Sunday. However, she felt that she did not belong there, and her feelings of disconnection from Christianity were commonly shared with other reading group members who had also been invited to churches after their arrival in the US. Once they started practicing Buddhism, they felt that they finally "went home."

Shuilian's way of "going home" was influenced by her mother and the hybrid communities around her. After her son was born in 1997, her parents came to help her. Her neighbor's mother believed in Tibetan Buddhism, and her neighbor knew of a professor who came to their town to give free lectures

"Going Home"   161

about Buddhism every month. After learning this, Shuilian and her neighbor alternated sending their parents to attend the lectures, and she also became interested in Buddhism.

In 2000 a master from Tiantai School started Buddhist summer camps in Florida, and Shuilian took her family to attend them. Each summer camp—organized once every year until 2019—lasted five days. They were very intense but beneficial to Shuilian and her family. Because various masters from different schools in Han Buddhism, Tibetan Buddhism, and Theravada Buddhism were invited to give lectures there, they were exposed to diverse Buddhist traditions. Meanwhile, lay Buddhists from different schools and Dharma centers distributed various materials at the camps. Shuilian's mother Wuchen got the TBC magazine, and when she saw a picture of the deceased master, she immediately responded and felt that the master was her teacher in her previous life. Wuchen returned to China in 2010, taking the magazine with her, and when she found out that the relics, or *śarīra*, of the master were in a Tibetan Buddhist monastery on a mountain, she went there with her son to pay homage. She also learned that the reincarnated master was in Nepal, so Wuchen contacted the teacher of the reincarnated master and started to study Tibetan Buddhism with him, calling him "grandmaster" (*shizu*). Shuilian said that her mother used to enjoy attending all kinds of activities and listening to all the masters who came to give lectures, but after the visit to the monastery, her mother only completed work assigned by her grandmaster.

Shuilian and her mother were exposed to diverse Buddhist traditions, but eventually they chose to follow one particular lineage of Tibetan Buddhism. From 2013 to 2015, masters from Longquan Monastery went to Florida and started to spread the Dharma there. Shuilian's family owned a big house, so she volunteered to host some activities. At that time, the masters taught *The Great Treatise on the Stages of the Path to Enlightenment: Tsongkhapa's Lamrim Chenmo (Puti Dao Cidi Guanglun)*. Shuilian listened to the lecture series and changed her view of Tibetan Buddhism. She found that Tibetan Buddhism was very systematic, and she could study it step by step, which was exactly what she needed at that moment.

After learning that her mother believed in Tibetan Buddhism, some "Buddhist friends" (*foyou*) forwarded Shuilian important information about various activities organized by the local TBC. Some masters from the TBC came to teach the Dharma to support the local center. Influenced by her mother, Shuilian started to go to the local TBC frequently in 2015. At that time, the master taught Green Tara Practice, and as Shuilian practiced this path she felt connected with Tara, who is the most beloved deity by Tibetans of all the female awakened beings, the Mother of all the Buddhas, and the actuality of wisdom and compassion, embodying one's Buddha nature.

In September 2015, Shuilian attended a special retreat organized by the TBC where the master who started TBC in the US taught *The Ocean Of Definitive Meaning*. The master used this retreat to reward Taiwanese people who donated tens of thousands of dollars to build the monastery in the US and made it open to Chinese speakers. The master gave lectures in the Tibetan language, and interpreters translated them into Chinese. It was the first time that Shuilian systematically studied Tibetan Buddhism in Chinese.

After coming back from her first retreat, Shuilian began going to the TBC for morning practice every Sunday. The morning practice often included three one-hour sessions: Introduction to Buddhism class, Dharma study and book reading, and Chaturbhuja Lokeshvara practice and meditation. Shuilian often invited her female friends to go with her. One day, a woman asked some challenging questions—Shuilian did not know how to answer them, so she invited Wenxin to join the TBC meeting and help her. The lama saw that many Chinese women were interested in studying Buddhism, and he recommended Shuilian organize the Chinese reading group.

After the Chinese reading group was founded in the spring of 2016, Shuilian and Wenxin introduced Buddhism to numerous Chinese women, and several of them continued their participation within the group. The impact of studying Buddhism was evident as many of the women shared how it positively transformed their relationships with family members, increased their happiness, and changed their perspectives. Chinese immigrant women were very diverse in Florida, and they often had different political backgrounds and standpoints. Despite these differences, Shuilian skillfully brought these women together, respecting their individual choices, and encouraging them to delve into Buddhism and pursue happiness in their lives. By creating hybrid communities, these women were able to connect with broader networks, engage in a range of activities, and provide mutual support during challenging moments in their lives. This nurturing environment fostered personal growth, resilience, and a sense of belonging among the women.

The individualized spiritual journey of "going home" is an ongoing process for Shuilian and many Chinese lay Buddhist women who have crafted hybrid communities in global contexts. In these communities, the dichotomy of "ethnic" and "convert" categories has been dissolved, and diverse interactions and hybridizations occur. A growing individualization and autonomy have made Chinese lay women more responsible for their own "combination of picking, choosing, mixing, hybridizing, and creolizing from different religious traditions" according to their needs in their "spiritual journey" (Rocha 2006, 120).

THE ROLE OF BUDDHISM IN COPING WITH THE PANDEMIC

The COVID-19 pandemic exaggerated social, cultural, political, and economic inequalities, which effectively privilege certain lives over others. It disproportionately devastated certain individuals, groups, and communities, especially the elderly, poor, sick, and disabled as well as immigrants, women, sexual minority communities, and communities of color. In my study, I asked my contributors if practicing Buddhism helped them cope with the pandemic. Shuilian said, "I think that concepts in Buddhism are helpful in many ways, because you would see problems from different perspectives . . . when you calm down, if you have the basic foundation in Buddhism, you would not have stronger attachments as you did before, and you would not be so emotional, or you would quickly be aware of it. Sometimes you would not have strong fear when seeing problems, or you would have less desire" (interview on November 19, 2021).

Amid the outbreak of COVID-19, Shuilian found herself deeply concerned about the health and well-being of her elderly parents, spouse, and children. Her worries escalated as her son resided in New York City, and after his roommate's colleague tested positive for COVID around March 2020, both her son and his roommate fell ill. However, testing options were unavailable to them at that time. In coping with the overwhelming anxiety and stress brought on by these circumstances, Shuilian found solace in her Buddhist practice, which she believed provided her with valuable support. She said,

> Whenever I feel anxious, first, I pray in my heart for the blessing of the Bodhisattva, for being blessed with compassion and wisdom to find the right way. Second, I accumulate merits and clear away karma [*ji zi jing zhang*]. Generally speaking, all Buddhist practices have two purposes, that is, to accumulate merits and to clear away karma. Thus, if I run into something urgent or troublesome, I will go to offer lamps [*gong deng*], make more offerings to the Triple Gem, and then recite more spells, practice Dharma, pray more, etc. Anyway, after you are done with these things, you feel less anxious.

Shuilian sought to accumulate more merits for her family by dedicating herself to studying the Dharma, reciting spells, and engaging in merit-accumulating charitable acts, including making various offerings to the Triple Gem—the Buddha, the Dharma, and the Sangha. Embracing Buddhism provided her with a sense of relief from stress amid the challenging circumstances brought on by the pandemic.

When reflecting on the role of Buddhism in coping with the pandemic, Fanghua found that many friends around her developed an interest in meditation and mindfulness practices. She experienced an increased opportunity for self-reflection and meditation while staying at home. A significant transformation occurred as she learned to relinquish attachments and control her desire to acquire material possessions. Fanghua realized that excessive consumerism did not bring her genuine joy or fulfillment. During the period of staying at home in 2020, she refrained from purchasing any new clothes, shoes, or bags and started to cook more meals at home. Consequently, she not only saved a considerable amount of money but also embraced a more tranquil and contented lifestyle.

Many contributors told me that the pandemic made them realize how fragile life was. They understood that impermanence was the cornerstone of Buddhist beliefs and practices, and everything was impermanent. In other words, nothing lasts, and thus nothing can be grasped or held onto. As the Buddha said before his nirvana: "All compounded things are subject to vanish. Strive with earnestness!" (Maha-parinibbana Sutta). When my contributors appreciated this simple but profound truth, they felt peace and remained calm. As Fanghua said, "When you study Buddhism, understand that everything is impermanent, and then look at what happened in your life, you could use Buddhist ideas to make yourself calm, or they help you see those changes differently" (interview on July 23, 2021).

Buddhist teachings and practices helped my contributors relieve anxiety and pain. Feeling the pain of impermanence was a profoundly important reminder for them of what it meant to exist. As Shuilian said, "Everything is unpredictable, so we should cherish what we have now and spend time and energy on meaningful things." Many reading group members were highly educated women, and they continued to live their meaningful lives during the pandemic. Moreover, they strived to understand impermanence at the deepest possible level, to merge with it fully, and to pursue the Buddhist path with diligence.

Shuilian, along with other lay Buddhist women, cultivated wisdom and compassion, and embraced equanimity, peace, and happiness. Shuilian said that she always wished she could be blessed with wisdom and compassion to face all her problems and all the different "realms." Although she still experienced anxiety, its intensity and frequency diminished through her Buddhist practices. She consistently reminded herself to remain mindful of her negative emotions and approach problems from the perspectives of impermanence and karma. Drawing from her Buddhist beliefs, she found solace in addressing negative emotions, reducing attachments, and uncovering practical solutions to the challenges she faced.

"Going Home" 165

Xianhong highlighted the considerable support Buddhism provided her during various challenging circumstances in her life. Throughout the pandemic, she faced numerous crises, prompting her to seek assistance from counselors. Her son, an only child, was studying in the US and faced difficulties securing air tickets to return to China between 2020 and 2021. In November 2021, she traveled to the US to visit him but was then unable to return to China until July 2022. Nonetheless, she continued her Dharma learning through online platforms while in America. Upon reflection, Xianhong acknowledged the significant role Buddhism played in navigating and coping with the trials in her life:

> It [Buddhism] gives me support, invisible support. When you encounter difficulties, you retreat to that point, you won't retreat to the endless abyss. You will retreat to that point, which is its point of support. You feel that when you have no way to go, you retreat, and retreat to that point, it can make you start over. I think that background is invisible, but it is huge. It will make you realize that many things are from your mind. Originally, when you retreat, you may retreat to rely on some people. They might be your parents, friends, or children. But the Dharma teaches you that you can only rely on yourself and your mind, and your mind is very powerful. (Interview on December 26, 2021)

Xianhong articulated the significance of self-empowerment in Buddhist teachings, and she relied on that power to help her make it through life crises and the pandemic. She and many lay Buddhist women devoted themselves to learning the Dharma, pursuing enlightenment, and achieving nirvana. They were often concerned with their existence and destinies and intended to make merit fields and pursue well-being for their families. In this process, they built a strong sense of belonging and empowered themselves to go through challenges in times of crisis.

The COVID-19 pandemic served as a revealing measure of how social actors turned to religions for symbolic resources to cope with the anxiety and distress brought about by the crisis. The stress caused by COVID-19 might have fueled the surge in interest in meditation and its mindfulness variation, although these "means of salvation" or spiritual techniques had already been spreading widely outside their places of origin before the pandemic (Obadia 2020). In the realm of spiritual well-being, Buddhism occupies a distinct space that aligns with the needs of a broad audience worldwide. Buddhism has experienced rapid and extensive growth globally, while meditation and yoga have seen a remarkable rise in popularity, both in terms of participant numbers and as part of a thriving service economy (Lange 2020). This growth mirrors the logics of global capitalism, a system in which Buddhism has become increasingly involved (Borup and Fibiger 2017).

The emphasis on asceticism, highlighted during the pandemic, is a significant aspect of Buddhist modernism (Lopez 2002). However, it is important to point out that Buddhism is not merely confined to meditation and scholarly pursuits in solitude, nor can it be reduced solely to its monastic variant, which is relevant to only about 1 percent of its followers (Harvey 2012). Buddhism also encompasses a complex religious framework that involves popular and unorthodox forms of religiosity practiced in various local cultures (Taylor 2015). A less noticed but noteworthy effect of the pandemic has been the emergence of religious responses beyond the well-known ascetic and meditative practices of "elite Buddhism." These responses, often overlooked in media portrayals of a modernist view of Buddhism, include popular, magical, and devotional practices, such as the use of amulets, talismans, and protective imagery, serving as symbolic defenses against pandemic risks (Salguero 2020).

Combating Anti-Asian Racisms and Facing Death

Buddhism became the victim of anti-Asian racisms and violence during the pandemic. As COVID-19 broke out in China, where Buddhism is one of the five official religions and among its three historical religions (alongside Confucianism and Daoism), the association between China and Buddhism represented a conflation of the coronavirus's origin with Buddhism. This association was particularly noted in the US and Europe, where Buddhism has been extensively culturally assimilated and is regarded as an integral part of the mainstream cultural landscape. However, the pandemic has exposed persistent anti-Asian racisms ironically aimed at a religion that is otherwise considered compatible with modern values in these Western regions (Obadia 2020).

In North America, there were acts of vandalism against Buddhist symbols, such as the beheading of Buddha statues in temples. Anti-Asian hate incidents included the vandalism at a Vietnamese temple in Montreal, Canada, in March 2020; the destruction of Buddha statues in a Laotian temple in Fort Smith, Arkansas, in April 2020; and attacks against a Thai Buddhist temple in Santa Ana, California, at the end of 2020 (Obadia 2020). These hate incidents, though isolated, reflect the linking of COVID-19 to its Asian origins, with Buddhism becoming a focal point for anti-Asian racisms. Buddhist communities, broadly categorized as Asian in a generalized ethnic labeling process, faced collective blame and imaginary responsibilities in a pandemic environment rife with misinformation and varying interpretations (Brouillette and Renner 2020).

In the reading group, many women did not experience racisms in person as they primarily stayed at home during the outbreak, but they were fully aware of what was happening to AAAPI communities. Shuilian mentioned that some CCA professors were discriminated against and treated unfairly. Wenxin chose to retire early after she saw how some CCA scientists and engineers were wrongly arrested by the Federal Bureau of Investigation and unfairly charged as "Chinese spies" by the US government. Among those CCA scientists who suffered from structural injustice and systematic racisms, the most well-known include (but are not limited to) Gang Chen, Carl Richard Soderberg Professor of Power Engineering at MIT; Xiaoxing Xi, Laura H. Carnell Professor of Physics at Temple University; and Sherry Chen, a hydrologist who once worked in the National Weather Service office in Wilmington, Ohio. Although all the charges against them were eventually dropped, they suffered from the long-term damage of structural injustice and systemic racisms. Their experiences also affected other CCA scientists and engineers, some of whom became fearful of political prosecution in America. As China-US relations deteriorated, some CCA scientists and engineers returned to China, including Shuilian's husband Yong, who went back in 2020 and worked as a full professor at a prestigious university in South China. After seeing her daughter get married in the US, Shuilian sold their house in Florida and moved to China in November 2021.

The move to China was very challenging for Shuilian as she had to give up almost all her belongings accumulated over thirty years in America. When packing up and selling her house, Shuilian experienced feelings of sadness and loss, and she felt trapped in negative emotions. She grappled with strong attachments to her belongings and the memories associated with them, making it difficult to let go and move on. She drew on Buddhist ideas and engaged in rituals like reading and practicing the Diamond Sutra when she felt sad— her religious practices became coping mechanisms that she employed to deal with her emotions.

Shuilian's decision to move back to China as an act of agency challenges Western feminist notions of agency, which often assume universally shared experiences of oppression and favor liberal and secular definitions as premised on free will, individualism, choices free from structural constraints, the satisfaction of personal preferences and desires, and capabilities for rational thought. These assumptions reveal the latent secularist, Western, and colonial biases of feminist thought where local, national, and cultural contexts are disregarded. Feminisms and agencies have different forms and meanings, and their understandings should be situated within particular social, cultural, economic, and political contexts. It is important to emphasize the primacy of "demarginalization" and the reconstruction of Asian Buddhist women's experiences, voices, and agencies in different cultural contexts (Cheng 2007), and to construct a postpatriarchal Buddhism to change patriarchal constraints and to empower women in both societies and Buddhist organizations (Gross 1993).

Shuilian's agencies are complicated, nuanced, and situational. When facing racisms in the US and after the Atlanta spa shootings, she joined her CCA communities to protest against anti-Asian hate. When her husband decided to go back to China, she followed him no matter how hard the international move was for her. She dared to protest against systemic racisms and also embraced the family and gender social structures that feminists might see as locations of oppression. Her fluid and generative agencies are situated in particular local, national, and global contexts. Her case illustrates the diverse agencies CCA women developed and exerted with their hybrid communities and Buddhist traditions.

When using the feminist decolonizing approach to interpret Chinese lay Buddhist women's diverse agencies, I highlight their subjectivities and their own constructions and perceptions of agencies. Different from clergies, they have not lost their strong connections with their own families. By making and sharing merits, they pursue worldly prosperity for their families and themselves. They consider their own needs, interests, and agendas, and also support each other to achieve enlightenment and fight for social goods. There are no universal yardsticks to define what "counts" as an agency and what does not. Decolonization returns CCA women the power to define their own agencies and decide how they want to live. Furthermore, decolonization provides the possibility of innovative and creative approaches to antiracisms and advocates for active grassroots movements at the social, political, economic, and cultural levels, creating alternate solidarities (McLaren 2017).

Feminists are very interested in the possibilities for and obstacles to social, political, cultural, and economic changes that promote gender equality, and many believe that they should also address unjust social structures that reproduce various forms of privilege and power (Avishai 2016). Feminist activisms are often integrated with racial, sexual, class, and national dynamics. During the pandemic, the surging anti-Asian racisms pushed Chinese lay Buddhist women to go out of their comfort zones and reconnect with broader CCA and AAAPI communities to fight for social justice.

Within CCA communities at Y City, many were first-generation immigrants and worked for University X and hospitals. Many CCA scholars, scientists, students, medical doctors, and health workers contributed tremendously to seeking solutions to respond to the global pandemic and making the US a better place for all. However, they were still seen as "foreigners forever," and sometimes were called "Chinese viruses" or "Chinese spies." The Atlanta spa shootings and Stop AAPI Hate (SAH) reports were a wake-up call for them, and they united to condemn all hate crimes against any groups of people, fight against systemic racisms, and make their campus and city a safe, healthy, welcoming community for all.

In Y City, CCA communities arranged two rallies: one led by University X professors, scholars, students, and residents on March 20, 2021, and the other engaging with broader AAAPI communities on March 27, 2021. The rallies condemned hate crimes against AAAPIs and any racist attacks against any group due to differences in sex, culture, language, appearance, religion, and beliefs. Moreover, they condemned the criminalization of Chinese scientists and engineers as "Chinese spies." On March 27, 2021, multiple AAAPI groups mobilized to participate in Protect AAPI Lives: A March and Vigil of Love and Solidarity, with over 250 protestors walking from a plaza to a central park in Y City. Shuilian—along with other lay Buddhist women and their children—participated in these protests and rallies.

Another group, the Anti-Hate Team, organized the vigil and encouraged participants to use their voices to condemn racisms against AAAPIs. Many CCA teenagers and young adults spoke out, and one young adult read aloud a poem titled "The Game Board: Second Generation Chinese American Female Edition" by Laura Lisa Ng, which uses the metaphor of a board game to describe female Asian American experiences during the pandemic. The poem detailed a process of moving forward on the "game board" when assimilating to American culture and moving backward when Asian American women encounter discrimination, hate, racism, and sexism. Throughout the vigil, people were encouraged to write personal notes describing racisms they experienced and promoting unity and solidarity. The notes were posted online by the Anti-Hate Team as part of a virtual "healing garden." When reflecting on her experiences of participating in the rallies, Shuilian said, "When I was discriminated against, I could easily understand the feelings of other people who were discriminated against. Meanwhile, I think that we should unite minority groups, let more people be aware of the existence of racisms, and combat racisms against any person."

Some Chinese lay Buddhist women and their family members experienced racisms in various forms in their lives. The Atlanta spa shootings filled them with anger and sadness. They joined the SAH protests and rallies to demand justice and accountability for the victims and their families and to raise awareness of the systemic racisms that plague US society. They have

170   Impacts of the COVID-19 Pandemic on Chinese and Chinese American Women

shown courage in fighting against racisms and demanding action from authorities. They have also shown solidarity with other marginalized communities who face discrimination and oppression. By embracing humanity, they have found healing and hope in these dark times. The rallies are a reminder that they are not alone and that they have strong allies and friends who care about them. By taking both big and small actions, they believe that they can stop AAPI hate and create a more just and inclusive society for all sentient beings.

Social activisms are enacted in multiple forms by Chinese lay Buddhist women. The practices of social activisms are not limited to recognizable civil organizations or political movements but also include the diverse ways that these women use their expressions to promote specific social and personal goals that create spaces for liberation. Here, the term *liberation* is defined in diverse ways and encompasses "a range of registers and experiences that are cocreated, including those of race, gender, sexuality, ethnicity, religion, (dis)ability, and national identity" (Otero and Martínez-Rivera 2021, 9).

During the pandemic, Buddhist funeral rites played important roles in building antiracist solidarities. After the Atlanta spa shootings, a group of CCA and AAAPI people held a special Buddhist funeral for Feng Daoyou, who was killed in Young's Asian Massage in Atlanta. While the stories of the other five Asian female victims were repeatedly told by their families and friends, Daoyou's body lay in the morgue for a week, with no trace of her life to be found. The Chinese embassy in the US contacted Ying Guangyong, a local Chinese community leader, to handle end-of-life affairs for Daoyou. Li Xiaosong, the director of a state hospital and a psychologist, took on the task of locating Daoyou's body. After making many calls, he found Daoyou's body and managed to contact her older brother Feng Daokun in China. After getting her brother's permission, Daoyou's body was cremated. Ying specifically chose a pink urn for her, thinking it was a color she would have liked as a woman (Wei 2021).

Lay Buddhist women in Atlanta helped organize Daoyou's funeral in early April 2021, and more than a hundred CCA and AAAPI community members attended it. Li Xiaosong was the first one to speak, and he introduced Daoyou's life stories. Daoyou was born in January 1977 into a poor peasant family in Lianjiang, Guangdong Province. She had two older brothers and an older sister, and she was the youngest child in her family. At about fourteen, she started to work in cities like Shenzhen, Guangzhou, and Shanghai, where she worked as a factory worker and later learned beauty care. In 2017, a good friend asked her if she wanted to go to the US, suggesting there might be better income and life opportunities. She came to the US without telling her friends and family. She worked in New York, Los Angeles, and Atlanta, mainly in salons and spas. She worked very hard and sent money back to her mother to purchase an apartment. She never started a family of her own. On March 16, 2021, the gunshots took away all her dreams and ended her life at the age of forty-four (Wei 2021).

Nobody knew how Daoyou came to the US. She barely spoke English and had no green card. However, despite difficulties in ascertaining details of Daoyou's background, CCA communities got together to commemorate her. Lay Buddhist women invited a monk to chant scriptures and perform rituals for her soul's transcendence. She was buried in a park-like cemetery in downtown Atlanta, a location chosen by Ying, as he passed by it every day on his way to and from work. His mother was also buried there, and he thought that in this way, she would have some company (Wei 2021).

For AAAPI communities across the US, particularly in Atlanta, the Atlanta spa shootings marked a pivotal moment in the national movement for racial justice, with millions of people taking to the streets to protest anti-Asian hate and racisms. The killing also brought profound grief, anger, and anxiety. At Daoyou's funeral, although no participants knew her personally, the collective commemoration served as a unifying force for CCA and AAAPI communities to come together, grieve, and advocate for social justice (Hinden, You, and Guo 2023). At the anniversaries of the Atlanta spa shootings, AAAPI communities continue to feel a loss and organize activities to commemorate the lives lost. Although healing from this collective trauma will be a long journey, there is a strong sense of solidarity and dedication within the communities to work through the pain and collaboratively build a better world for all.

Conclusion

In Buddhism, women were often viewed as sources of pollution and spiritual regression, especially in early Buddhist scriptures. This dynamic existed despite the fact that "Buddha recognized that women had the ability, just like men, to practice the Dharma and achieve enlightenment" (Yü 2020, 219). Chinese Buddhism was not misogynistic, but it was shaped within Confucian patriarchal moralism in history. The climate of rapid social, cultural, political, and economic changes in the modern world has allowed Chinese lay Buddhist women to take new chances and reassert their creative agencies in transnational contexts. Despite ideology-laden structures, Chinese lay Buddhist women have exerted their creative agencies in their everyday practices of self-identification, community building, and social engagement. I highlight their innovative agencies in self-empowerment and social justice in times of crisis by practicing Buddhism despite all restrictions and challenges.

From a decolonizing perspective, I use *hybrid communities* to refer to the diverse communities that CCA women have crafted. Here the notion of being or becoming hybrid signifies the act of creating a sense of belonging or home in an unfamiliar or foreign environment. This concept is imbued with ideas of creativity, agency, and innovation, unveiling a dynamic process of identity construction and negotiation. The notion represents a type of energy field in which various forces interact. It encapsulates both relationships of dominance and resistance to domination.

Chinese lay Buddhist women exercise diverse agencies in going through life crises, the pandemic, and anti-Asian racisms and creatively transform those crises into opportunities. I examine spiritual, social, and political dimensions of newly emerging powerful agencies of Chinese lay Buddhist women in transnational contexts. Women's religious agencies emerge in different forms and are constructed differently within different social, political, cultural, and historical contexts (Hüsken 2022). No one size can fit all at the same time. This study contributes to the ongoing dialogues about feminist agencies that go beyond religious, racial, ethnic, national, and gendered paradigms and boundaries, not overlooking differences in perspectives and views.

What can we do to support Chinese lay Buddhist women in the US? First, we could help them strengthen hybrid Buddhist communities that specifically address their needs and experiences, support their livelihoods, facilitate opportunities for networking and mentorship, and promote cultural exchanges and understanding between Buddhists and non-Buddhists. Second, local communities and organizations could create platforms for Chinese lay Buddhist women to develop leadership skills and empower them to take on more active roles within their communities and beyond. Within Buddhist communities, these women should be encouraged to speak out and make their voices heard in the decision-making processes. Third, we should combat discrimination against diverse Buddhist traditions and practitioners, ensuring that those traditions and practitioners are respected and valued. Fourth, we should advocate for gender equality within Buddhist institutions, and make sure that Chinese lay Buddhist women have equal opportunities for leadership and participation. Fifth, we should challenge and debunk stereotypes and stigmas associated with Buddhism and Chinese lay Buddhist women, and promote religious diversity and inclusivity. I hope that the strategies and considerations presented herein will inform policymakers, religious leaders, community organizations, and individuals working toward supporting the diverse experiences and aspirations of Chinese lay Buddhist women. Ultimately, by valuing and supporting diverse voices and agencies of Chinese lay Buddhist women, we all could foster a more inclusive and equitable society that combats racisms and embraces religious diversity.

NOTE

1. First-generation immigrants are individuals who have moved from their country of birth to another country, where they settle permanently or for an extended period. These individuals are the first in their family to make this transition, differentiating them from second-generation immigrants, who are the children of first-generation immigrants born in the new country.

6

FLUID FOODWAYS, RACISMS, AND EVERYDAY LIVES

THIS CHAPTER OFFERS A SNAPSHOT of how the pandemic changed fluid foodways and everyday lives of Chinese and Chinese American (CCA) women and communities by integrating eighty-three interviews, virtual ethnography, virtual panels, and class surveys, exploring complicated, nuanced, and situational relationships between racisms, foodways, and gender in the US. It tells the stories of how foodways contribute to our identity formation, social advocacy, community building, and personal well-being.

The term *foodways* embraces "a wide range of activities, from producing, procuring, preserving, and transforming foodstuffs to presenting, sharing, consuming, and disposing of what is not eaten" (M. Jones 2022, x). The topic of foodways also encompasses individuals' perceptions, such as meanings, values, beliefs, and aesthetics, everyday routines and special occasions for food preparation and consumption, and communications about self and others (M. Jones 2022). Due to its association with hearth and home, the significance of foodways is often overlooked or undervalued in understanding human interactions and addressing broader concerns like health, politics, and (dis)identifications, which are central themes explored in this book.

In this study, the concept of "fluid foodways" is inspired by Zygmunt Bauman's theory of "liquid modernity." Bauman ([2000] 2012, foreword) defines "liquid modernity" as follows:

> Forms of modern life may differ in quite a few respects—but what unites them all is precisely their fragility, temporariness, vulnerability and inclination to

constant change. To "be modern" means to modernize—compulsively, obsessively; not so much just "to be," let alone to keep its identity intact, but forever "becoming," avoiding completion, staying underdefined. . . . What was some time ago dubbed (erroneously) "post-modernity," and what I've chosen to call, more to the point, "liquid modernity," is the growing conviction that change is *the only* permanence, and uncertainty *the only* certainty. A hundred years ago "to be modern" meant to chase "the final state of perfection"—now it means an infinity of improvement, with no "final state" in sight and none desired.

Similarly, the concept of "fluid foodways" presents the "fragility, temporariness, vulnerability and inclination to constant change" of foodways, "forever becoming" and never ending, especially during the COVID-19 pandemic when our daily lives were full of uncertainties and unpredictability. As Bauman emphasizes, "Flexibility has replaced solidity as the ideal condition to be pursued of things and affairs" (ibid.).

Foodways have long been included in folklore studies and have been used to examine the dynamics of folk groups, ethnicity and regionalism, identity construction, artistic expression, and power hierarchies (Bell and Valentine 1997; Bourke 1895; Brown and Mussell 1984; Camp 1989; Gabaccia 1998; Georges 1984; Humphrey and Humphrey 1988; M. Jones 2007; Jones, Giuliano, and Krell 1983; Long 2004, 2009; Mirsky 1981; Yoder 1972). Lucy Long (2018) identifies three areas of emphasis that characterize folkloristic perspectives on foodways: the personal (as in individual agency within larger structures), aesthetics (artistry and creativity as a part of that agency, and aesthetic experience as a motivation for engaging in cultural forms), and meaningfulness (sense of connectedness between individuals and their pasts, places, and other people). Foodways are seen as cultural, social, and personal constructions and as performance of identities. Folkloristic approaches to foodways can be applied to issues within food systems and to broader questions such as nationalism, cultural appropriation, authenticity, social inequalities, and community building (Long 2018).

Foodways as a medium for constructing and negotiating group and individual identities have been examined closely by folklorists. Contemporary scholarship also highlights the critical role of power dynamics in shaping these identities. Margaret Magat (2019) and LuAnne Roth (2006) have shed light on the influence of power structures and their impact on the representation and perception of food-related identities. Moreover, folkloristic research on gender and food has experienced notable advancements, showing how foodways are frequently used subversively. Through coded communication, foodways become a tool for expressing covert messages and assertions, especially for women who find agency within this seemingly trivialized domain.

Roth (2014) and Diane Tye (2010) are among the folklorists contributing to this line of inquiry, exploring the ways in which women use foodways to assert themselves and navigate societal norms. As folklorists delve deeper into the intricate intersections of foods, identities, and power, the dynamics of foodways continue to unfold. Acknowledging the influence of power dynamics and the subversive potential of foodways offers fresh perspectives on how individuals and groups navigate, resist, and assert their identities through the medium of food.

The pandemic exaggerated the social, cultural, political, and economic inequalities in our daily lives globally. In addition to the unequal access to health care, the unequal access to food became a serious problem. Food shortages and hunger caused by the strict lockdowns and other policies occurred in many parts of the world. In March and April 2022, when Shanghai was locked down, isolated residents struggled to get access to food, medicine, and other necessities. Many Shanghai residents had to get up at 6:00 a.m. in the hope of being able to order vegetables and meat online before stock ran out, but most were unsuccessful and had to get by on one or two meals a day. The food supply chain was interrupted under the strictest conditions. Unreliable deliveries of government food packages and difficulties in securing food orders through online shopping apps caused Shanghai residents to organize group purchases directly from suppliers. The food crisis during Shanghai lockdowns made residents in other Chinese cities stockpile food, and refrigerators and freezers sold out in some places (Yeung 2022).

In addition to food shortages and supply chain issues that worsened globally during the pandemic, our normal ways of purchasing, cooking, and consuming foods were changed, deconstructed, and reconstructed based on public health protocols enacted to contain the coronavirus, such as wearing masks, social distancing, and conforming to lockdown, quarantine, stay-at-home, and self-isolation measures. In this book, I illustrate how the pandemic changed the ways CCA women grow, buy, cook, and consume foods as well as their concepts and understandings of fluid Chinese foodways in the US. Breaking with norms of conceptualizing foods as fixed markers of national, regional, and cultural identities, I study how CCA women use foodways to create their fluid racialized, gendered, religious, and individualized identities in their everyday lives.

The COVID-19 outbreaks affected our lives and livelihoods in unprecedented ways. During early lockdowns, many restaurants and businesses were forced to close, and some were closed permanently. Many women had to engage in labor-intense cooking and serving at home. The COVID-19 outbreaks created new barriers for CCA women to purchase, cook, and consume foods, and worldwide many people faced hunger, unemployment, poverty, sickness, and other issues exacerbated by the pandemic. In *Gender, Food and COVID-19: Global Stories of Harm and Hope*, a group of scholars, practitioners, and community members from across the globe provide on-the-ground accounts and personal reflections on the impacts of the COVID-19 pandemic on gender, agriculture, food systems, and individual lives (Castellanos, Sachs, and Tickamyer 2022). They discussed the pervasiveness of food insecurity, the ubiquity of women's care work, food justice, and policies and research that can contribute to building a more equal and just future.

To gain a comprehensive understanding of individuals' experiences of foodways during the pandemic, Lucy Long developed an international oral history project that resulted in an archive of documentation from over sixty-five interviews, a website with extensive resources (www.foodandcul ture.org), an online exhibit, a virtual symposium, a journal special issue, and community workshops (Long et al. 2021; Long 2022, 2023). The project aimed to broaden the understanding of "comfort food" by encompassing various activities within foodways and delving into the diverse meanings associated with this concept, highlighting the cultural and social constructs of both "food" and "comfort." The project serves as a public folklore presentation of folkloristic concepts and materials while also exploring the implications of comfort foodways during the pandemic through the lens of public humanities.

In this chapter, my key themes are (1) the dissemination of fluid Chinese foodways to the US; (2) the common experience of the lunchbox incident, Chinese/Asian American identities, and youth activisms; (3) fluid foodways of Chinese adoptees, authenticity, and vernacular culture; (4) Chinese women students' dietary changes and comfort foodways; and (5) fluid foodways of Chinese lay Buddhist women and vegetarianism.

The Dissemination of Fluid Chinese Foodways to the US

Food is related to all aspects of Chinese history and culture, and cooking and eating play a vital role in Chinese cultural and social life. As the old saying goes: "To the people, food is the Heaven." Chinese foodways are rooted in the civilization of antiquity (Anderson 1988; K. Chang 1977). Throughout history, many Chinese people left their ancestral homelands for new settings. In the nineteenth and early twentieth centuries, numerous Chinese immigrants left behind their homes and families to pursue a fresh start in the US. This journey exposed them to different cultures and unfamiliar plants, animals, challenges, and diseases. These new surroundings exerted unique pressures on their bodies and spirits, and they had to acclimate themselves to new habitats as quickly as possible. As they carried traditional recipes and some foodstuffs to the US, they were able to continue their traditional foodways, which helped them maintain their physical and spiritual well-being, but they also created new ways to develop their food traditions and adapt to the new society and culture.

Chinese restaurants in the US have faced ongoing prejudice despite their appeal to Americans. The Chinese Exclusion Act (1882) limited Chinese immigration and anti-Chinese sentiments grew with the boycott of American goods in China in 1905 and riots in San Francisco in 1906 (Tung 1974). In 1924 Chinese immigration to the US was further restricted based on the belief that the Chinese were unassimilable, and popular magazines reiterated the widely held view that one reason why the Chinese could not be assimilated was because of their eating habits (J. A. G. Roberts 2002). Despite such prejudice, Chinese restaurants gradually spread across the US and became important places where people from diverse cultural backgrounds could come together. This unique aspect made Chinese restaurants and their culinary practices ideal locations to examine intercultural interactions and conflicts (Cho 2018). For instance, due to the varied clientele and the presence of an "alien" culinary tradition, Chinese restaurants were often associated with the spread of menacing diseases (N. Shah 2001; M. Li 2023).

In the 1990s, CCA people in the US underwent significant economic and cultural changes due to domestic and global factors. Chinese restaurants adapted to American tastes and business ethics, and Chinatowns were transformed to attract tourists, offering a chance to experience the "exotic Orient" without traveling to China (Lin 1998, 171). Jing Fong, a beloved landmark in Manhattan's Chinatown, opened in 1978, obtained a loan from the Bank of China, and relocated to a spacious banquet hall in 1993, accommodating 1,100 guests (Lin 1998). It was permanently closed in March 2021 due to anti-Asian racisms and pandemic-related challenges. Its closure symbolizes the plight of numerous restaurants, bars, and nightclubs that succumbed to the pandemic. When COVID-19 emerged, the bustling crowds vanished, and Jing Fong closed for six months during the indoor dining ban. Although it reopened at limited capacity, the significant decline in customers made its survival difficult. Upon learning of its closure, customers flocked to have their final meals, expressing their sadness and emphasizing the restaurant's importance to themselves and their communities (Hu, Tsui, and Guerrero 2021).

At the time of completing this manuscript in July 2023, it became clear that the COVID-19 pandemic accelerated various trends that were already in motion. As the broader implications and impacts of the pandemic started to be understood, various arguments were made concerning a wide array of matters—from racial, economic, and health inequality and the forms of intersectional violence the pandemic created to the ongoing rise of state surveillance (Abedi et al. 2021; Shepherd 2023; Winter 2023). The question is how the issues of accelerated changes pertain to CCA communities in their everyday lives.

THE LUNCHBOX INCIDENT, CHINESE/ASIAN AMERICAN IDENTITIES, AND YOUTH ACTIVISMS

In early March 2021, the Parents and Children Education (PCE) Club invited nine CCA young adults to discuss identifications in a special panel. The panelists were second-generation Chinese American college students and working professionals from all over the US, with majors covering education, media studies, political science, economics, anthropology, sociology, computer science, and more. They shared their own experiences and challenges growing up as ethnic minorities, the disadvantages and stereotypes that Asian American and Pacific Islanders (AAPIs) had to face in personal development, and the lack of attention mainstream culture and education systems gave to AAPI culture and identities. One of the key themes in the panel was the commonly experienced lunchbox incident and various responses to it. Kyle, a recent graduate from Southern Methodist University who studied computer science, talked about the first time he experienced the lunchbox incident he experienced in school, when his White classmates made fun of his food:

> I brought dumplings to lunch, and people told me it smelled. And I started crying because I was like . . . so one of the incidents is that somebody made fun of my lunch, I started crying. And then eventually, one of my friends, was also trying to help me get over it. But then looking back, I realized that like, one of the things that you could do is you can offer them to try it, because then later on, people started asking me like, "Oh, hey, you brought dumplings, can I have one?" Because they really like them.

While that early experience was traumatizing, Kyle believes that younger generations of Americans are "more open-minded" and "willing to try new things," and exposing people to new cultures at a young age can make them more tolerant. Kyle has experienced racisms throughout his life, and it has taken him quite a while to figure out how to respond to them. By sharing his personal experiences of being racially discriminated against and stereotyped as an Asian American, he highlighted the various ways in which Asian Americans respond to racisms and offered a possible solution to it. He also encouraged calling out and explaining to White people why their behavior was wrong. He stressed the importance of embracing one's identity, accepting one's cultural heritage and roots, and not trying to conform to societal expectations of being White or Americanized.

Frequently, food has become a marker of the other, especially the inferior other, and its consumption is racialized. As David Arnold (2019, 126) writes, "Food perennially served as a moral marker for something beyond itself—for race and physique, for climate and disease, for colony and nation." The connection between food as a marker of the other and its racialization is evident in the school lunchbox incident that Kyle and many CCA children experienced—food choices became a basis for racial stereotypes and hierarchies, perpetuating the notion of the "inferior other." At schools, food consumption was used by White children as a means to marginalize and stigmatize CCA cultural practices, perpetuating harmful notions of superiority and inferiority based on food choices.

Other young CCA panelists responded to the lunchbox incident that Kyle experienced in different ways. Alia, a third-year student at Occidental College, was working with elementary school students in Eagle Rock County to help with their education. Based on her training in education, she stated that the lunchbox incident often occurred to Chinese/Asian American children in elementary schools and further articulated the feelings of rejection and isolation associated with it:

> It's around elementary school when I think most Asian Americans experience what I like to call the lunchbox incident, which is exactly what Kyle explained, like, you have dumplings, or you have this weird, like Asian snack that you think is normal. And the food is a symbol and a representation of your Chinese heritage. And you grow up proud and happy that you have such a unique culture with such wonderful food and wonderful traditions. But once that incident occurs, where peers that you might consider friends, that you might want to be friends with, like, they voiced the rejection to it: "That's weird, that's gross, how can you eat that? Like, that looks so weird, how can you possibly find that appealing?" Things like that. And so that creates an association, a negative association with your food, which is your culture, and other people, and by other people, I mean, rejection, isolation, that sort of thing, rejection of peers. And so that can oftentimes manifest itself into a rejection of culture, which is what Kyle stated.

Alia also discussed the evolving images of Asian Americans in popular culture, including Korean popular culture and Japanese anime, and the negative impacts of the COVID-19 pandemic on Asian American identities. She thought that it was important to combat anti-Asian racisms, overcome negative associations with Asian American identities, and bring positive associations back.

Associated with the lunchbox incident, young panelists addressed the complexities and challenges of growing up and living as Chinese Americans between two different cultures and the difficulties of feeling that they do not fit in with either group completely. Annie was a fourth-year student at Vassar College, double majoring in education and media studies. She articulated the paradoxes of becoming Chinese American this way:

> Our lived experiences as adolescents are very complicated because we grow up in a constant back and forth between bicultural Chinese and American settings. Some people might call it code-switching. I don't—, I don't personally call it that. But I can understand why. So because we're growing up, and we're going to school, we're too Chinese to be American, right? Other students make fun of our lunches, they ask us to parrot words in Chinese just to prove that we can, because it's, we're so foreign to them, even though we were born and raised in the US just like them, you know, we are not represented in school curriculum like at all, we are not represented in the US history. . . . And that environment is often pretty harsh for us, because it makes it difficult for us to want to be Chinese when we're young, because we want to fit in and be accepted by our non-Asian peers, but we inherently can't, because we don't look like them. But then, on the other hand, with relatives we are too American to be Chinese. Sometimes we speak broken Chinese, but we essentially carry our Americanness with us. And even though we are welcomed by our relatives to a certain degree, there are things that we're not that make us different. So we don't completely interact fluidly with them. So I guess this process of bicultural thing is kind of how we end up becoming Chinese American.

By explaining her experiences of moving between two cultures and languages and noting that she did not personally use the term "code-switching," Annie suggests that there were different ways of conceptualizing the experiences of navigating multiple cultural identities. These experiences highlight how racisms and cultural exclusion have impacted young AAPIs' identifications and sense of belonging. However, when interacting with Chinese relatives, Annie felt "too American to be Chinese." Thus, the process of becoming a Chinese American is to navigate two different cultures and form multiple identities, and this process has been impacted by different forms of anti-Asian racisms. Eventually, Annie felt proud to be a Chinese American, but she hoped that young CCAs could get strong support from an early age:

> I'm proud to be a Chinese American now. But I think growing up, it would have been much easier to arrive at the state that I'm in if more people around me had told me that it was okay to be Chinese and American at the same time . . . just accepting that I have had a different lived experience than one side or the

182   Impacts of the COVID-19 Pandemic on Chinese and Chinese American Women

other. And I think it's especially important now in the time of the COVID-19 pandemic, with the rise of anti-Asian sentiments, that we really need to have solidarity with our Asian communities, and especially with other communities of color, too.

Annie articulated the complexities, struggles, and challenges of growing up biculturally and the conflicts and tensions between being "too Chinese to be American" and "too American to be Chinese." As the process of becoming a Chinese American is very challenging, she has encouraged CCA parents to help their children navigate cultural conflicts at an early age and to recognize the advantages in finding solidarities with other underrepresented groups.

The lunchbox incident did not happen to all CCA children, and some panelists have embraced their Chinese food traditions and Chinese American identities without problems. Yihan graduated from college in 2021 and was a product manager at DoorDash living in San Francisco with her husband and their two cats. She felt fortunate to have a lot of great Chinese supermarkets nearby, and she loved cooking Chinese dishes, such as fish-flavored eggplant, dan dan noodles, and mapo tofu. She did not spend much time thinking about being Chinese American as she was very comfortable with who she was. Being Chinese American is a part of her identity just as being a woman in a male-dominated business world is also a part of her identity. She said, "I feel very lucky to be in a place where there are a lot of Asian Americans [and] working at a company where there are Chinese Americans and Indian Americans in leadership. And to be in a world today where I think there's a lot more Asian representation in media and Asians in leading roles in media where they're not defined by being Asian, they're just another person on the show with a lot of different aspects of their identity."

Jinmu enjoyed Chinese food very much as she was born and raised in China; she later moved to the US in her teens. She shared her unique experiences as follows:

> As I was growing up, everything that I did or all the foods that I ate were considered the majority. So I never felt that I was left out. I never felt that my culture was less than or like my food was disgusting. But after I came to the US when I was fourteen, I started high school in the Deep South. That was quite a culture shock because I was the only Asian kid in my very, I guess, prestigious southern private school. Everyone else is White. So that was a very special and interesting experience for me, because all of a sudden, everything that I know, my culture, my food, my holidays, all of a sudden, all those things were considered the minority. So I had to figure out a way to fit in, but also keep that pride in me of who I am, keep that pride, make sure that I still feel proud of me and my culture and just being a Chinese person—that went on for four years. That was a very special time. I was confused for quite some time, but eventually, I did make my

Fluid Foodways, Racisms, and Everyday Lives   183

way to college in the north, in New Jersey. So after I came to New Jersey, that was quite a liberating experience, because I got to know more people with the same background like me, people that are born and raised in China or Chinese Americans that grew up in the Chinese culture. So I feel like, once again, I'm able to enjoy all the things that I used to enjoy with other people that I know they're enjoying the same thing as me. That was like I said, a very enjoyable and liberating experience.

The culture shocks Jinmu experienced when she moved from China to the American South affected her deeply, and she struggled to fit in while maintaining her pride in her Chinese culture. Once she found her communities of support in college, she regained her joy in eating Chinese food and being Chinese. Because of these situations, she hoped that the school systems in the US would be able to better support Asian and Asian American students. She knew that school staff only had minimal experience or training in multicultural conversations, and so many were not prepared to have those types of conversations with AAPI students. She encouraged CCA parents to reach out to schools and advocate for their children: "I think it's really up to us to encourage your children's school, to facilitate these types of conversations and encourage these conversations to happen, reach out to your children's teachers, reach out to the school counselors, reach out to the principal, do whatever we can to have these types of conversations happen and encourage the students to be proud of who they are and to continue and facilitate these types of conversations in mainstream American schools to better support our Chinese American students." The recommendations made by Jinmu were in alignment with the thoughts of numerous AAPI activist mothers. Subsequently, similar recommendations were implemented in the state of New Jersey as well as in some other states.

Alan graduated from Columbia University in 2017 and used to volunteer for PCE Club in high school. He emphasized the importance of focusing on strategies and solutions rather than hardships faced by CCAs and AAPIs. Based on his individual experiences, he encouraged CCA parents to raise children with strong characters and virtues:

My experience has shown me that what a child is raised well means . . . that you end up with a strong child, and by strong I mean all these following characteristics: virtuous, capable, competent, emotionally regulated, high EQ, and that manifests as, for example, like being able to take individual responsibility for your actions and your outcome, being able to aim at the highest version of yourself, being able to make friends easily and rely on those relationships for help, and being able to make promises or keep to your promises so that other people learn to rely on you and trust you.

To raise strong children, Alan recommended that CCA parents embody all these values and build strong relationships with their children.

Michelle, a senior at Rutgers University, majoring in cultural anthropology and minoring in journalism, really loves being Chinese American and is very proud of it. It took her a while to get to this point, but since then she has been very happy to primarily eat Chinese foods, speak Chinese in public, and hang out with other Chinese Americans. She agreed with Alan about staying strong and taking individual responsibilities, but she also wanted to work with her community to create some structural changes:

> Because you can tell anybody you need to be strong, but it's also about what can we do together as a community to make it so that kids don't need to always have their barriers up, because I think that's a really unfortunate way to have to grow up. And I don't think the world should be as cruel and hateful as it is. And I think that if we were to come together, we can definitely change that. So what can you do? Jinmu talked about this a little bit earlier with getting more involved in the education system and everything like that. When I was in high school, I was really determined. I lobbied the board of education of my town for two years to recognize the Lunar New Year as an official district holiday. At the end of the two years, I was a senior and I graduated, so I didn't get to enjoy the fruits of my labor. But it worked. So I've been out of high school for like four years now, time goes by so quickly, I didn't even realize it. But for the past four years, students have had time off on the Lunar New Year to be able to actually celebrate that with their families and sit down and be able to make food with their families, and watch the Chinese TV [Spring Festival Gala] . . . and just engage in that culture. It's something that I didn't have access to. But I made it my mission to ensure that other children in the community would be able to have access to that. And I think you can also take it a step further. There is so much Asian American activist history. We have a legacy in this country of activism, and we don't know about it. And that's why it's so hard for us to continue that legacy. . . . Like Asian American, it always feels as if it's a new identity, but the reality is that it's not, we have a history in this country and we belong here, and we deserve to feel like we belong here, but it's really important to even know that.

Michelle emphasized the importance of crafting communities of support for CCA children and creating social changes to make this world a better place for all. She inherited the legacy of Asian American activism, which manifested in her work to have the Lunar New Year recognized in her school district, and hoped that more young CCAs would know and continue that legacy.

Young CCA panelists consider education, supportive parenting, and community engagement to be good solutions to combat anti-Asian racisms.

They think that it is important for CCA parents to educate themselves and their children about racisms, have conversations about these issues from early on, make them visible in the local communities, and advocate for inclusive curriculums in schools so that future generations of CCAs and Asian, Asian American, and Pacific Islanders (AAAPIs) do not have to experience the same discrimination and exclusion again. Furthermore, they state that CCA parents and children should not only talk about these issues, but also take active roles in ensuring that anti-Asian racisms are addressed from individual to structural levels, and important social changes are made by joint efforts.

The final panelist, Raymond, was the student body president at Washington University in St. Louis, where he was a sophomore studying political science and sociology. He emphasized the importance of acknowledging the impacts of racisms on Asian Americans and promoting structural changes to combat them:

> We know that we are viewed in certain ways when we go into certain rooms. And we know that we face these consistent racist actions across the board, right? We all share these different experiences that are very, very similar. The idea of people looking at our lunches and thinking that it looks gross; people who might look at us differently, who ask us if we have COVID-19 because of our skin color—this consistency in experience shows that there is a form of racism that we do all experience. So I think instead of shying away from that and trying to say that we need to live our lives ignoring that, we should address it head-on and try to create the structural changes that many of our panelists have been talking about.
>
> On race, I really want to talk about a few pieces of this. I'm very similar to Michelle. I'm very proud of my Asian identity. And when I ran for student body president, I made it very clear that I am someone who is both Asian and gay, and I'm at this school on a lot of financial aid. Those are all characteristics that I'm not shy about and things that I'm actually very proud about, because I think they inform who I am and make me a stronger and more resilient person. Then I want us to be able to acknowledge these identities, because I think they all impact and inform the way that we are treated in society, and teaching our kids that they are growing up in a society that will look at them differently will be the best way to prepare them to be resilient in the face of that adversity.

Raymond was passionate in his viewpoint on how to address racisms, and he also discussed the need for more genuine representations of Asian Americans in media, governments, and positions of power. He further suggested that activism should not subjugate others and that the struggles for Asian American rights are tied to the liberation struggles of all people:

Asian American rights in the United States actually came from a lot of activism, like previous speakers mentioned, of Black people, of Latinx people, undocumented people, LGBTQ+ rights—the fact that our rights are tied to the liberation struggles of all people should cause us to be allies in their struggles as well. . . . I don't think any of us want to live in a society when you are oppressed and denied potential because of the way that you look, because of who you love, because of the gender that you are. I think embracing this type of vision for the Asian community will both make us more politically engaged and make us more visible in the public sphere.

If we want to raise healthy, productive, and moral children, I think we have to start at the roots of why we face discrimination and why we experience pain in the first place and working together to build a society that reflects our values and allowing our children to flourish as themselves as opposed to trying to fit them into these boxes that society has told us Asian Americans are.

The young panelists emphasized that CCA parents' acceptance, care, and empathy were crucial for building their children's self-confidence. They advised CCA parents not to deny their children's experiences and feelings as ethnic minorities, even if parents grew up in China. They recommended that CCA parents should lead by example by actively embracing both Chinese and American cultures; working with their children to demonstrate initiative, leadership, and creativity; and gradually guiding schools and communities to be more inclusive and diverse.

Some action plans proposed by young panelists were implemented by AAAPI activist mothers and their allies through national movements to develop AAPI curriculums in different states after the Atlanta spa shootings on March 16, 2021. In New Jersey, AAAPI youth participated in the legislative process of advancing AAPI curriculum bills. On the PCE Club panel on February 5, 2022, one of those young people—Christina Huang—shared her personal motivation as follows:

I got involved because I was very passionate about political science and social justice work. I talked to my teachers a lot about it. I didn't plan on like any of this. I guess there are just little steps at a time. I spoke at a rally, and seeing all the things that went on in the news made me feel very sad, very frustrated. I think I wanted to get involved and tried to make a change where I thought that there wasn't any. I think the whole thing, the bill, a big part of it was, I guess as like an Asian American student, I often felt that I guess my history wasn't seen and I didn't really see much of it, of Asian American history until last year [2021], my junior year [in high school], and I did a research paper last year on like racism in the education system and looking at some of that and it kind of like inspired me to also get involved in that since then.

Christina was a junior high school student when she participated in advocating for AAPI curriculum bills in 2021 in New Jersey. What happened to AAAPIs in 2020 and 2021 was disheartening to her but also motivated her to get involved and make important social changes. She reflected on youth participation in the legislative process, noting,

> I think it's very important that we have more youth speakers because it's about taking control of the classroom that we should be getting involved in what we learn. We should have people that look like us in our textbooks. I think as Asian American students, we share a lot of stories and experiences, but we don't talk about them. I think I grow up sometimes feeling ashamed of some of the things. No one talks about it, like for instance, mental health, or if something happens in class or someone calls something, kind of pretend that it doesn't happen and you move on. But I think it's the point that we talk about it, and kind of like lead this movement, I guess, as students.

Christina noted that there were not enough resources to support CCA parents and children to talk about racisms together; however, being able to participate in advancing the bills helped change realities for herself, her peers, and future generations of CCA youth. The experience meant a lot to her, and she said, "I think it showed me that if you're very passionate about something or you see something that is wrong or things that could be changed, do get involved and advocate for yourself."

Christina received strong support from activist mothers, including her mother Ke Yongxi, who was an active member in local communities. Christina considered her mother as her "No. 1 supporter" or "biggest supporter," and her mother was always there to help her when she needed it. For example, when Christina testified for the education committee hearing in the state house, her mother left everything and drove her for two hours to attend the hearing. Christina felt empowered by her mother's support, which enabled her to give back to the world as well.

To advance the AAPI curriculum bills in New Jersey, Kani, Ying, Christina, and other Make Us Visible New Jersey (MUVNJ) leaders started with a statewide open letter calling for participation; they also built connections with almost all AAPI communities and organizations in New Jersey. They thought geographically and strategically about where to find AAPIs in the state. One of their main sources was Ballotpedia, which provides information on the legislative districts and their demographics. Another important source was the school enrollment data published by the Department of Education. They wrote to local AAPI groups and civil rights groups to ask for partnership and allyship.

AAPI youth have played important roles in advocating for AAPI inclusions and visibilities in New Jersey and other states. For instance, AAPI Youth Rising (AYR) is a student-led organization whose mission is to take small actions to make positive changes in AAPI communities. Its founder, Mina, told her stories as follows:

> I spoke about the rise in xenophobia against the AAPI community due to COVID-19 at my school assembly at the beginning of the pandemic back in 2020, at a time when no one was talking about it. After a year of witnessing the increase in anti-Asian sentiment and violence toward my community, I decided to take more action. Originally I had a little idea to hang a sign in support of the AAPI community over the I-80, one of the busiest intersections in California. This small idea evolved into the AAPI Youth Rising Rally.
>
> On March 28, 2021, community members representing the diversity of the Bay Area came together in solidarity with the AAPI community at our rally in Berkeley, California. Originally, I had hoped for seventy participants. To my surprise, over 1,200 participants joined the crowd. On a bright and sunny day, we heard from many brave youth as we raised our voices. A first-grader even spoke up! We then marched to the San Francisco Bay Pedestrian Footbridge and hung our signs on the overpass while we heard motorists honk in support. It was an inspirational day for all of us. In that moment, we realized that even as middle-schoolers, we can make a difference. These small actions add up. (AAPI Youth Rising n.d.)

Because of its great work, AYR was honored by President Biden at the United We Stand Summit at the White House on September 15, 2022, and on May 4, 2023, it was chosen as one of the ten statewide civil rights organizations to collaborate with the California Civil Rights Department to launch California vs. Hate Resource Line and Network to report and address hate across the state. In March 2023, AYR presented its work to the President's Advisory Commission on Asian Americans, Native Hawaiians, and Pacific Islanders (AANHPI): Commission Subcommittee for Health, as part of the White House Initiative on AANHPI. AYR members were invited by Dignity.us, a bipartisan initiative to combat the rise in hate-fueled violence in America, to share their youth perspectives. AYR was also named a 2023 Asia Game Changer West Honoree by the Asia Society Northern California and received the 2023 Allied Organization of the Year and the 2022 Changemaker of the Year awards from Act to Change. The group was selected as the 2022 Girl of the Year Partner Organization by American Girl for the first Chinese American Girl of the Year, Corinne Tan. Through this partnership announcement, AYR's message reached more than 1.3 billion impressions in 2022 (AYR 2022).

Asian Youth Act (AYA) is another student-led civic organization founded in the summer of 2020. Although its founders are from New Jersey, its members are from all over the world. AYA seeks to promote the political and civic engagement of Asian youth through informative and research-centered posts and personal narratives. It is a nonpartisan organization constructed to be an open-minded space where youth can seek empathy, understanding, and collaboration. AYA seeks to empower global Asian students to not only be proactive and informed world citizens but also to inspire change in all generations of AAPI communities.

From May 2021, MUVNJ worked with AYR, AYA, and the Livingston AAPI Youth Alliance in advocating for the New Jersey legislative bills S4021 and A6100, and youth leaders contributed to the passing of both bills. In particular, youth leaders delivered speeches at various webinars hosted by MUVNJ, reached out to New Jersey state legislators to solicit support for the bills, and created/presented written and video testimonies to the New Jersey State Senate and Assembly Education Committees in support of the bills. After the passing of these bills, more individuals from younger generations became involved in advocacy for AAPI visibilities and implementation of the bills in public schools not only in New Jersey but also in other states.

The lunchbox incident and racisms that CCA students experienced have led to a series of youth activisms that aimed to assert and celebrate AAPI cultures and identifications. By collaborating with activist mothers and broader allies, AAPI youth activists have cocreated and sustained diverse communities of support, advocated for AAPI visibilities and inclusions, challenged stereotypes and discrimination, and worked toward social justice for all. As Kyle said, CCA children should feel proud of the cultural foods that they bring with them in their lunchboxes and be open-minded in their interactions with people from other cultures. By working together, they can have the best lunchboxes that they could possibly have in the future.

Fluid Foodways of Chinese Adoptees, Authenticity, and Vernacular Culture

Existing scholarship on Chinese foodways in the US often focuses on the foodways of adult Chinese immigrants and the role of Chinese restaurants (Y. Chen 2014; H. Liu 2015); little attention has been paid to the foodways of Chinese adoptees, who were often brought from China at a young age and rarely carried any memories about their lives in China. They were often raised in White American families and had little or limited exposure to Chinese foodways—therefore, Chinese adoptees' relationships with Chinese foodways are very complicated. Their dietary changes are both similar to and different from adult Chinese immigrants. When adult Chinese immigrants came to the US, there were three kinds of relationships with Chinese foodways: (1) they kept the original recipes and rarely changed them; (2) they abandoned them for an American food lifestyle, or (3) they prepared and ate both Chinese and Western foods, the latter being the most common. As time went by, younger generations became more used to a Western style of eating, which was seen as unhealthy by older generations, who believed that Chinese cuisines were much healthier and more natural than American cuisines (Lv and Cason 2004). Contrastingly, most Chinese adoptees swiftly embraced American foodways upon arriving in the US with their White adoptive families, lacking the opportunity to fully experience traditional Chinese foodways during their upbringing. Consequently, they never truly "abandoned" Chinese foodways, as they had limited exposure to them. If given the chance, many Chinese adoptees express a desire to integrate both Chinese and American foodways into their daily lives.

Among my twenty-six adoptee contributors, twenty-three said that they mainly ate American foods at home, and three said that they ate both American and Chinese or Asian foods. Some thought that American foodways were a mixture of different food traditions. Some did not know what Chinese food was. Carsen, born in 1999 and adopted by a White couple when she was eight months old, explained why she was not familiar with Chinese foodways:

> Growing up my parents never shielded me or tried to keep me away from Chinese culture, but I was literally in the middle of a cornfield most of my childhood. So there wasn't an opportunity. Even in SD, I don't know anything that would let me be introduced to genuine Chinese food or any other food. Specifically, I haven't been going to restaurants a whole lot because of the pandemic. And also, I try to save money. But I know my parents talk about how good Chinese food is, and how it's healthy and things like that. And I like rice. (Interview on February 24, 2021)

Carsen's experiences are very common among my adoptee contributors. As AAAPI history and cultures were excluded from textbooks for a long time, Chinese adoptees didn't have enough opportunity to learn much about China and Chinese cultures at schools. Many Chinese adoptees have never been to China, and their White adoptive parents often do not make enough effort to learn about Chinese cultures and cook Chinese dishes for them. Some Chinese adoptees go to Chinese restaurants with their White adoptive parents once a week or once every few weeks, but they understand that foods in Chinese restaurants in America are different from foods in China.

In Carsen's interview, she mentioned that her White family members teased her about her rice diet. Actually, the racial aspects of rice consumption are embedded in large political and economic contexts. In general, rice diets are common in many Asian societies and thus are perceived as Asian (Bray 2019). In colonial India, rice was once seen to be a "bad" food as it was believed to be less nutritious and less healthy than European staple foods such as wheat; this view contributed to what was conceptualized "to be the moral weakness as well as physical inferiority of the many Indians for whom it constituted the principal diet" (Arnold 2019, 112). Therefore, rice became a racial marker of the inferior others and was used to delineate between not just Europeans and Asians but also Asia's different races and geographical zones. The racialization of rice consumption has persisted to the present, and it has affected my contributors' daily encounters. One contributor mentioned that some White boys shouted "rice" at her on the freeways. The perception of rice as a "bad" food has been further complicated by its association with anti-Asian racisms in everyday lives.

Little or limited exposure to Chinese foodways has made many Chinese adoptees' connection to their cultural roots and heritage even more fragile. The loss of connection to Chinese cultures is very painful for some adoptees, and they have to rebuild those connections, explore their own cultural roots, and remake their own identities. Some Chinese adoptees have learned to cook Chinese dishes by themselves, some have learned to make Chinese foods with their Chinese professors or friends, and some eat frequently in Chinese or Asian restaurants. For example, Helen, a vegetarian, learned to cook Chinese dishes by herself, focusing on rice and vegetable dishes and taking into account the many different ways these ingredients were cooked and seasoned within the variety of local, regional, and national cuisines. Grace learned how to make dumplings with her Taiwanese professor, who invited several students to her house to celebrate the Lunar New Year in February 2020. While her professor made the fillings and dumpling skins, Grace and the other students wrapped them; Grace got the recipe from her professor and was later able to replicate it on her own.

Having experienced both Chinese and American foodways, Grace rejects the notion of viewing them as binary opposites. Instead, she perceives them as existing on a spectrum and positions them at considerable distances from each other in terms of freshness and quality. Grace firmly believes that Chinese cuisines embody greater diversity, flavor, color, freshness, and overall healthiness compared to American foods. As a result, she began incorporating more Chinese dishes into her diet, particularly during the pandemic.

Yang Ji reconnected with Chinese foodways during the pandemic through the family of Eric, her Chinese American boyfriend. Ji was born in Guangdong Province, China, in 1996, and was adopted at eleven months old by her White American parents. She lived in Washington until she went to college in Oregon. After graduating, she worked for two years until losing her job due to lockdowns. The three-month unemployment period was challenging for her as it impacted her sense of self-worth and limited her interactions with family and friends. She chose not to visit her elderly adoptive parents for Thanksgiving and Christmas as a precautionary measure to ensure their safety.

Ji moved in with Eric's family after losing her job. Eric's mother lived in a Chinese village in Vietnam for the first fifteen years of her life before coming to the US, and Eric's father came from mainland China. During the Lunar New Year in January 2020, Ji celebrated with Eric's family for the first time, experiencing traditional Chinese cultures and foodways. It was a joyous occasion for her to connect with Eric's extended family, who warmly welcomed her. Ji felt touched and valued during this gathering, which became a cherished memory as it was their last gathering before the pandemic.

During the pandemic, Ji had the opportunity to consistently eat Chinese foods, which was a new experience for her. Growing up in her White adoptive family, she mostly had American foods like hamburgers and hot dogs. Both of Eric's parents were good cooks, and living with his family, Ji was amazed by the variety of dishes his mother cooked for them every day. It felt like a feast with multiple dishes for each meal, unlike her upbringing with one dish per meal. Ji appreciated the care and effort put into the meals by Eric's mother. Ji's favorite food was homemade *hum bao* (steamed BBQ pork buns), which Eric's mother made for her after realizing her love for it. Ji felt grateful to be in an environment where people expressed their care and concern through food.

During the pandemic was also the first time that Ji looked closely at herself as an adoptee and came out of "the fog." For instance, she became aware of her Asian looks while going out in public. Although she and other adoptees grew up in the US their whole lives, because of their appearances, they were still seen as "permanent foreigners." She thought a lot about Asian American experiences and knew that inequities were evident in how the judicial systems were reacting to the surging anti-Asian hate crimes—too often they did not even see them as hate crimes or racisms at the beginning. Moreover, Ji realized how the myth of the "model minority" harmed AAAPI more than it helped them. She reflected on what it meant to be an Asian American in a difficult time and connected with other Asian adoptees online. She joined the Subtle Asian Adoptee Traits Facebook group, followed different Instagram accounts with resources for adoptees, and had an adoptee pen pal; these groups exposed her to people who validated different experiences that she felt were unique to Asian adoptees.

Ji contemplated her Chinese identity and acknowledged that she hadn't been raised in Chinese cultures, leading her to question what it truly meant to be Chinese. She felt that she hadn't "earned" it as she lacked a deep understanding of Chinese history, and she wanted to approach it with respect. In her perspective, being Chinese involved understanding the culture, learning the language, enjoying Chinese foodways, and immersing oneself while maintaining humility and respect.

Ji often faced the question "Where are you really from?" in conversations, but she questioned the significance of it. By the time of our interview on February 21, 2021, Ji had spent twenty-four years of her life in America. She believes that being born in China and spending only the first eleven months there doesn't negate her American identity. Ji held the belief that anyone could be American, as this was the message America had promoted worldwide with the allure of the American dream. However, she recognized that in reality the American dream was racialized and limited to specific groups, as evidenced by immigration bans and the perception of AAAPIs as perpetual foreigners in America, rather than recognized as true American citizens.

The everyday lived experiences of Chinese adoptees and notions of authenticity are often intertwined. Race, ethnicity, and foodways are used to mark differences and reinforce social boundaries. This differentiation and boundary setting is inconsistent with the value placed on diversity, equality, and inclusiveness. Chinese adoptees encounter notions and questions of authenticity because they feel that they have been seen as "fake" Chinese and "forever foreigners" who are unlikely to be fully integrated into American society. Questions about authenticity and the immigrant condition concern origins, thus Chinese adoptees are often asked the same question: "Where do you come from?" followed by "Where do you *really* come from?"

Authenticity—whether it applies to people, foodways, or other experiences—centers on the notions of origins or roots (Manalansan 2013). It has racist implications when placing it in the lived experiences of Chinese adoptees. For White Americans, being able to set people and things in certain places is a way to legitimize their White supremacy and assess the differences or acceptability of people and things in question. Thus, authenticity conveys the ideas of essence and purity of origins and roots, which are conventionally viewed as fixed, static, and unchanging.

Regina Bendix (1997) sought to problematize the fundamental concept of authenticity in folklore studies by arguing that the "search of authenticity" had emerged as one of the most questionable legacies, which persisted in shaping both the field and its subjects. She argued that the shift toward performance merely transitioned authenticity from a material attribute to an experiential dimension. She suggested that comprehending the field's history of constructing authenticity held great potentials for liberation: once we are free of the key dichotomy of authentic versus inauthentic, we can commence an examination of this dichotomy itself as a subject of analysis.

Authenticity is socially and culturally constructed. Foodways are often used by "foodies"—people who love to prepare, talk, think, and learn about food—to shed light on the relationships between symbolic boundaries, authenticity, exoticizing of others, social inequality, and environmental politics. Josée Johnston and Shyon Baumann (2009) link authenticity to exoticism, which represents a cosmopolitan approach to broadening the culinary canon and forming intercultural connections but masks an orientalist and racist discourse of othering, discrimination, and a process of status creation. Rather than foster democracy and equality, authenticity and exoticism facilitate differentiation, distinction, and perpetuation of hierarchies in American society.

I intend to dismantle the White logic of authenticity and propose to use the concept of "the vernacular" as an important lens to examine the fluid foodways of Chinese adoptees in the US. The vernacular has attracted attention since the late nineteenth century, particularly in the field of architecture, as a means of identifying alternatives to modernity. Renewed interests in the vernacular in recent years within more diverse and interdisciplinary discourses indicate the renewed significance of the term in exploring the culture in terms of what has been dismissed and excluded within the modern paradigm of universal enlightenment (Konagaya 2023).

Folklorist Leonard Primiano (1995, 43) defines the vernacular as the "personal, aesthetic, cultural, and social investment . . . as well as the way individuals privately and creatively adapt to their specific life needs." Richard Bauman (2008, 32–33) defines the vernacular as "a communicative modality characterized by: (1) communicative resources and practices that are acquired informally, in communities of practice, rather than by formal instruction; (2) communicative relations that are immediate, grounded in the interaction order and the lifeworld; and (3) horizons of distribution and circulation that are spatially bounded, by locality or region. The vernacular, furthermore, can only be understood in dynamic relation to the cosmopolitan." With "vernacular turns" in folklore studies and the increasing visibility of the vernacular in public culture, Diane Goldstein (2015) suggests folklorists pay close attention to how the vernacular is used, abused, appropriated, celebrated, critiqued, and discarded within particular contexts.

The vernacular has now enhanced its critical perspectives, particularly within the decolonial and global contexts, by dismantling the dominant, official, Western, and elitist assumptions of culture and identifications, and highlighting the marginalized, unofficial, non-Western, excluded, and so on (Konagaya 2023). Ben Bridges, Ross Brillhard, and Diane E. Goldstein (2023, 5) define the vernacular "as a broad category of local knowledge production and action that is reflective of a particular group or region and focused on community-based forms of expression." They consider vernacular culture to "be flexible, dynamic, multi-sourced, and global" (5).

Vernacular culture, which may align or contrast with mainstream narratives, often integrates elements from dominant ideologies, using them in ways such as borrowing, adapting, or commodifying. It is deeply rooted in local experiences and can be best understood within its cultural contexts. The COVID-19 pandemic has shed light on the diverse faces of vernacular culture and how it is utilized, appropriated, celebrated, or even discarded (Bridges, Brillhard, and Goldstein 2023). It has underscored themes like community, creativity, fluidity, traditions, resistance, and resilience. This study captures these themes and illustrates Chinese adoptees' discourses, practices, and actions to cope with anti-Asian racisms and the pandemic. In chapter 4, I examine how Chinese adoptees drew on diverse vernacular cultural forms to articulate and exert their creative agencies in building communities of support, fighting for social justice, and remaking their identities. Furthermore, some Chinese adoptees use disidentification as a strategy to express their agencies in articulating their feelings and combating racisms (Muñoz 1999). Chinese adoptees, often navigating complex identities within predominantly White society, also employ creative foodways as a form of disidentification. This strategy involves neither assimilating into the dominant culture nor rejecting it entirely but instead engaging with it critically and creatively to articulate one's agency and challenge systemic inequalities.

For Chinese adoptees, creative foodways serve as a nuanced form of disidentification. Foodways, often tied to culture and identities, offer a tangible medium through which these individuals express and explore their creative agencies. The act of disidentification through foodways does not conform to the dominant cultural narratives about authenticity; instead, it allows Chinese adoptees to articulate their feelings, combat racisms, and challenge stereotypes. By choosing how to (dis)integrate Chinese foodways into their lives, they can subtly yet powerfully critique and reshape the dominant White cultural logics from within. Moreover, these creative foodways embody the daily acts of resistance Muñoz describes. Every meal or food-related interaction becomes an opportunity to assert agency, celebrate heritage, and challenge monolithic narratives. These acts might seem small in isolation, but collectively, they contribute to broader structural changes by fostering understanding, challenging stereotypes, and creating spaces for nuanced expressions of agencies and identities. It shows the power and fluidity of the vernacular and their resistance on the ground.

Chinese Women Students' Dietary Changes and Comfort Foodways

Comfort foodways are traditionally linked to American culture, embodying a distinct food ethos (Long 2022), but it is evident that the idea of seeking comfort through foodways exists in other cultures as well. Considering the profound connections between foodways and cultural identities, it is natural to explore the diasporic aspects when investigating comfort foodways across diverse cultures. In Chinese communities worldwide, comfort foodways are practiced differently by different people in different places. For instance, what qualifies as comfort foodways for individuals residing in China might differ significantly from those of Chinese descent residing elsewhere. This aligns with common observations of ethnic foodways, where individuals and communities must adapt their foodways to the particular cultural environments they inhabit (Mehravari 2022, 11). Building on the existing scholarship but complicating our understanding of comfort foodways, this section illustrated how Chinese women students in the US experienced and reflected on dietary changes and comfort foodways during the pandemic.

Chinese women students—facing racisms, discrimination, exclusions, and mental health issues—drew on Chinese foodways to rebuild their homes as imaginary landscapes and connect with their cultural traditions. In my interviews, they often reflected on their foodways and dietary changes during the pandemic. Sixteen women students started cooking for themselves during the lockdowns, and their cooking skills were improved by this experience. Some contributors found comforts in cooking delicious Chinese dishes while in isolation, and some emphasized the significance of maintaining healthy and balanced diets to strengthen their immune systems.

Qin meticulously planned her daily meals and recorded them on a small blackboard in her apartment. For breakfast, she liked to cook Wuhan hot dry noodles, a renowned and popular dish with an eighty-year history. Being from Wuhan, she frequently enjoyed this dish for breakfast back in China. Her preference for Wuhan hot dry noodles as breakfast highlights the significance of this food as part of comfort foodways for her and reflects her desire to connect with her cultural and culinary roots. Similarly, for lunch, Qin liked to cook red braised eggplant, a dish that holds cultural and sentimental value for her. Her nutritious and balanced dinner, once consisting of salmon, baked potato, fried green lentils with salmon sauce, and a slice of watermelon, demonstrated her focus on maintaining a healthy diet while still incorporating comforting elements. Overall, Qin's meal choices illustrate how comfort foodways play a role in providing a sense of comfort, nostalgia, home, and well-being within her daily life.

During the pandemic, Qin tried many new recipes and learned to cook several special dishes, including red braised beef (*hong shao niu rou*), fried salmon, red braised pig trotter (*hong shao zhu ti*), and others. She also learned to bake potatoes, pork chops, and chicken drumsticks, along with scones, bread, and cakes. Qin felt that cooking eased her stress and made her enjoy her life, noting, "After I spent a lot of time cooking, my happiness in life was immediately brought up, and I was very happy" (interview on June 16, 2020).

The pursuit of a "balance of nutrients" (*ying yang jun heng*) and a "combination of meat and vegetables" (*hun su da pei*) was a common goal among many women students, driven by their desire to strengthen their immune systems and maintain a healthy body. Due to limited control over their diets in college dining halls, some often relied on consuming ample vegetables and fruits to maintain a balanced diet. During lockdowns in early 2020, some students chose to move out of their dorms, rent apartments near campus, and cook meals for themselves. Meng and Rong, for instance, rented an apartment together and began cooking and dining together. Meng learned to cook during junior high school and improved over time, eventually cooking delicious meals for her Chinese friends in college. Meng said that the biggest life change for her during the pandemic was that she did not eat in the dining hall but ate more meals cooked by herself. She felt good choosing what she ate every day and eating whatever she wanted. By controlling the amounts of oil and carbohydrates in her diet, Meng successfully lost weight, in contrast to many who experienced weight gain while staying at home. She and Rong kept healthy diets with a "combination of meat and vegetables." Their typical daily meal included rice or noodles, a dish of meat, a dish of vegetables, and soup. For instance, one day their dinner included fat beef in sour soup (*suan tang fei niu*), stir-fried eggs with Chinese chives (*jiu cai chao dan*), and pork rib soup (*pai gu tang*). With Meng's cooking skills, Rong gladly took on errands and dishwashing responsibilities. During busy school periods, Meng sometimes prepared two days' worth of meals at once, allowing her to save time for studying.

Proficiency in culinary skills holds significant value for Chinese students studying abroad due to limited access to desired dishes in the US and the high costs associated with dining out. Despite the presence of student dining facilities at American colleges and universities, female Chinese students often expressed dissatisfaction with the available meals. This sentiment arose from their upbringing in China, where they were immersed in the rich culinary traditions of their homeland. Consequently, their palates, affectionately referred to as "Chinese stomachs" (*zhongguo wei*), exhibited strong preferences for Chinese cuisines regardless of their geographic locations. To prepare Chinese meals that cater to their discerning palates, some female students proactively pursued culinary education at specialized culinary schools, often facilitated by their international high schools in China, before they studied abroad, whereas others received culinary training from their mothers or other family members in China. Frequently, they improved their cooking skills through diverse means such as educational videos on platforms like YouTube or TikTok or by closely following recipes available on Xiachufang, a renowned Chinese application known for its extensive collection of millions of recipes and a vibrant culinary community.

If they tested positive for COVID-19, Chinese female students immediately transformed their dietary practices. Students were often required to be quarantined if they tested positive for COVID-19, and so they often had to resort to online meal orders, receiving their sustenance directly at their doorstep. One female student said that her college allocated a daily stipend of sixty dollars to cover the costs of three meals during her hotel quarantine. Alternatively, if the affected students resided in rented apartments, their roommates sometimes assumed the responsibility of cooking meals for them. For example, Shan, a graduate student enrolled in a prominent public research university and living in an apartment with two roommates, tested positive for COVID-19 on November 18, 2021, and remained confined to her room until November 27. During this period, Shan experienced several symptoms, including high fever, diarrhea, cough, and fatigue. To alleviate her discomfort, she resorted to medications such as fever reducers and over-the-counter cold remedies, namely, DayQuil and NyQuil. One of Shan's roommates also received positive test results, necessitating her self-isolation within the apartment. While Shan rested, her Chinese roommate Yao—fully vaccinated and unaffected—took on the responsibility of grocery shopping and cooking meals. Shan's Chinese friends also generously delivered food items to her doorstep, and Yao prepared nourishing pork rib soup with daikon (*luobo paigu tang*), accompanied by porridge, and also offered pickled vegetables (*xue li hong*) to aid Shan's recovery. Despite her diminished appetite and reluctance to eat, Shan compelled herself to eat meals to facilitate a speedy recuperation.

Some individuals infected with COVID-19 encountered a notable reduction or complete loss of smell and taste, with the duration of this impairment ranging from a span of two days to two weeks. While many eventually regained their sense of smell and taste, a subset of patients endured persistent long-term deficiencies in these sensory faculties. For female students who experienced such loss, the inability to perceive flavors and aromas made the act of cooking difficult at best and transformed the act of eating into a necessity for sustenance rather than a source of pleasure. Scientists identified the loss of smell and taste as prevalent symptoms among adolescents who tested positive for COVID-19, often exhibiting spontaneous recovery within a few weeks alongside the resolution of other associated symptoms (Kumar et al. 2021).

In my study, I asked Chinese women students to reflect on the foods of great significance to them during the pandemic. Among various responses, hotpot emerged as the most popular comfort food. Xia reminisced about the routine practice of indulging in hotpot with her Chinese friends every Friday evening in their dormitory, following the reopening of their college in the fall of 2020. During these gatherings, each participant contributed a food item, resulting in a collaborative culinary experience. For instance, on one given occasion, one student brought two cans of tomatoes to create the soup base, while another procured beef balls from an Asian grocery store. Additional offerings included meat, crab legs, cabbages, and an assortment of vegetables. With a simmering pot positioned at the center of their dining table, the group engaged in cheerful conversations while simultaneously cooking individual portions of meat, seafood, and vegetables in the flavorful broth. As the hotpot transformed into an aromatic concoction infused with the essence of the various ingredients, the participants further enhanced their dining experience by engaging in lively group activities. The combination of delectable cuisine and the companionship of friends cultivated a highly enjoyable communal dining atmosphere, offering Xia comfort and support during challenging times.

Another important comfort foodways practice for Chinese women students is making and eating dumplings. In the north of China, dumplings are often made at family reunion dinners during the Spring Festival because of the auspicious meanings they bear—dumplings are symbols of good fortunes as well as the passing of the old days and the coming of new happy days. The making of dumplings has been very popular among Chinese students to celebrate the Spring Festival. The skills, materials, forms, and meanings of making dumplings are interwoven with their community lives and cultural traditions. Meng said that the pandemic made her like eating dumplings more because they were always delicious and represented "a taste of home."

The concept of "comfort food" is a familiar one to folklorists, whether such foods "generate feelings of comfort or cause distress, unite families or produce conflict, celebrate tradition or challenge it, remind individuals of pleasant experiences or force them to confront painful memories" (M. Jones and Long 2017, 13). Comfort foods and foodways are often explored in American contexts, but here I examine them among Chinese women students in transnational contexts. During the pandemic, making and having hotpots, dumplings, and other comfort foods with friends helped Chinese women students combat stress and feelings of loneliness and isolation, create connections with their homeland, and build new communities in America. For many Chinese women students who had to stay in the US, traditions and connections satisfied through comfort foodways are not only related to their homeland but also to the community that they created after they studied abroad. The comforts offered by Chinese foodways represent how they wanted to live before, during, and after the pandemic.

The emphasis on age and gender differences has been a major trend in the study of comfort foods among scholars in different fields. Laurette Dubé, Jordan LeBel, and Ji Lu (2005) found that men's comfort food consumption was motivated by positive emotions, whereas women's consumption was triggered by negative effects, and younger participants reported more intense negative emotions before consuming comfort foods. Jayanthi Kandiah and colleagues (2006) explored the impacts of stress on appetite and eating habits related to comfort foods in American women college students (seventeen to twenty-six years old), finding that American women students with an increased appetite chose significantly more types of sweet foods and mixed dishes when stressed. Sweet foods commonly eaten were desserts, chocolate/candy bars, candy, ice cream, muffins/sweet bread, and fresh or canned fruit, whereas mixed dishes commonly eaten were burgers or sandwich meat items, pizza, casseroles, tacos, ethnic foods, and fast food.

Different from their American peers, Chinese women students often chose foods from their hometowns for comfort, such as hot dry noodles, crossing-the-bridge noodles (*guoqiao mixian*), rice noodle rolls (*chang fen*), Beijing roast duck (*Beijing kaoya*), dim sum, and savory soy milk and fried breadstick (*doujiang youtiao*) as well as special foods cooked by their mothers or grandmothers. For instance, Yue took a gap year before coming back to the US in 2021, and she appreciated all the delicious foods made by her grandmother and mother at home. She could not eat those dishes in the US, and when she tasted them at home, she burst into tears from happiness. She said, "The taste of home makes me feel greatly comforted."

The pandemic challenged the fundamental human needs to belong and to make social connections. Feelings of loneliness and a lack of social connections caused many problems for Chinese women students, including anxiety, depression, and other mental health issues. For them, comfort food-ways served as "social surrogates" that derive their unique emotional power from their connections to home and existing relationships, and reduced their feelings of loneliness, isolation, and exclusion (Troisi and Gabriel 2011).

Being far away from their homeland, struggling with COVID-19 and racisms continually, feeling "overwhelmed" or "abandoned" in both host and home societies, and many other circumstances made Chinese women students feel alone, isolated, excluded, and depressed. In this context, the embrace of comfort foodways has been particularly healing for them. These types of foodways provide comfort for not only their bodies but also their souls.

Comfort foods carry different perceptions of health in American and Chinese foodways. While comfort foods are often viewed as unhealthy in America, they hold a different significance in Chinese culinary traditions. In America, comfort foods are often associated with indulgence, high-calorie content, and potential negative health effects (M. Jones and Long 2017). However, in Chinese foodways, comfort foods are more closely aligned with nourishment, balance, and the promotion of overall well-being. Chinese foodways emphasize the use of fresh ingredients, a variety of veg-etables, and cooking techniques that retain nutritional value, and practices of eating together. These stark contrasts in the perceptions of comfort foods reflect the cultural and dietary differences between the two cultures, which reminds us that our understanding of what constitutes comfort foodways is influenced by our cultural perspectives and societal norms. Recognizing and appreciating the diversity in how comfort foodways are viewed can broaden our understanding of healthy eating practices and encourage a more inclu-sive approach to food studies.

In addition, the American approaches to comfort foodways often focus on individuals seeking emotional support or satisfaction. However, these foodways could also serve as a means to alienate people or highlight their lack of belonging. Jerry Reed (2022) reflects on how dietary restrictions pre-vent certain individuals from finding comforts in food, underscoring their differences from the prevailing norms. While Reed's interviewees managed to overcome these obstacles, he points out that others were not as fortunate, emphasizing the fact that not everyone has the privilege of finding comfort through food. On the other hand, some individuals intentionally utilize comfort foodways to spark social change. Christine J. Widmayer (2022) dis-cusses a community group in Minnesota called Sweet Potato Comfort Pie that bakes and distributes sweet potato pies to bring solace to those affected by racial violence or other adversities and to express gratitude to activists dedicated to racial justice. Moreover, the pies foster an environment of care and support within the group's initiatives, which facilitate challenging conversations about White supremacy and systemic racisms in times of crisis.

The complexities of comfort foodways were amplified during the pandemic, leading folklorists to recognize the power of foodways in carrying memories, fostering and validating relationships, and enriching our sense of belonging (Long 2022). The future significance of comfort foodways remains uncertain and open to exploration. As our society evolves and adapts to new circumstances, the role of comfort foodways may continue to evolve as well. It is crucial to recognize the dynamics of our relationships with foodways and remain open to potential changes and developments that lie ahead.

Fluid Foodways of Chinese Lay Buddhist Women and Vegetarianism

The way people interact with foodways plays a crucial role in shaping, performing, and resisting various conceptualizations of gender in the US. Foodways can either reinforce conservative ideologies that uphold unequal social hierarchies where gender intersects with other identifications like race, ethnicity, class, ability, and sexuality, or they can be employed by individuals of all genders to challenge inequitable gender systems and create alternative spaces and expressions of identifications. Folklorists, both in academia and public settings, recognize and value the creativity and cultural contributions of marginalized individuals, shedding light on women and others who are often overlooked or oppressed. Moreover, they critically examine the construction and perpetuation of gender systems, while also exploring how folklore can be harnessed for positive social transformation (Gilman 2018).

In chapter 5, I have illustrated how Buddhism empowers Chinese lay Buddhist women to express their creative agencies within particular contexts. Ina Marie Lunde Ilkama (2022, 53) writes, "We need to acknowledge different types of female ritual agency—as agency is more than resistance against oppressive structures and taking over roles traditionally reserved for men," and she defines "religious agency" as "the power of creativity and innovation." She continues, "Religious agency is about gaining and exercising the power to influence how things happen, and this may take many forms; from subtle to more overt, the agents oscillate from audience to main ritual performers" (61). The interpretations and definitions of agencies are contextually grounded in the lives and concerns of Buddhist women, highlighting that their religious agencies might either reinforce gender norms or challenge and transform them.

Vegetarianism serves as a significant avenue through which Chinese lay Buddhist women in the US negotiate their identities and exercise their creative agencies. Although vegetarianism existed in China before the introduction of Buddhism during the Han Dynasty (202 BCE–220 CE), its religious significance surged with the spread of Buddhism. By the tenth century, vegetarianism had become a standard practice in Chinese Buddhism, distinguishing it from Buddhism in other regions where such practices were less common (Kieschnick 2005). The adoption and adherence to vegetarianism within Chinese Buddhism stemmed from broader moral concerns regarding the killing of animals for food, sentiments shared by other religious and philosophical traditions, including Confucianism and Daoism (Klein 2016). The association of meat consumption with immoral excess played a pivotal role in promoting the acceptance of vegetarianism within Chinese Buddhist communities. In addition to karmic retribution and Buddhist ethical precepts, the concept of Buddhist vegetarianism also intersected with modern scientific discourses, particularly the Western biomedical notion of hygiene (Lu 2021).

In the US, although vegetarianism was often associated with the 1960s and 1970s, a burgeoning vegetarian movement occurred in the early nineteenth century, with advocates focused mainly on the moral and physiological rationales for vegetarianism instead of ethical concerns for the treatment of animals (Puskar-Pasewicz 2010). American vegetarianism did not exist in isolation from the rest of the world, and it was largely influenced by vegetarianism in other cultures. With the coming of tens of thousands of Chinese immigrants after the changes in immigration law in the 1960s, Chinese Buddhists started to influence the dynamics of Buddhism in America (Seager 2012). As many lay Buddhists attempted to maintain vegetarian diets, they brought their unique foodways to America.

Vegetarianism plays an important role in the formation of Chinese laywomen's personal and religious identities as Buddhists and provides them with a sense of belonging and continuity. It also appears to be a fluid, subjective category that is "good to think" (Tambiah 1969; Twigg 1979, 31), with some laywomen identifying themselves as vegetarian while staying flexible in their daily lives, especially when their family members are not vegetarians. For instance, Shuilian was first introduced to vegetarian diets when she attended Buddhist summer camps in Florida in 2001. Many Taiwanese laywomen worked there as volunteers and cooked a variety of vegetarian meals for the participants. Those meals were delicious, and Shuilian happily enjoyed them. She managed to maintain a vegetarian diet shortly afterward. Shuilian liked to cook vegetarian dishes for her and her husband, but when her children were back home, she cooked meat for them. Her vegetarian meals were very diverse. For breakfast, she liked to cook porridge and vegetable pancakes or toast bread, and for lunch and dinner, she made noodles, fried rice, steamed buns with fillings, or dumplings. She also liked to add in winter melon soup, seaweed soup, or other vegetable soups for lunch and dinner.

The relationships between vegetarianism and identities are complicatedly constructed in particular social and cultural contexts. Food choices and identities are mutually constitutive, with identities both derived from and influenced by food choices. Identities are also affected by other personal situations, social and physical environments, and communities and are consequently both stable and fluid. Over time, food choices foster self-images and are an ongoing source of self-reflection and self-evaluation. For instance, Chinese adoptee Sarah's journey toward vegetarianism commenced during her high school years when she embraced Buddhism. Although she did not disclose the original impetus behind her decision to her White Christian adoptive parents, she informed them that she chose vegetarianism due to its perceived sustainability. Sarah's family supported her choice and began preparing one or two vegetarian dishes for her at home. Meanwhile, during school hours, she opted for vegetarian meals provided in the dining hall or purchased vegan foods from stores. She particularly enjoyed pasta with spinach, a tofu rice vegetable mix, and fruits in season; she also liked to drink green tea.

For many Chinese lay Buddhist women in the US, vegetarianism provides a profound means of forging and reinforcing connections with their broader social, cultural, and religious communities. As these women navigate their roles in a constantly changing world, their commitment to vegetarianism embodies deliberate and meaningful interactions with their hybrid communities. This conscious engagement with vegetarianism allows for the creation of reciprocal relationships, enriching their connections and fostering a sense of belonging. It is through these daily, deliberate food choices that these women articulate and reaffirm their agencies and identities, weaving together the threads of their personal beliefs and spiritual aspirations. In doing so, they not only nurture their individual selves but also contribute to the vibrancy and resilience of their communities. Thus, for these Chinese lay Buddhist women in the US, vegetarianism is a powerful medium, integrating the personal with the communal and the spiritual with the societal, in their pursuit of a balanced and interconnected existence.

Conclusion

Integrating eighty-three interviews, virtual ethnography, virtual panels, and class surveys, this chapter examines the impacts of the COVID-19 pandemic on CCA communities in their fluid foodways and everyday lives, and the interplay of racisms, foodways, and gender. The analysis begins with the lunchbox incident, which serves as a pivotal moment in the experiences and narratives of CCA young adults, encapsulating their struggles around identification and belonging. For some CCA youth, the lunchbox incident ignited an engagement with political activism to advocate for racial justice and systemic change. Furthermore, this chapter delves into the fluid foodways of Chinese adoptees, revealing how culinary practices are intertwined with changing notions of authenticity and vernacular culture. It illustrates how foodways become a medium for adoptees to connect with their cultural heritage, negotiate their identities, and navigate the nuances of cultural belonging. Moreover, the chapter examines dietary changes and comfort foodways of Chinese women students, highlighting how food choices are influenced by and reflective of changing environments, racialized and gendered experiences, psychological needs, and the quest for a taste of home. Last, the chapter explores fluid foodways of Chinese lay Buddhist women, with a focus on the intersection of vegetarianism, identification, and spirituality. In short, this chapter presents a snapshot of the diverse and fluid foodways of CCA women and communities in the US. Through the lens of foodways, we gain profound insights into the complexities of identity formation, community building, and social engagement in times of crisis.

During the pandemic, the disruption of supply chains, economic instability, social restrictions, and anti-Asian racisms significantly impacted CCA women's abilities to maintain consistent and culturally meaningful foodways and everyday lives. They faced numerous challenges in sustaining livelihoods, maintaining well-being, and fostering a sense of belonging. In a way, the sense of precariousness made CCA young adults like Kyle reflect on the lunchbox incidents and racisms they experienced in school and find the best strategies to combat racisms. It made Qin, Meng, Rong, Xia, and other Chinese women students use hotpot, dumplings, and other foods to connect with home, craft new communities, and seek comfort to reduce their feelings of loneliness, isolation, and exclusion. It made Yang Ji and other Chinese adoptees reconnect with their cultural heritage and negotiate their racial, ethnic, and cultural (dis)identifications. It made Shuilian and other Chinese lay Buddhist women reaffirm their personal and social identities as Buddhists and strengthen their sense of belonging and compassion.

Precariousness is often used to describe our experiences during the pandemic, with various affects and emotions accompanying this sense of "precariousness": "fear, vulnerability, a sense of the fragility of hope, a certain foreclosing of future dreams and aspirations, a sense of foreboding" (Shepherd 2023, 7). Living with precariousness, uncertainty, and instability is not new for many people in the Global South and in marginalized communities in the Global North. As decolonial thinkers such as Walter Mignolo, Gloria Anzaldúa, Enrique Dussel, Arturo Escobar, and others point out, colonialism has ingrained precariousness into the lives of conquered populations and territories through actions like genocide, resource extraction, and the eradication of cultural practices (Fforde et al. 2023). The systematic creation of precariousness has been an integral part of modern history, alongside narratives of progress, development, and scientific advancements. During the COVID-19 pandemic, a sense of precariousness was perceived as a shared human experience. Attempts by some governments to impose travel bans and quarantines could not fully respond to the pandemic, which required global collective action. Beyond these specific issues, there may be a broader underlying logic at play—a result of centuries of history. The capitalist frontiers historically followed the colonial frontiers, wreaking devastating violence on various populations and territories they encountered (Butler 2009, 2012; Fforde et al. 2023; Gnecco 2023; Waterton, Saul, and Tolia-Kelly 2023). As new frontiers for conquest and exploitation become scarce, we could envision the frontiers encircling the globe and returning to their origins in the Global North. This shift coincides with the widespread recognition of precariousness as a universal human condition.

Anna Tsing (2015, 2) articulates the complexities of precarity in our everyday lives and writes, "Precarity once seemed the fate of the less fortunate. Now it seems that all our lives are precarious—even when, for the moment, our pockets are lined. In contrast to the mid-twentieth century, when poets and philosophers of the global north felt caged by too much stability, now many of us, north and south, confront the condition of trouble without end." Tsing further explains that her book does not critique the dreams of modernization and progress that promised stability in the twentieth century as many scholars have already analyzed those dreams in detail. Instead, she intends to "address the imaginative challenge of living without those handrails, which once made us think we knew, collectively, where we were going" (2). She explains, "This book tells of my travels with mushrooms to explore indeterminacy and the conditions of precarity, that is, life without the promise of stability" (2). By drawing on the metaphor of a matsutake mushroom emerging from the ruins of Hiroshima, a city devastated by an atomic bomb in 1945, Tsing emphasizes that if we do not hold on to the belief of a global revolution that would transform our future, we have to face the reality of living in the present. She continues, "To live with precarity requires more than railing at those who put us here (although that seems useful too, and I'm not against it). We might look around to notice this strange new world, and we might stretch

Fluid Foodways, Racisms, and Everyday Lives   207

our imaginations to grasp its contours" (3). We are challenged to make sense of "this strange new world," a world without guiding frameworks that once provided stability. This sense of precarity has been intensified since the outbreak of the COVID-19 pandemic. As we are constantly living in a precarious world, we have to cherish what we have, appreciate every meal, and do the best we can to live a meaningful life.

7

CONCLUSION

THIS BOOK PRESENTS DIVERSE LIVED experiences, struggles, actions, and achievements of Chinese immigrant mothers, women international students, transracial adoptees, and lay Buddhist women in the US during the COVID-19 pandemic. Theoretically, I integrate decolonizing, antiracist, global feminist, and anti-oppressive approaches to deconstruct White Western colonial matrixes of power, exploitation, misrepresentation, and knowledge production (Fivecoate, Downs, and McGriff 2021; González-Martin, Martínez-Rivera, and Otero 2022; Otero and Martínez-Rivera 2021; Strega and Brown 2015). In addition, I let Chinese and Chinese American (CCA) women define, articulate, and exert their own strengths, agencies, and strategies that allow their marginalized and oppressed communities to survive, succeed, and thrive, despite the risks, challenges, and uncertainties they face.

In particular, I explore how the COVID-19 pandemic affected CCA women and how they coped with anti-Asian racisms and multiple crises of the pandemic. My main purpose is to dismantle the White Western logic of feminist agency, which values individualization, self-reliance, self-direction, free will, personal choice, and rational thinking. Instead, I illustrate how CCA women define, articulate, and cultivate their diverse forms of creative agencies within their communities during the pandemic. Chinese immigrant mothers, women students, adoptees, and lay Buddhist women struggled with the pandemic in both similar and different ways. This study aims to offer important findings and discussions on the racialized and gendered aspects of the pandemic to governments, institutions, policymakers, activists, and

209

scholars, and make concrete and actionable recommendations to better serve the needs of CCA women and their communities.

Racisms, Antiracisms, and Political Activisms of CCA Women

Racisms have different forms across time, space, and culture and have been defined in many different ways (P. Collins 2009; J. Jones 1997; Rattansi 2020). The widely accepted definition of racism characterizes racial prejudices and discrimination as the manifestation of contaminated "hearts and minds" of perpetrators and many contemporary theories about racism locate the problems of racial discrimination and inequality within personal agents and assume that "if there is racism, there must be racists" (Goff, Steele, and Davies 2008, 91). This perspective is often reflected in discussions about combating racisms, wherein the emphasis is placed on eradicating hatred and ignorance from individual "hearts and minds." However, this definition is not well grounded, as research has shown that attitudes are unreliable indicators of behavior (Goff, Steele, and Davies 2008, 91). During the pandemic, Asian, Asian American, and Pacific Islander (AAAPI) communities did not go into the streets to demand that White people love them more; instead, they marched to end the violence caused by racisms. Therefore, the focus is on actions rather than feelings only. If the definition of a form of racism prioritizes the intentions of perpetrators over the harm inflicted on victims, it is inherently racist. If we redefine racisms from the perspective of the vernacular and situate them within particular contexts, we could transform them into solvable problems and provide space to empower marginalized individuals, groups, and communities to fight for their rights, equality, and inclusion. Those people that we define as "the vernacular" have the power to decide how they dismantle the White Western colonial logics of hegemony and supremacy, and how they make both top-down systemic reforms and bottom-up grassroots changes to make this world a better place for all. Changing our understanding of the problems is the first step to forming better solutions.

Facing surging anti-Asian racisms, diverse AAAPI communities have proposed different action plans and solutions. The first major solution is related to the hate crime report system—for example, the Stop AAPI Hate (SAH) report on hate crime statistics—but some contributors do not trust the official report systems. The second is related to grassroots activisms, such as rallies, bystander trainings, and self-defense trainings, but AAAPI communities also need long-term goals and action plans. The third is related to education. In some states, AAAPI communities have advocated for and facilitated the passage of AAPI (Asian American and Pacific Islander) curriculum bills, and AAPI history has been required in K–12 education in public schools. However, it is not easy to put together the curriculum and decide who would be best suited to teach it. Emily, an adoptee and educator teaching young children, emphasized the importance of starting conversations about race and racisms with children at an early age. She did not think that children were colorblind and believed that they learned biases very early. Although teachers could not have the same discussions about race and racisms with children as they did with young adults, they could change the narratives and introduce children to people who did not look like them or who ate different foods. Emily believed that children could be exposed to cultural and racial equity and inclusion at an early age, with the support of parents, teachers, schools, and communities.

The SAH movement emerged as a crucial force in addressing and combating the surging anti-Asian racisms during the pandemic, and played a pivotal role in advocating for policy changes and legislation. Recognizing the need for comprehensive actions, AAAPI activists and organizations collaborated with lawmakers and community leaders to push for legislation addressing hate crimes and education and to provide resources for AAAPIs. By championing these efforts, the movement sought to create a more equitable and inclusive society where AAAPIs can live without fear. Furthermore, the significance of the SAH movement lies in its long-term impacts on social consciousness. It challenged existing narratives and misconceptions about AAAPIs, debunking harmful stereotypes and fostering a deeper understanding of the diverse experiences and contributions of AAAPIs. Through education and advocacy, the movement sought to dismantle the harmful structures that perpetuate racisms, hate, and violence.

The SAH movement stands as a testament to the resilience, strengths, and agencies of AAAPI women and serves as a call to action for building a more just and equal society for all. As shown in earlier chapters, CCA women played important roles in organizing and participating in the SAH movement in different places, along with mobilizing diverse forms of political activisms to challenge and change the racisms, stereotypes, violence, and exclusion they face in their everyday lives. In particular, Chinese immigrant mothers, women international students, adoptees, and lay Buddhist women have utilized different strategies and actions to combat racisms at different levels. They challenged stereotypes or misinformation about AAAPIs in education or media, promoted representation and leadership of AAAPIs in various sectors, and celebrated the contributions and achievements of AAAPIs in American society. Most importantly, these actions live beyond the pandemic and continue today.

Decolonization and Diverse Voices from the Margins

Decolonization challenges hegemonic and dominant theories of knowledge, languages, power, and politics that prevail in mainstream American society. It differs from postcolonialism as it goes beyond simply acknowledging the aftermaths of colonization. Decolonization aims to break free from colonial structures, including values, methods, and knowledge. However, decolonizing is not limited to theoretical and epistemological realms; it is an active and ongoing struggle for social justice across various dimensions such as economic, political, cultural, racial, and gender equality (McLaren 2017). Decolonization opens up the possibility for innovative solutions to contemporary issues.

In this study, the decolonizing approach represents a vital and transformative process that challenges the entrenched power structures, knowledge systems, and ideologies that have been shaped by colonialism and racisms in the US. By addressing economic inequalities, political injustices, cultural erasure, racial discrimination, and gender disparities, decolonization strives to create a more equitable and inclusive world. It encourages the exploration of alternative perspectives, methodologies, and approaches to problem-solving, fostering creativity and innovation in response to contemporary challenges. It seeks to restore autonomy, agencies, and self-determination to marginalized communities whose voices have been historically silenced or ignored. Decolonization is a collective endeavor that requires ongoing commitment and action at all levels and in every arena. It necessitates critical reflection, unlearning entrenched biases, and reimagining new possibilities rooted in justice and equality. By engaging in the decolonization process, marginalized communities have the opportunity to redefine their identities, remake their cultural traditions, and create inclusive spaces that celebrate diverse ways of knowing and being. Ultimately, decolonization offers hope for a future where power is decentralized, knowledge is deconstructed and reconstructed, and the wounds of colonialism and racisms are healed. It is a journey toward a more just and equitable world, where the dignity and contributions of all individuals and communities are recognized and celebrated.

By employing a feminist decolonizing approach, I am not only addressing the subject matter of my study—the lived experiences and actions of Chinese immigrant mothers, international students, transracial adoptees, and lay Buddhist women—but also challenging the traditional structures and paradigms through which this knowledge has been historically understood and disseminated. The feminist decolonizing approach integrates feminist theories with decolonizing frameworks. Feminist theories critique the structures of power that have traditionally marginalized women's voices whereas decolonizing frameworks challenge the Eurocentric and often patriarchal perspectives that dominate mainstream discourses and practices. By combining these, I emphasize a shift in perspectives that seeks to center and uplift the voices and experiences of women, particularly those from marginalized communities. This approach is crucial in reevaluating and challenging the dominant discourses that have often overlooked or misrepresented these individuals and communities.

My research specifically highlights Chinese immigrant mothers, women international students, transracial adoptees, and lay Buddhist women. These groups and communities face both similar and different challenges and have diverse experiences shaped by intersections of gender, race, class, culture, immigration status, and religious practices. By focusing on these groups and communities, I am acknowledging and exploring the complex experiences, stories, and actions that are often ignored or underrepresented in mainstream folklore studies. It is important to note that this study does not claim to be comprehensive, as certain issues faced by various groups of CCA women could not be addressed due to my inability to meet with or reach specific groups as well as various other obstacles to gathering information during the pandemic. However, this study emphasizes the urgency of gender-responsive research and policies firmly rooted in decolonizing, antiracist, and global Asian feminist approaches.

The challenges faced by CCA women during the pandemic were significant, testing their strength and well-being. However, they were not deterred by these challenges but rather used them as opportunities for growth and transformation. Through their resilience, empathy, and determination, these women have found innovative ways to connect, support, and uplift one another and their broader communities. They have demonstrated their creative agencies and the profound impacts they could have in times of crisis.

The voices of Chinese immigrant mothers, women international students, adoptees, and lay Buddhist women hold immense significance in Global Asian Folklore Studies (GAFS), but their voices have been historically overlooked and marginalized in existing Asian, Asian Diaspora, Asian American, and folklore studies. By focusing on their voices, this book aims to embrace inclusive integrated approaches to illuminate their diverse lived experiences and make their contributions known in academia and society at large.

Here I adopt inclusive, integrative, and decolonizing approaches that start from my contributors' subjective and affective experiences. Through this approach, I remain attentive to the intricate interplay of diverse frameworks they draw on to construct self and communities, which allows me to

Conclusion   213

avoid the determinism associated with privileging any single preconceived symbolic structure. Rather than treating affective life as a mere byproduct of abstract social theories, my study seeks to embrace mixed methods and their capacity to challenge preconceived notions about the practical implications of selfhood, gender, class, place, sexuality, race, religion, work, nation, and other aspects of social existence. As emphasized by Avery F. Gordon (2008), our experiences and affective responses do not typically conform to the rational and objective frameworks we tend to depict them with, and truly grasping the complexity of subjectivity and social life requires our willingness to be surprised and to grapple with the difficulties of imagining beyond the limits of our existing understanding.

Future Directions for Research

While I have proposed various policy recommendations to support and empower Chinese immigrant mothers, international students, adoptees, and lay Buddhist women, I also believe additional research is needed to further our understanding of the impacts of the COVID-19 pandemic on diverse gendered groups and global Asian communities as well as their responses to anti-Asian racisms and the multiple crises of the pandemic. I have emphasized the importance of GAFS and global Asian feminisms for future research. It is also important to embrace a more thoughtful approach to study design, participant selection, and analysis, ensuring that the voices and experiences of diverse gendered groups and global Asian communities are heard and valued. Acknowledging this, future research could benefit from including a broader spectrum of participants, encompassing various socioeconomic statuses, education levels, racial and ethnic identities, gender and sexual orientations, occupations, religions, and so on.

Gender is not a binary construct but a more fluid social construct situated within particular contexts. Current studies have not fully investigated the impacts of the COVID-19 pandemic on LGBTQIA+ individuals, groups, and communities and their responses to racisms and other forms of oppression. Future research can be conducted to examine the impacts of the pandemic on global Asian LGBTQIA+ communities and their diverse political activisms. This study was conducted between 2020 and 2023 and primarily focuses on CCA women who are often well educated and have access to the internet and online communities, although they were multiply marginalized because of anti-Asian racisms, sexism, geopolitical conflicts, and other problems the pandemic exacerbated. There is a clear need for additional studies to understand the impacts of the pandemic and grassroots responses through diverse gender identities on the gender spectrum.

Although the media and scholarly literature suggest that the COVID-19 pandemic has negatively impacted women's and girls' education, health, livelihoods, psychological and mental well-being, unpaid care work, careers, and so on, it is important to explore the comparative lived experiences of men to understand how divergent their experiences are from women. Particularly related to this study, researchers could examine the lived experiences of AAAPI fathers, male international students, male adoptees, and male religious practitioners to compare experiences with the contributors in this study and extend the current research on the impacts of the COVID-19 pandemic on CCA women.

Finally, while this study lays the foundation for the examination of the impacts of the COVID-19 pandemic on CCA women in the US, future studies may focus on CCA women who left the US during the pandemic, as this was not fully covered in the current study. Furthermore, examining how the lived experiences of these women differed based on various factors would enhance the findings of this study. For instance, were the experiences of Chinese immigrant mothers with full-time jobs notably different from those without full-time jobs? Did the different responses of the diverse higher education institutions affect international students' experiences? Did the ages of adoptees affect their responses to the pandemic and anti-Asian racisms? Did middle-class lay Buddhist women have particularly different experiences than those from other social classes or those who believed in other religions? Such detailed analysis would shed light on the key variables influencing the responses of AAAPI individuals and communities in larger social, political, and cultural contexts.

"How Do We Want To Live?"

This book presents how CCA women in the US experienced and responded to anti-Asian racisms and multiple crises of the pandemic. In closing the book, I would like to return to the voices of my contributors who reflected on their personal experiences, conceptualized the meaning of life, and envisioned their lives with hope after the pandemic.

> I personally believe that health and life are the most important things. All the fame and wealth, in my opinion, are not as valuable as living a down-to-earth and healthy life in this world. (Wu Meili, unemployed, mother, interview on May 18, 2020)

> The life I envision is one where I can give back more to society and the country, where I can engage in more charitable activities and make greater contributions ... whether it is during or after the pandemic, if we continue to contribute

to this country, gradually, the country will accept us. History will remember us. (CP, nurse practitioner, mother, interview on July 4, 2020)

After the pandemic ends, I hope to resume a normal life and have the freedom to travel between China and the United States without the need for quarantine. (Shuilian, lay Buddhist, interview on November 19, 2021)

It's a significant question, and I believe it revolves around how to make the most of each day. One aspect is reminding myself to consider the meaning of life, such as contemplating life and death. . . . I want to stand on the right side of history and genuinely contribute to resolving issues. (Xu, graduate student, interview on June 5, 2020)

If the pandemic comes to an end, I still want to go out and explore, see distant mountains and seas, and listen to other people's poetry and songs. It would be great to sit on the edge of a cliff and gaze at the moon. (Liu, undergraduate student, interview on June 30, 2022)

I will definitely not be taking being able to go out to restaurants and stuff and like traveling, I won't take that for granted as much because I definitely miss doing that a lot. And then also taking for granted being able to hang out with friends. I definitely really miss the social aspects prior to the pandemic and so I want to be able to just kind of enjoy the life that I have through this either sort of traveling or just like eating out, or just simply going over to a friend's house without like having this like either guilt or fear of what if I give them something, or what if they give something to me. I miss that guilt-free hanging out with people. (Yang Ji, adoptee, interview on February 21, 2021)

Hopefully, in the years to come, the events of the pandemic are not forgotten but used as a motivator towards better things. It is important to remember both the negative and positive moments of the pandemic to truly grasp what next steps can be taken locally, regionally, and nationally to move forward as a community. (Emily, undergraduate student, class survey, March 2022)

Once the pandemic is over, I hope to have more interaction with people just to see people, but also, I really hope that people are more cognizant and aware of racial discriminations, especially in the United States, and also just financial inequalities. I think that we're definitely headed in that direction, but there's definitely a lot more work to be done. I'm hoping the awakening of people's awareness continues to expand. (Melody, adoptee, interview on February 26, 2021)

After the pandemic, I hope our lives will return to be expected, and we won't have to wear masks and worry about infection. If I had the chance, I would like to travel to Wuhan, the city that was "hurt" the most because of COVID-19, to see the people and places in Wuhan. Besides that, I would cherish the time I spend with my family and friends. Finally, I hope that the world will become a kinder and better place. In a world with an epidemic, all people should come together and help each other instead of leading to more racism and prejudice. (Xinyan, undergraduate student, class survey, March 2022)

The life that I desire to live after the pandemic . . . is passing people on the sidewalks on campus and being able to smile at them and see them smile back. I long for human connection in a way that I feel unsafe to do in the midst of a global pandemic. I miss meeting new people and making new friends. I miss being invited to parties, and gatherings of people outside my small circle of friends. (Grace, undergraduate student, class survey, March 2022)

Once this pandemic ends, I want to continue my work in community building and advocacy through the creation of an intercultural organization committee here at CoW so that we can facilitate conversations about equity and what it means to be antiracist in an active capacity. It's incredibly important that we create stronger bonds between multi-cultural orgs on campus to unify the student voice to be more efficient to pushing for change on campus. I also hope to continue my studies on how my racial, cultural, and ethnic identit[ies] fuse and interact with my queer and neurodivergent identities through sculpture, ceramics, visual art, fashion, and dance. (M, undergraduate student, class survey, March 2022)

I hope that the society after the epidemic can be more harmonious, better, and more equal. For Asian Americans, we must also grasp our position, actively fight for our own power, and use this opportunity to let everyone see us, see our ability and the unfair treatment. . . . Asians should let the world see their difference, their bravery and super execution in the face of the epidemic. I hope that after the pandemic, we can see a better society, and this is what each of us should strive for. (Ruohan, undergraduate student, class survey, March 2022)

The ideal life that I want to live once, or if depending on the severity of the virus in the future, is one where everyone in our nation can accept each other as equals and that nations will actually cooperate with each other rather than petty rivalries and hostilities. . . . I guess mostly I just want people to care about what is happening to Asians and Asian Americans because they are an integral part of our nation and our history. (V, class survey, March 2022)

A healthy society should not have only one voice. From the early stage to the middle stage to the late stage of the pandemic, it is important to be inclusive and allow different voices to be heard. (C, mother, interview on May 28, 2020)

Once I have thought about things I want to do, places I want to go, or people I want to meet, I immediately put them into action without waiting. (Q, interview on May 14, 2020)

I really want to go to events. I've been missing going to concerts so bad and fairs and festivals. I love going to those and just eating food there, I love food.

I want to travel. I really want to travel just anywhere, because I know that's been difficult. I want to get married and I want to get married when there's not a pandemic and I can hug everyone, and we can not wear masks anymore. . . . I hope that the government and society understand more how to prepare for a pandemic. And I hope, especially with the new president, if there's anything that happens again if something else hits or in the future, maybe the president will be more proactive about it, and maybe we will not be in this situation, so we don't have history repeat itself. (Mia, adoptee, interview on May 28, 2021)

Our journey to explore the question "How do we want to live?" is endless, and the COVID-19 pandemic prompted us to reflect on the meaning of life and how we face death, uncertainties, and social injustice individually and collectively. Diverse acts of support like what CCA women and communities have done, though seemingly small, can ripple through the fabric of our society with profound and lasting impacts. These acts ignite hope, cultivate resilience, and rebuild diverse communities, reminding us that we are not alone in our struggles. Together, we can make the beautiful life that we want to live come true.

APPENDIX
Contributors

CHINESE IMMIGRANT MOTHERS

1. MN, born 1980, university professor, married with a daughter and a son, interviewed on May 15, 2020.

2. Wu Meili, born 1972, accountant (laid off), married with a daughter, interviewed on May 18, 2020.

3. MY, born 1982, stay-at-home wife and mother of two sons, married to YZJ, born 1977, university faculty (laid off), interviewed on May 25, 2020.

4. LJL, born 1984, married with two sons and a daughter, interviewed on May 27 and June 3, 2020.

5. C, born 1980, freelancer, married with a daughter, interviewed on May 28, 2020.

6. GM, forty-three years old, stay-at-home wife and mother of three children, interviewed on June 16, 2020.

7. LQ, born 1983, stay-at-home wife and mother of one daughter, interviewed on June 17, 2020.

8. YMZ, born 1960, stay-at-home wife and mother of two sons and one daughter, interviewed on June 18, 2020.

9. LYM, born 1977, working in the hospital, married with two sons, interviewed on June 19, 2020.

10. Amy, born 1981, stay-at-home wife and mother of two sons, interviewed on June 20, 2020.

11. LYL, born 1962, accountant, married with a daughter and a son, stayed at home for thirteen years until her son went to high school, interviewed on July 3, 2020.

12. CP, born 1981, nurse practitioner, married with a daughter and a son, interviewed on July 4, 2020.

13. Lin, born 1979, restaurant owner, married with a daughter and a son, interviewed on August 6, 2020.

14. Tan, born 1985, university lecturer, divorced with a daughter, interviewed on August 7, 2020.

15. YY, born 1981, university professor, married with a son and a daughter, interviewed on August 12, 2020.

16. PP, born 1981, university professor, married with a daughter and a son, her husband is also university faculty, interviewed on June 11, 2021.

17. Vivien, born 1984, activist, married with a son, interviewed on February 8, 2022.

18. Shuilian, born 1966, retired, lay Buddhist, married with a daughter and a son, interviewed on November 19, 2021.

CHINESE IMMIGRANT FATHERS

1. YZJ, born 1977, university faculty (laid off), married to MY with two sons, interviewed on May 25, 2020.

2. Rong, born 1955, entrepreneur and Chinese community leader, married with three children, his daughter has two daughters, interviewed on May 25, 2020.

3. Andy Dai, born 1977, president of Huagen Chinese School, married with a daughter and a son, interviewed on May 28, 2020.

4. Mai, born 1973, entrepreneur and Chinese community leader, married with a daughter and two sons, interviewed on June 9, 2020.

CHINESE INTERNATIONAL STUDENTS

1. NA, female, born 1990, interviewed during her quarantine in Shijizhuang on May 22, 2020.

2. HU, male, born 2000, undergraduate, interviewed on May 30, 2020.

3. Zhan, male, born 2000, undergraduate, interviewed on June 1, 2020.

4. Hang, female, born 1997, college graduate, interviewed during her quarantine in Shanghai on June 3, 2020.

5. Qing, female, born 1998, college graduate, interviewed during her quarantine in Shijiazhuang on June 4, 2020.

6. Xu, male, born 1996, graduate student, interviewed on June 5, 2020.

7. Qin, female, born 1996, graduate student, interviewed on June 16, 2020.

8. XI, male, born 2001, undergraduate, interviewed on August 5, 2020.

9. Meng, female, born 1999, undergraduate, interviewed on May 19, 2021.

10. Rong, female, born 1999, undergraduate, interviewed on May 19, 2021.

11. WY, female, born 1999, undergraduate, interviewed on May 19, 2021.

12. TL, female, born 2000, undergraduate, interviewed on May 19, 2021.

13. Ting, female, born 1999, college graduate, interviewed on May 31, 2021.

14. Yin, female, born 2000, undergraduate, interviewed on August 13, 2021.

15. Niu, female, born 1999, undergraduate, interviewed on August 17, 2021.

16. Miao, female, born 1999, undergraduate, interviewed on December 10, 2021.

17. Shan, female, born 1990, graduate student, interviewed on December 21, 2021.

18. Caiwei, female, born 2000, undergraduate, interviewed on June 17, 2022.

19. Yinuo, female, born 2000, undergraduate, interviewed on June 21, 2022.

20. Tian, female, born 2000, undergraduate, interviewed on June 21, 2022.

21. Xia, female, born 1998, graduate student, interviewed on June 22, 2022.

22. Z, female, unknown birth year, graduate student, interviewed on June 22, 2022.

23. Wanru, female, born 2001, undergraduate, interviewed on June 23, 2022.

24. Yue, female, born 1999, undergraduate, interviewed on June 23, 2022.

25. Xin, female, born 2002, undergraduate, interviewed on June 28, 2022.

26. Fei, female, born 2001, undergraduate, interviewed on June 29, 2022.

27. Liu, male, born 2000, undergraduate, interviewed on June 30, 2022.

28. Coco Liu, female, born 1999, undergraduate, coleader of March for Asian Lives, full story presented in chapter 3, and her speech is available here: https://youtu.be/Gwp8ZWhVxyY.

Chinese Adoptees

1. Eva, born 1998, single, undergraduate, interviewed on February 17, 2021.

2. Gwei, born, 1999, single, undergraduate, interviewed on February 21, 2021.

3. Ni Zhuhua, born 1993, single, undergraduate, interviewed on February 21, 2021.

4. Yang Ji, born 1996, single, graduated from college, HR coordinator, interviewed on February 21, 2021.

5. Carsen, born 1999, married, graduated from college, interactive designer, interviewed on February 24, 2021.

6. Jade, born 1998, single, graduated from college, retail associate at a bakery, musician, interviewed on February 24, 2021.

7. Ella, born 2000, single, undergraduate, interviewed on February 25, 2021.

8. Melody, born 2001, single, undergraduate, interviewed on February 26, 2021.

9. Rose, born 1996, single, undergraduate, interviewed on February 27, 2021.

10. Annie, born 1999, single, undergraduate, interviewed on February 28, 2021.

11. LiEllen, born 1998, single, undergraduate, interviewed on February 28, 2021.

12. Katara, born 1998, single, undergraduate, interviewed on March 3, 2021.

13. Jiang Liang-Liang, born 2000, single, undergraduate, interviewed on March 4, 2021.

14. Daisy, born 1993, married, graduate student, interviewed on March 5, 2021.

15. Helen, born 1996, single, graduate student, interviewed on March 10, 2021.

16. Nina, born 1998, married, undergraduate and mom, interviewed on March 10, 2021.

17. Grace, born 1999, single, undergraduate, interviewed on March 12, 2021.

18. Elise, unsure about gender, born 2000, single, undergraduate, interviewed on March 31, 2021.

19. Madelyn, born 2001, single, undergraduate, interviewed on May 18, 2021.

20. Emma, born 1996, married, graduated from college, photographer, repair technician, interviewed on May 20, 2021.

21. Zoe Seymore, born 2000, single, undergraduate, interviewed on May 23, 2021.

22. Emily B., born 2000, single, undergraduate, interviewed on May 24, 2021.

23. Mia, nonbinary, born 1998, single, undergraduate, interviewed on May 28, 2021.

24. Sydney, born 2000, single, undergraduate, interviewed on May 31, 2021.

25. Callie, born 1997, single, graduated from college, interviewed on July 14, 2021.

26. Sarah, born 2001, single, undergraduate, interviewed on August 11, 2021.

CHINESE LAY BUDDHIST WOMEN

1. Ning, born 1971, music teacher, married, interviewed on June 16, 2020.
2. Jingshu, born 1962, accountant, interviewed on July 3, 2020.
3. Fanghua, born 1990, graduate student, interviewed on July 23, 2021.
4. Shuilian, born 1966, retired, interviewed on November 19, 2021.
5. Xianhong, born 1968, divorced with a son who studied and worked in the US, interviewed on December 26, 2021.
6. Sarah, born 2001, undergraduate, interviewed on August 11, 2021.
7. Lama Kate, the resident teacher of a TBC in central Ohio, guest lecturer in fall 2021.
8. Lan, Wenxin, and other women in the Chinese Buddhist reading group.
9. 20 contributors that I interviewed during my fieldwork in China in summer 2019.
10. 368 members in three Buddhist WeChat groups (2020–2023).

MISCELLANEOUS CONTRIBUTORS

1. Q, female, born 1987, economist, married with a daughter (born in 2021), interviewed on May 14, 2020.
2. XY, female, born 1976, university professor, married, interviewed on May 27, 2020.
3. LLL, female, born 1986, GIS analyst and programmer, married, interviewed on June 21, 2020.
4. ZF, female, born 1973, waitress (laid off), married, interviewed on July 2, 2020.
5. XU, male, born 1971, restaurant owner, married, interviewed on July 7, 2020.
6. Kyle and eight other CCA young adults who participated in the PCE virtual panel in early March 2021.
7. Twenty-one students in my CHIN-21300-01 (31778) Anti-Asian Racism class in the spring of 2022, including two Asian American student leaders, two Chinese adoptees, four female Chinese students, six male Chinese students, and many other amazing students.
8. Twenty students in my CHIN-29902-01 (30605) Food & Religion in China class in the fall of 2021.
9. Numerous contributors from Ohio Contemporary Chinese School, Huagen Chinese School, and Parents and Children Education Club.

BIBLIOGRAPHY

AAPI Youth Rising (AYR) website. 2022. "About Us." https://aapiyouthrising.org/about/.
———. n.d. "About Mina." Accessed October 25, 2023. https://aapiyouthrising.org/about/mina/.
Abedi, Vida, Oluwaseyi Olulana, Venkatesh Avula, Durgesh Chaudhary, Ayesha Khan, Shima Shahjouei, Jiang Li, and Ramin Zand. 2021. "Racial, Economic, and Health Inequality and COVID-19 Infection in the United States." *Journal of Racial and Ethnic Health Disparities* 8 (3): 732–42.
Access to Insight (BCBS Edition). 2013. "Maha-parinibbana Sutta: Last Days of the Buddha" (DN 16). Translated from the Pali by Sister Vajira and Francis Story. November 30, 2013. http://www.accesstoinsight.org/tipitaka/dn/dn.16.1–6.vaji.html. Accessed May 5, 2023.
Adeola, Ogechi, ed. 2021. *Gendered Perspectives on Covid-19 Recovery in Africa: Towards Sustainable Development*. Cham, Switzerland: Springer International.
Agamben, G. 2003. *Stato di eccezione*. Torino, Italy: Bollati Boringhieri.
Ahmed, Sara, 2000. *Strange Encounters: Embodied Others in Post-coloniality*. London: Routledge.
Anagnost, Ann. 2000. "Scenes of Misrecognition: Maternal Citizenship in the Age of Transnational Adoption." *Positions: East Asia Cultures Critique* 8 (2): 389–421.
Anderson, Eugene Newton. 1988. *The Food of China*. New Haven, CT: Yale University Press.
Arnold, David. 2019. "The Good, the Bad, and the Toxic: Moral Foods in British India." In *Moral Foods: The Construction of Nutrition and Health in Modern Asia*, edited by Angela Ki Che Leung and Melissa L. Caldwell, 111–29. Honolulu: University of Hawai'i Press.
Asian American Federation (AAF). 2014. *The State of Asian American Children*. https://www.aafederation.org/doc/AAF_StateofAsianAmericanChildren.pdf.
Asian Women United of California (AWUC). 1989. *Making Waves: An Anthology of Writing by and about Asian American Women*. Boston: Beacon.
Association of Religion Data Archives (ARDA). n.d. "First Buddhist Temples Built—Timeline Event." US Religion: American Religion Timelines. Accessed October 25, 2024. https://www.thearda.com/us-religion/history/timelines/entry?etype=1&eid=354.

Aughinbaugh, Alison, and Donna S. Rothstein. 2022. "How Did Employment Change during the COVID-19 Pandemic? Evidence from a New BLS Survey Supplement." *Beyond the Numbers: Employment & Unemployment* 11 (1). U.S. Bureau of Labor Statistics. https://www.bls.gov/opub/btn/volume-11/how-did-employment-change-during-the-covid-19-pandemic.htm.

Avishai, Orit. 2016. "Theorizing Gender from Religion Cases: Agency, Feminist Activism, and Masculinity." *Sociology of Religion* 77 (3): 261–79.

Ayeshah, Émon, and Christine Garlough 2015. "Refiguring the South Asian American Tradition Bearer: Performing the 'Third Gender' in Yoni Ki Baat." *Journal of American Folklore* 128 (510): 412–37.

Azuma, Eiichiro. 2021. "The Challenge of Studying the Pacific as a 'Global Asia': Problematizing Deep-Rooted Institutional Hindrances for Bridging Asian Studies and Asian American Studies." *Journal of Asian Studies* 80 (4): 1023–31.

Baldassar, Loretta. 2002. *Visits Home: Migration Experiences between Italy and Australia.* Carlton South, Australia: Melbourne University Press.

Banerjea, Niharika, Paul Boyce, and Rohit K. Dasgupta, eds. 2022. *Covid-19 Assemblages: Queer and Feminist Ethnographies from South Asia.* Ethnographic Innovations, South Asian Perspectives. Abingdon, UK: Routledge.

Bardwell-Jones, Celia T. 2017. "'Home-Making' and 'World-Traveling': Decolonizing the Space-Between in Transnational Feminist Thought." In *Decolonizing Feminism: Transnational Feminism and Globalization*, edited by Margaret A. McLaren, 151–76. London: Rowman and Littlefield.

Bashford, Alison. 2020. "Beyond Quarantine Critique." Somatosphere, March 6, 2020. http://somatosphere.net/forumpost/beyond-quarantine-critique/.

Bauman, Richard. 2008. "The Philology of the Vernacular." *Journal of Folklore Research* 45 (1): 29–36.

Bauman, Zygmunt. (2000) 2012. *Liquid Modernity.* Cambridge: Polity Press.

Beck, Ulrich. 1999. *World Risk Society.* Cambridge: Polity Press.

Belford, Nish, and Reshmi Lahiri-Roy. 2019. "(Re)negotiating Transnational Identities: Notions of 'Home' and 'Distanced Intimacies.'" *Emotion, Space and Society* 31:63–70.

Bell, David, and Gill Valentine. 1997. *Consuming Geographies: We Are Where We Eat.* New York: Routledge.

Bender, Mark, ed. 2017. *The Borderlands of Asia: Culture, Place, Poetry.* Cambria Sinophone World Series. Amherst, NY: Cambria Press.

Bendix, Regina. 1997. *In Search of Authenticity: The Formation of Folklore Studies.* Madison: University of Wisconsin Press.

Billé, Franck, and Sören Urbansky, eds. 2018. *Yellow Perils: China Narratives in the Contemporary World.* Honolulu: University of Hawaiʻi Press.

Black, Kelly. 2018. "6 Statistics about China International Adoption." *International Adoption* (blog). Accessed May 22, 2023. https://internationaladoption.org/6-statistics-china-international-adoption/#:~:text=A%20total%20of%2078,257%20children,China%20came%20home%20to%20America.

Blank, Trevor J., and Andrea Kitta, eds. 2015. *Diagnosing Folklore: Perspectives on Disability, Health, and Trauma.* Jackson: University Press of Mississippi.

Boccagni, Paolo. 2017. *Migration and the Search for Home: Mapping Domestic Space in Migrants' Everyday Lives.* New York: Palgrave Macmillan.

Boche, Laura. 2022. "Giving a Lot of Ourselves: How Mother Leaders in Higher Education Experienced Parenting and Leading during the COVID-19 Pandemic." *Frontiers in Education (Lausanne)* 7:1–17.

Bodner, John, Wendy Welch, Ian Brodie, Anna Muldoon, Donald Leech, and Ashley Marshall, eds. 2021. *COVID-19 Conspiracy Theories: QAnon, 5G, the New World Order and Other Viral Ideas*. Jefferson, NC: McFarland.

Boellstorff, Tom, Bonnie Nardi, Celia Pearce, and T. L. Taylor. 2012. *Ethnography and Virtual Worlds: A Handbook of Method*. Princeton, NJ: Princeton University Press.

Borup, Jørn, and Mariann Qvortrup Fibiger, eds. 2017. *Eastspirit: Transnational Spirituality and Religious Circulation in East and West*. Leiden, Netherlands: Brill.

Bourdieu, Pierre. 1977. *Outline of a Theory of Practice*. Translated by Richard Nice. Cambridge: Cambridge University Press.

Bourke, John G. 1895. "Folk-Foods of the Rio Grande Valley and of Northern Mexico." *Journal of American Folklore* 8 (28): 41–71.

Bradsher, Keith, Chang Che, and Amy Chang Chien. 2022. "China Eases 'Zero Covid' Restrictions in Victory for Protesters." *New York Times*, December 8, 2022. https://cn.nytimes .com/china/20221208/china-zero-covid-protests/dual/.

Bray, Francesca. 2019. "Health, Wealth, and Solidarity: Rice as Self in Japan and Malaysia." In *Moral Foods: The Construction of Nutrition and Health in Modern Asia*, edited by Angela Ki Che Leung and Melissa L. Caldwell, 23–46. Honolulu: University of Hawaiʻi Press.

Bridges, Ben, Ross Brillhard, and Diane E. Goldstein, eds. 2023. *Behind the Mask: Vernacular Culture in the Time of COVID*. Denver: University Press of Colorado.

Briggs, Charles L. 2021. *Unlearning: Rethinking Poetics, Pandemics, and the Politics of Knowledge*. Logan: Utah State University Press.

Briggs, Charles L., and Clara Mantini-Briggs. 2003. *Stories in the Time of Cholera: Racial Profiling during a Medical Nightmare*. Berkeley: University of California Press.

———. 2016. *Tell Me Why My Children Died: Rabies, Indigenous Knowledge, and Communicative Justice*. Durham, NC: Duke University Press.

British Broadcasting Company (BBC). 2020. "Coronavirus: The World in Lockdown in Maps and Charts." April 7, 2020. https://www.bbc.com/news/world-52103747.

Brouillette, Monique, and Rebecca Renner. 2020. "Why Misinformation about COVID-19's Origins Keeps Going Viral?" *National Geographic*, September 18, 2020. https://www .nationalgeographic.com/science/article/coronavirus-origins-misinformation-yan -report-fact-check-cvd.

Brown, Linda Keller, and Kay Mussell, eds. 1984. *Ethnic and Regional Foodways in the United States: The Performance of Group Identity*. Knoxville: University of Tennessee Press.

Brunsting, Nelson C., Corinne Zachry, and Risa Takeuchi. 2018. "Predictors of Undergraduate International Student Psychosocial Adjustment to US Universities: A Systematic Review from 2009–2018." *International Journal of Intercultural Relations* 66:22–33.

Buccitelli, Anthony Bak. 2020. "(Folk)Life, Interrupted: Challenges for Fieldwork, Empathy, and Public Discourse in the Age of Trump." *Journal of American Folklore* 133 (530): 412–29.

Bureau of Consular Affairs. 2019. "Graph Illustration and Chart of Adoption Statistics 1999–2019." Adoption Statistics. U.S. Department of State. Accessed October 25, 2024. https://travel.state.gov/content/travel/en/Intercountry-Adoption/adopt_ref/adoption -statistics.html.

Burton, David. 2017. *Buddhism: A Contemporary Philosophical Investigation*. New York: Taylor and Francis.

Butler, Judith. 1999. *Gender Trouble: Feminism and the Subversion of Identity*. Florence: Taylor and Francis. 10th anniversary ed., New York: Routledge.

———. 2009. "Performativity, Precarity and Sexual politics." *AIBR: Revista de Antropologia Iberoamericana* 4(3): i–xiii.

———. 2012. "Precarious Life, Vulnerability, and the Ethics of Cohabitation." *The Journal of Speculative Philosophy* 26(2): 134–51.

Camp, Charles. 1989. *American Foodways: What, When, and How We Eat in America*. Little Rock, AR: August House.

Cantwell, Cathy. 2009. *Buddhism: The Basics*. New York: Routledge.

Carlitz, Katherine. 1994. "Desire, Danger, and the Body: Stories of Women's Virtue in Late Ming China." In *Engendering China: Women, Culture, and the State*, 101–24. Cambridge, MA: Harvard University Press.

Carter, Zoe B. 2022. "The Scars of China's One-Child Policy and the Birth of a New Reality: A Feminist Rhetorical Analysis Of Chinese Netizens' Reactions to the Three-Child Policy." Senior Independent Study Theses. Paper 10024. College of Wooster. https://openworks.wooster.edu/independentstudy/10024.

Castellanos, Paige, Carolyn E. Sachs, and Ann R. Tickamyer, eds. 2022. *Gender, Food and Covid-19: Global Stories of Harm and Hope*. Abingdon, UK: Routledge.

Centers for Disease Control and Prevention (CDC). 2021. "CDC Updates and Shortens Recommended Isolation and Quarantine Period for General Population." December 27, 2021. https://www.cdc.gov/media/releases/2021/s1227-isolation-quarantine-guidance.html. Accessed May 5, 2023.

Chang, Iris. 2003. *The Chinese in America: A Narrative History*. New York: Penguin Books.

Chang, Kwang-chih, ed. 1977. *Food in Chinese Culture: Anthropological and Historical Perspectives*. New Haven, CT: Yale University Press.

Chao, Mary. 2021. "Asian American Curriculum Bill Passes NJ Legislature, Murphy Signature Is Final Hurdle." NorthJersey.com, last modified December 22, 2021. https://www.northjersey.com/story/news/2021/12/22/asian-american-history-schools-law-nj-legislature-aapi/8985403002/.

Chawla, Devika, and Stacy Holman Jones, eds. 2015. *Stories of Home: Place, Identity, Exile*. Lanham, MD: Lexington Books.

Che, Chang. 2022. "COVID Is Spreading Rapidly in China, New Signs Suggest." *New York Times*, December 26, 2022. https://cn.nytimes.com/china/20221226/covid-spreading-china/dual.

Chen, Carolyn. 2005. "A Self of One's Own: Taiwanese Immigrant Women and Religious Conversion." *Gender & Society* 19 (3): 336–57.

Chen, Juliet Honglei, Yun Li, Anise M.S. Wu, and Kwok Kit Tong. 2020. "The Overlooked Minority: Mental Health of International Students Worldwide under the COVID-19 Pandemic and Beyond." *Asian Journal of Psychiatry* 54:102333.

Chen, Kuan-Hsing, and Chua Beng Huat, eds. 2007. *The Inter-Asia Cultural Studies Reader*. New York: Routledge.

Chen, Tina. 2018. "Always Verging on the (Im)possible: The Structural Incoherence of Global Asias." *Social Text*, May 14, 2018. https://socialtextjournal.org/periscope_article/always-verging-on-the-impossible-the-structural-incoherence-of-global-asias.

———. 2021. "Global Asias: Method, Architecture, Praxis." *Journal of Asian Studies* 80 (4): 997–1009.

Chen, Tina, and Eric Hayot. 2015. "Introducing Verge: What Does It Mean to Study Global Asias?" *Verge: Studies in Global Asias* 1 (1): vi–xv.

Chen, Yong. 2014. *Chop Suey, USA: The Story of Chinese Food in America*. New York: Columbia University Press.

Cheng, Wei-Yi. 2007. *Buddhist Nuns in Taiwan and Sri Lanka: A Critique of the Feminist Perspective*. New York: Routledge.

China's State Council Information Office (CSCIO). 2020. "Fighting Covid-19: China in Action." State Council Information Office of the People's Republic of China, June 7, 2020. http://english.www.gov.cn/news/topnews/202006/07/content_WS5edc559 ac6d066592a449030.html.

Cho, Lily. 2018. *Eating Chinese: Chinese Restaurants and Diaspora*. Toronto: University of Toronto Press.

Chou, Rosalind S., and Joe Feagin. 2016. *Myth of the Model Minority: Asian Americans Facing Racism*. 2nd ed. New York: Routledge.

Choy, Catherine Ceniza. 2013. *Global Families: A History of Asian International Adoption in America*. New York: New York University Press.

Civil Aviation Administration of China (CAAC). 2020. "Notice on Further Reducing International Passenger Flights during the Epidemic Prevention and Control Period." http://www.caac.gov.cn/en/XWZX/202003/t20200326_201748.html. Accessed May 5, 2023.

Cohen, Geoffrey. 2022. *Belonging: The Science of Creating Connection and Bridging Divides*. New York: W. W. Norton.

Cohen, Patricia. 2020. "Recession with a Difference: Women Face Special Burden." *New York Times*, November 17, 2020, updated March 8, 2021. https://www.nytimes.com/2020 /11/17/business/economy/women-jobs-economy-recession.html.

Cohen, Patricia, and Tiffany Hsu. 2020. "Pandemic Could Scar a Generation of Working Mothers." *New York Times*, June 3, 2020. https://www.nytimes.com/2020/06/03 /business/economy/coronavirus-working-women.html.

Collins, Caitlyn, Leah Ruppanner, Liana Christin Landivar, and William J. Scarborough. 2021. "The Gendered Consequences of a Weak Infrastructure of Care: School Reopening Plans and Parents' Employment During the COVID-19 Pandemic." *Gender & Society* 35 (2): 180–93.

Collins, Patricia Hill. 2009. *Black Feminist Thought: Knowledge, Consciousness, and the Politics of Empowerment*. 2nd ed. New York: Routledge.

Committee of 100. 2023. "AAPI and Ethnic Studies Requirements for K-12 Students in America's Public Schools." August 7, 2023. https://www.committee100.org/wp-content /uploads/2023/12/C100.23_AAPIEd_K-12_Report_V1.pdf.

Constante, Agnes. 2020. "In Connecting Chinese Adoptees to Birth Families, Couple Makes Discovery about China's One-Child Policy." NBC News, March 30, 2020. https://www .nbcnews.com/news/asian-america/connecting-chinese-adoptees-birth-families-couple -makes-discovery-about-china-n1172301.

Crenshaw, Kimberlé. 1991. "Mapping the Margins: Intersectionality, Identity Politics, and Violence against Women of Color." *Stanford Law Review* 43 (6): 1241–99.

Cummins, Molly Wiant, and Grace Ellen Brannon. 2022 "Mothering in a Pandemic: Navigating Care Work, Intensive Motherhood, and COVID-19." *Gender Issues* 39:123–41.

Davidson, Joyce, and Christine Milligan. 2004. "Embodying Emotion, Sensing Space: Introducing Emotional Geographies." *Social and Cultural Geography* 5:523–32.

Delgado, Richard. 1989. "Storytelling for Oppositionists and Others: A Plea for Narrative." *Michigan Law Review* 87 (8): 2,411–41. https://repository.law.umich.edu/cgi/viewcontent .cgi?article=3419&context=mlr.

DeVido, Elise Anne. 2010. *Taiwan's Buddhist Nuns*. Albany: State University of New York Press.

Di, Di. 2021. "Gendered Paths to Enlightenment: The Intersection of Gender and Religion in Buddhist Temples in Mainland China and the United States." *Social Currents* 8 (4): 341–57.

Bibliography   227

Dias, Felipe A., Joseph Chance, and Arianna Buchanan. 2020. "The Motherhood Penalty and the Fatherhood Premium in Employment during Covid-19: Evidence from the United States." *Research in Social Stratification and Mobility* 69:100542.

Domosh, Mona, and Joni Seager. 2001. *Putting Women in Place: Feminist Geographers Make Sense of the World*. New York: Guilford Press.

Dorow, Sara K. 2006. *Transnational Adoption: A Cultural Economy of Race, Gender, and Kinship*. New York: New York University Press.

Douglas, Susan, and Meredith Michaels. 2004. *The Mommy Myth: The Idealization of Motherhood and How It Has Undermined Women*. New York: Free Press.

Dubé, Laurette, Jordan L. LeBel, and Ji Lu. 2005. "Affect Asymmetry and Comfort Food Consumption." *Physiology & Behavior* 86:559–67.

Dugarova, Esuna. 2020. "Unpaid Care Work in Times of the Covid-19 Crisis: Gendered Impacts, Emerging Evidence and Promising Policy Responses." Paper prepared for the UN Expert Group Meeting "Families in Development: Assessing Progress, Challenges and Emerging Issues. Focus on Modalities for IYF+30." June 16–18, 2020. https://www.un.org/development/desa/family/wp-content/uploads/sites/23/2020/09/Duragova.Paper_.pdf.

Durkheim, Emile. (1912) 1995. *The Elementary Forms of Religious Life*. Translated by Karen E. Fields. New York: Free Press.

Embassy of the People's Republic of China in the United States of America. 2020–22. Notices. Accessed October 25, 2024. http://us.china-embassy.gov.cn/eng/zytz/.

———. 2022. Notice on New Testing Requirements for China-bound Passengers. April 15, 2022. http://us.china-embassy.gov.cn/eng/zytz/202204/t20220415_10668662.htm.

Fenster, Tovi. 2005. "The Right to the Gendered City: Different Formations of Belonging in Everyday Life." *Journal of Gender Studies* 14:217–231.

Fernandes, Leela. 2013. *Transnational Feminism in the United States: Knowledge, Ethics, and Power*. New York: New York University Press.

Ferrari, Laura, Rosa Rosnati, Elena Canzi, Anna Ballerini, and Sonia Ranieri. 2017. "How International Transracial Adoptees and Immigrants Cope with Discrimination? The Moderating Role of Ethnic Identity in the Relation between Perceived Discrimination and Psychological Well-Being." *Journal of Community & Applied Social Psychology* 27 (6): 437–49.

Fforde, Cressida, Steve Hemming, Merata Kawharu, Lia Kent, Laura Mayer, Daryle Rigney, Laurajane Smith, and Paul Tapsell. 2023. "Heritage, Reconciliation and Peacebuilding in Australia and New Zealand." In *Rethinking Heritage in Precarious Times: Coloniality, Climate Change, and Covid-19*, edited by Nick Shepherd, 233–60. London: Routledge.

Fincher, Leta Hong. 2014. *Leftover Women: The Resurgence of Gender Inequality in China*. London: Zed Books.

Fisher, Gareth. 2016. "Mapping Textual Difference: Lay Buddhist Textual Communities in the Post-Mao Period." In *Recovering Buddhism in Modern China*, edited by Jan Kiely and J. Brooks Jessup, 257–90. New York: Columbia University Press.

Fivecoate, Jesse A., Kristina Downs, and Meredith A. E. McGriff, eds. 2021. *Advancing Folkloristics*. Bloomington: Indiana University Press.

Fleming, P. 2021. *Dark Academia: How Universities Die*. London: Pluto Press.

Ford, James Ishmael. 2006. *Zen Master Who?* Wisdom Publications.

Foster, Michael Dylan. 2020. "Cultural Heritage in the Age of Pandemic: A Review Essay." *Journal of Folklore Research*, September 3, 2020. https://jfr.sitehost.iu.edu/review.php?id=2318. Accessed July 31, 2021.

Franceschini, Ivan. 2021. "The Work of Culture: Of Barons, Dark Academia, and the Corruption of Language in the Neoliberal University." *Made in China Journal* 6 (2): 241–49.

Franceschini, Ivan, and Nicholas Loubere. 2022. *Global China as Method.* Cambridge: Cambridge University Press.

Francisco-Menchavez, Valerie. 2018. *The Labor of Care: Filipina Migrants and Transnational Families in the Digital Age.* Urbana: University of Illinois Press.

Frandy, Tim, and B. Marcus Cederström, eds. 2022. *Culture Work: Folklore for the Public Good.* Madison: University of Wisconsin Press.

Fujiwara, Lynn, and Shireen Roshanravan. 2018. *Asian American Feminisms and Women of Color Politics.* Seattle: University of Washington Press.

Gabaccia, Donna R. 1998. *We Are What We Eat: Ethnic Food and the Making of Americans.* Cambridge: Harvard University Press.

Gabbert, Lisa. 2011. *Winter Carnival in a Western Town: Identity, Change, and the Good of the Community.* Logan: Utah State University Press.

———. 2018. "American Festival and Folk Drama." In *The Oxford Handbook of American Folklore and Folklife Studies*, edited by Simon J. Bronner, 277–97. New York: Oxford University Press.

George, Irene, and Moly Kuruvilla, eds. 2021. *Gendered Experiences of COVID-19 in India.* Cham, Switzerland: Springer International Publishing.

Georges, Robert A. 1984. "You Often Eat What Others Think You Are: Food as an Index of Others' Conceptions of Who One Is." *Western Folklore* 43 (4): 249–56.

Giddens, Anthony. 1976. *New Rules of Sociological Method.* New York: Harper and Row.

———. 1979. *Central Problems in Social Theory.* Berkeley: University of California Press.

Gilbert, J., and L. Von Wallmenich. 2014. "When Words Fail Us: Mother Time, Relational Attention, and the Rhetorics of Focus and Balance." *Women's Studies in Communication* 37 (1): 66–89.

Gilman, Lisa. 2018. "Folklore and Folklife of Women, Men, and Other Gendered Identities." In *The Oxford Handbook of American Folklore and Folklife Studies*, edited by Simon J. Bronner, 917–36. New York: Oxford University Press.

———. 2021. "A Message from the Editor." *Journal of American Folklore* 134 (533): 249–51.

Gnecco, Cristóbal. 2023. "Entries in an Apocryphal Diary: Heritage, Crisis, Turbulent Times." In *Rethinking Heritage in Precarious Times: Coloniality, Climate Change, and Covid-19*, edited by Nick Shepherd, 221–32. London: Routledge.

Goertz, Gary, and Amy Mazur, eds. 2008. *Politics, Gender, and Concepts: Theory and Methodology.* Cambridge: Cambridge University Press.

Goff, Phillip Atiba, Claude M. Steele, and Paul G. Davies. 2008. "The Space between Us: Stereotype Threat and Distance in Interracial Contexts." *Journal of Personality and Social Psychology* 94 (1): 91–107.

Goldstein, Diane. 2015. "Vernacular Turns: Narrative, Local Knowledge, and the Changed Context of Folklore." *Journal of American Folklore* 128 (508): 125–45.

Goldstein, Diane E., and Amy Shuman, eds. 2012. *The Stigmatized Vernacular: Where Reflexivity Meets Untellability.* Special issue, *Journal of Folklore Research* 49 (2).

González-Martin, Rachel Valentina. 2020. "Latinx Publics: Self-Documentation and Latina Youth Activists." *Journal of American Folklore* 133 (530): 430–51.

González-Martin, Rachel Valentina, Mintzi Auanda Martínez-Rivera, and Solimar Otero, eds. 2022. "Redirecting Currents: Theoretical Wayfinding with Latinx Folkloristics and Women of Color Transnational Feminisms." Special issue, *Journal of American Folklore* 135 (536).

Gordon, Avery F. 2008. *Ghostly Matters: Haunting and the Sociological Imagination*. 2nd ed. Minneapolis: Minnesota University Press.

Gorman-Murray, Andrew. 2011. "Economic Crises and Emotional Fallout: Work, Home and Men's Senses of Belonging in post-GFC Sydney." *Emotion, Space and Society* 4:211–220.

Goss, Devon R. 2017. "'People's Heads Do Not Even Go There': Public Perceptions to Transracial Familial Intimacy." *Sociological Quarterly* 59 (1): 111–27.

Green, Fiona Joy. 2015. "Re-conceptualising Motherhood: Reaching Back to Move Forward." *Journal of Family Studies* 21 (3): 196–207.

Gross, Rita M. 1993. *Buddhism after Patriarchy: A Feminist History, Analysis, and Reconstruction of Buddhism*. Albany: State University of New York Press.

Grotevant, Harold D., Nora Dunbar, Julie K. Kohler, and Amy M. Lash Esau. 2000. "Adoptive Identity: How Contexts within and Beyond the Family Shape Developmental Pathways." *Family Relations* 49 (4): 379–87.

Grugel, Jean, Matt Barlow, Tallulah Lines, Maria Eugenia Giraudo, and Jessica Omukuti. 2022. *The Gendered Face of Covid-19 in the Gobal South: The Development, Gender and Health Nexus in the Global South*. Bristol, UK: Bristol University Press.

Hall, Stuart. 1980. "Race, Articulation and Societies Structured in Dominance." In *Sociological Theories: Race and Colonialism*, edited by UNESCO, 305–45. Paris: UNESCO.

Hallstein, D. Lynn O'Brien. 2008. "Silences and Choice: The Legacies of White Second Wave Feminism in the New Professoriate." *Women's Studies in Communication* 31 (2): 143–50.

———. 2010. *White Feminists and Contemporary Maternity: Purging Matrophobia*. New York: Palgrave Macmillan.

———. 2017. "Introduction to Mothering Rhetorics." *Women's Studies in Communication* 40 (1): 1–10.

Hamilton, Walter. 2013. *Children of the Occupation: Japan's Untold Story*. New Brunswick, NJ: Rutgers University Press.

Hanh, Thich Nhat. 2000. *Going Home: Jesus and Buddha as Brothers*. New York: Riverhead Books.

———. 2016. *At Home in the World: Stories and Essential Teachings from a Monk's Life*. Berkeley, California: Parallax Press.

Harvey, Peter. 2012. *An Introduction to Buddhism: Teachings, History and Practice*. Cambridge: Cambridge University Press.

Hays, Sharon. 1996. *The Cultural Contradictions of Motherhood*. New Haven, CT: Yale University Press.

Heggeness, M. L. 2020. "Estimating the Immediate Impact of the COVID-19 Shock on Parental Attachment to the Labor Market and the Double Bind of Mothers." *Review of Economics of the Household* 18 (4): 1053–78.

Hershatter, G. 2007. *Women in China's Long Twentieth Century*. Berkeley: University of California Press.

Hesketh, Therese, Liu Lu, and Zhu Wei Xing. 2005. "The Effect of China's One-Child Family Policy after 25 Years." *New England Journal of Medicine* 353 (11): 1171–76.

Hickey, Wakoh Shannon. 2010. "Two Buddhisms, Three Buddhisms, and Racism." *Journal of Global Buddhism* 11 (February): 1–25.

Higginbotham, Eve, and Maria Lund Dahlberg, eds. 2021. *The Impact of COVID-19 on the Careers of Women in Academic Sciences, Engineering, and Medicine*. Washington, DC: National Academies Press.

Hinden, Adam, Ziying You, and Zhen Guo. 2023. "Online Activism and Grassroots Memorialization in the Age of COVID-19: Dr. Li Wenliang's Virtual Wailing Wall." *Cultural*

Analysis, Forum Series 1: Pandemics and Politics, 1–22. https://www.ocf.berkeley.edu/~culturalanalysis/series/1/HindenYouGuo.html.

Hine, Christine. 2000. *Virtual Ethnography*. London: SAGE.

Ho, Jennifer, ed. 2024. *Global Anti-Asian Racism*. New York: Columbia University Press.

Holt International. n.d. About page. Accessed October 25, 2024. https://www.holtinternational.org/about/.

hooks, bell. 2014. *Yearning: Race, Gender, and Cultural Politics*. New York: Routledge.

Horigan, Kate Parker. 2018. *Consuming Katrina: Public Disaster and Personal Narrative*. Jackson: University Press of Mississippi.

Hsu, Madeline Y. 2016. *Asian American History: A Very Short Introduction*. 2nd ed. Oxford: Oxford University Press.

Hswen, Yulin, Xiang Xu, Anna Hing, Jared B. Hawkins, John S. Brownstein, and Gilbert C. Gee. 2021. "Association of '#covid19' versus '#Chinesevirus' with Anti-Asian Sentiments on Twitter: March 9–23, 2020." *American Journal of Public Health* 111 (5): 956–64.

Hu, Winnie, Anjali Tsui, and Melissa Guerrero. 2021. "Closing of Beloved Dim Sum Hall Leaves a 'Crater' in Reeling Chinatown." *New York Times*, March 11. https://cn.nytimes.com/usa/20210311/chinatown-restaurant-closures-coronavirus/dual/.

Hu, Yang, Cora Lingling Xu, and Mengwei Tu. 2020. "Family-Mediated Migration Infrastructure: Chinese International Students and Parents Navigating (Im)Mobilities during the COVID-19 Pandemic." *Chinese Sociological Review* 54 (1): 62–87.

Hua, Grace, Jess Huang, Samuel Huang, and Lareina Ye. 2021. "COVID-19's Impact on Asian American Workers: Six Key Insights." McKinsey & Company, May 6, 2021. https://www.mckinsey.com/featured-insights/diversity-and-inclusion/covid-19s-impact-on-asian-american-workers-six-key-insights.

Hua, S., Hao, K., and Korn, M. 2022. "Chinese Student Visas to U.S. Tumble from Prepandemic Levels; Global Competition, Strained Political Ties Lead to Drop That Hits Revenue at Big and Small Colleges and Universities." *Wall Street Journal* (Online), August 11, 2022. https://www.wsj.com/articles/chinese-student-visas-to-u-s-tumble-from-prepandemic-levels-11660210202.

Humphrey, Theodore C., and Lin T. Humphrey, eds. 1988. *"We Gather Together": Food and Festival in American Life*. Ann Arbor: University of Michigan Research Press.

Hune, S., and Gail M. Nomura, eds. 2003. *Asian/Pacific Islander American Women: A Historical Anthology*. New York: New York University Press.

Hüsken, Ute, ed. 2022. *Laughter, Creativity, and Perseverance: Female Agency in Buddhism and Hinduism*. New York: Oxford University Press.

Hutcheson, Cory Thomas. 2018. "Home and Vehicle in American Folklore and Folklife." In *The Oxford Handbook of American Folklore and Folklife Studies*, edited by Simon J. Bronner, 625–42. New York: Oxford University Press.

Ignatieff, Michael. 1994. *Blood and Belongings: Journeys into the New Nationalism*. London: Vintage.

Ilkama, Ina Marie Lunde. 2022. "'This Is Not a Home, It Is a Temple': Creative Agency in Navarāttiri Kolu." In *Laughter, Creativity, and Perseverance: Female Agency in Buddhism and Hinduism*, edited by Ute Hüsken, 52–63. New York: Oxford University Press.

Ingram, Shelley, Willow G. Mullins, and Todd Richardson. 2019. *Implied Nowhere: Absence in Folklore Studies*. Jackson: University Press of Mississippi.

Institute of International Education (IIE). 2022. *Open Doors 2022 Annual Report on International Educational Exchange*. November 14, 2022. https://opendoorsdata.org/data/international-students/.

Jacobson, Heather. 2008. *Culture Keeping: White Mothers, International Adoption, and the Negotiation of Family Difference*. Nashville, TN: Vanderbilt University Press.

Ji, Zhe. 2012. "Chinese Buddhism as a Social Force: Reality and Potential of Thirty Years of Revival." *Chinese Sociological Review* 45 (2): 8–26.

Ji, Zhe, Gareth Fisher, and André Laliberté, eds. 2019. *Buddhism After Mao: Negotiations, Continuities, and Reinventions*. Honolulu: University of Hawai'i Press.

Jiang, Liang-Liang. 2022. "Being Asian during Covid-19: A Cross-Sectional Study of Domestic and International Identities." Senior Independent Study Theses. Paper 9966. College of Wooster. https://openworks.wooster.edu/independentstudy/9966.

Johnson, Kay Ann. 1983. *Women, the Family, and Peasant Revolution in China*. Chicago: University of Chicago Press.

———. 2016. *China's Hidden Children: Abandonment, Adoption, and the Human Costs of the One-Child Policy*. Chicago: University of Chicago Press.

Johnson, Lili. 2018. "Searching in Photographs: Photography and the Chinese Birth Parent Search." *Adoption & Culture* 6 (1): 116–34.

Johnston, Josée, and Shyon Baumann. 2009. *Foodies: Democracy and Distinction in the Gourmet Foodscape*. Cultural Spaces Series. New York: Routledge.

Jones, James M. 1997. *Prejudice and Racism*. New York: McGraw-Hill.

Jones, Michael Owen. 2007. "Food Choice, Symbolism, and Identity: Bread-and-Butter Issues for Folkloristics and Nutrition Studies (American Folklore Society Presidential Address, October 2005)." *Journal of American Folklore* 120 (476): 129–77.

———. 2022. *Frankenstein Was a Vegetarian: Essays on Food Choice, Identity, and Symbolism*. Jackson: University Press of Mississippi.

Jones, Michael Owen, Bruce Giuliano, and Roberta Krell, eds. 1983. *Foodways and Eating Habits: Directions for Research*. Los Angeles: California Folklore Society.

Jones, Michael Owen, and Lucy M. Long, eds. 2017. *Comfort Food: Meanings and Memories*. Jackson: University Press of Mississippi.

Kalčik, Susan. 1975. "'. . . Like Ann's Gynecologist or the Time I Was Almost Raped': Personal Narratives in Women's Rap Groups." *Journal of American Folklore* 88:3–11.

Kandiah, Jayanthi, Melissa Yake, James Jones, and Michaela Meyer. 2006. "Stress Influences Appetite and Comfort Food Preferences in College Women." *Nutrition Research* 26: 118–23.

Khan, Fariha. 2015. "The Dars: South Asian Muslim American Women Negotiate Identity." *Journal of American Folklore* 128 (510): 395–411.

———. 2018. "Asian American Folklore and Folklife." In *The Oxford Handbook of American Folklore and Folklife Studies*, edited by Simon J. Bronner, 741–55. New York: Oxford University Press.

Kieschnick, John. 2005. "Buddhist Vegetarianism in China." In *Of Tripod and Palate: Food, Politics and Religion in Traditional China*, edited by Roel Sterckx, 186–212. New York: Palgrave Macmillan.

Kim, Elaine H., Lilia V. Villanueva, and Asian Women United of California (AWUC), eds. 1997. *Making More Waves: New Writing by Asian American Women*. Boston: Beacon Press.

Kim, Sojin, and Mark Livengood. 2015. "Ramen Noodles and Spam: Popular Noodles, Significant Tastes." In *The Food and Folklore Reader*, edited by Lucy Long, 205–14. London: Bloomsbury.

King, Martin Luther, Jr. 1965. "Our God is Marching On (How Long, Not Long)." Speech, Selma, Alabama, March 25, 1965. https://speakola.com/ideas/martin-luther-king -jr-how-long-not-long-1965.

Kitta, Andrea. 2019. *The Kiss of Death: Contagion, Contamination, and Folklore.* Logan: Utah State University Press.

Klein, Jakob A. 2016. "Buddhist Vegetarian Restaurants and the Changing Meanings of Meat in Urban China." *Ethnos* 82 (2): 252–76.

Konagaya, Hideyo. 2023. "Vernacular Politics in Urban Civic Festivals: Tourism, Policy, and Alternative Publics." Paper presented at the Association for Asian Studies annual conference, virtual, February 17, 2023.

Kornfield, S. 2014. "Pregnant Discourse: 'Having It All' While Domestic and Potentially Disabled." *Women's Studies in Communication* 37 (2): 181–201.

Krasny, Elke. 2023. *Living with an Infected Planet: COVID-19, Feminism, and the Global Frontline of Care.* Bielefeld, Germany: Transcript.

Ku, Robert Ji-Song, Martin F. Manalansan IV, and Anita Mannur, eds. 2013. *Eating Asian America: A Food Studies Reader.* New York: New York University Press.

Kumar, Lakshit, Namrata Kahlon, Avani Jain, Jasleen Kaur, Mitasha Singh, and A. K. Pandey. 2021. "Loss of Smell and Taste in COVID-19 Infection in Adolescents." *International Journal of Pediatric Otorhinolaryngology* 142:110626.

Kundakovic, Marija, and Devin Rocks. 2022. "Sex Hormone Fluctuation and Increased Female Risk for Depression and Anxiety Disorders: From Clinical Evidence to Molecular Mechanisms." *Frontiers in Neuroendocrinology* 66:101010.

Lange, David. 2020. "Yoga—Statistics & Facts." Statista. https://www.statista.com/topics /3229/yoga/.

Lawless, Elaine J. 2001. *Women Escaping Violence: Empowerment through Narrative.* Columbia: University of Missouri Press.

———. 2011. "Folklore as a Map of the World: Rejecting 'Home' as a Failure of the Imagination (AFS 2009 Presidential Address)." *Journal of American Folklore* 124:127–46.

Layman, Emma. 1976. *Buddhism in America.* Chicago: Nelson Hall.

Leary, James P. 1999. "Joua Bee Xiong, Hmong Musician." In *Wisconsin Folklore,* 292–304. Madison: University of Wisconsin Press.

Lee, Erika. 2003. *At America's Gates: Chinese Immigration during the Exclusion Era, 1882–1943.* Chapel Hill: University of North Carolina Press.

———. 2015. *The Making of Asian America: A History.* New York: Simon and Schuster.

———. 2019. *America for Americans: A History of Xenophobia in the United States.* New York: Basic Books.

Lee, Erika, and Judy Yung. 2010. *Angel Island: Immigrant Gateway to America.* Oxford: Oxford University Press.

Lee, Jonathan H. X., and Kathleen Nadeau, eds. 2010. *Encyclopedia of Asian American Folklore and Folklife.* 3 vols. Santa Barbara, CA: ABC-CLIO.

———, eds. 2014. *Asian American Identities and Practices.* Lanham, MD: Lexington Books.

Lee, Richard M. 2003. "The Transracial Adoption Paradox: History, Research, and Counseling Implications of Cultural Socialization." *Counseling Psychologist* 31 (6): 711–44.

Leong, Andrew Way. 2021. "Bridging Work and Global Asias: Stars and Sandbars." *Journal of Asian Studies* 80 (4): 1011–21.

Li, Mu. 2023. "Reencountering Chinese Restaurant Legends during the COVID-19 Pandemic." In "Folklore of Epidemics," edited by Juwen Zhang. Special issue, *Journal of Folklore Research* 60 (1).

Li, Yuhang. 2020. *Becoming Guanyin: Artistic Devotion of Buddhist Women in Late Imperial China.* Premodern East Asia: New Horizons. New York: Columbia University Press.

Lim, Adelyn. 2015. *Transnational Feminism and Women's Movements in Post-1997 Hong Kong: Solidarity beyond the State.* Global Connections. Hong Kong: Hong Kong University Press.

Bibliography   233

Lim, Shirley, and Mayumi Tsutakawa, eds. 1989. *The Forbidden Stitch: An Asian American Women's Anthology*. Corvallis, OR: Calyx Books.

Lin, Jan. 1998. *Reconstructing Chinatown: Ethnic Enclave, Global Change*. Minneapolis: University of Minnesota Press.

Lindahl, Carl. 2012. "Legends of Hurricane Katrina: The Right to Be Wrong, Survivor-to-Survivor Storytelling, and Healing." *Journal of American Folklore* 125 (496): 139–76.

Lindahl, Carl, Michael Dylan Foster, Kate Parker Horigan, Yutaka Suga, Yoko Taniguchi, Kōji Katō, Amy Shuman, Gloria M. Colom Braña, and Georgia Ellie Dassler. 2022. *We Are All Survivors: Verbal, Ritual, and Material Ways of Narrating Disaster and Recovery*. Bloomington: Indiana University Press.

Liu, Haiming. 2015. *From Canton Restaurant to Panda Express: A History of Chinese Food in the United States*. New Brunswick, NJ: Rutgers University Press.

Liu, Liangni Sally. 2014. "A Search for a Place to Call Home: Negotiation of Home, Identity and Senses of Belonging among New Migrants from the People's Republic of China (PRC) to New Zealand." *Emotion, Space and Society* 10:18–26.

Liu, Lisong. 2023. "'Virtual Ethnic Town Hall': WeChat and Suburban Chinese Migrants' Multidirectional Activism." *Journal of American Ethnic History* 42 (3): 5–39.

Lloyd, Timothy, ed. 2021. *What Folklorists Do: Professional Possibilities in Folklore Studies*. Bloomington: Indiana University Press.

Long, Lucy M., ed. 2004. *Culinary Tourism*. Lexington: University of Kentucky Press.

———. 2009. Introduction to *Journal of American Folklore* 122 (483): 3–10.

———. 2018. "American Food, Foodways, and Eating." In *The Oxford Handbook of American Folklore and Folklife Studies*, edited by Simon J. Bronner, 470–91. New York: Oxford University Press.

———, ed. 2022. "Folkloristic Perspectives on Foodways and Comfort during the COVID-19 Pandemic." Special issue, *Digest: A Journal of Foodways and Culture* 9 (2). https://scholar works.iu.edu/journals/index.php/digest/index.

———. 2023. "Refrigerators, Cupboards, and Canning Jars: Emergent Meanings and Subversive Practices in Food Preservation and Storage during the COVID-19 Pandemic." In "Pandemics & Politics." Special issue, *Cultural Analysis* Forum Series 1:1–21.

Long, Lucy M., Jerry Lee Reed III, John Broadwell, Quinlan Day Odum, Hannah M. Santino, and Minglei Zhang. 2021. "Finding Comfort and Discomfort through Foodways Practices during the COVID-19 Pandemic: A Public Folklore Project." *Digest: A Journal of Foodways and Culture* 8 (1/2): 5–25. https://scholarworks.iu.edu/journals/index.php /digest/article/view/33644.

Lopez, Donald, Jr., ed. 2002. *Modern Buddhism: Readings for the Un-enlightened*. London: Penguin.

Louie, Andrea. 2015. *How Chinese Are You?: Adopted Chinese Youth and Their Families Negotiate Identity and Culture*. New York: New York University Press.

Lu, Lianghao. 2021. "The Confluence of Karma and Hygiene: Vegetarianism with Renewed Meanings for Modern Chinese Buddhism." *Journal of Chinese Religions* 49 (1): 75–108.

Lv, Nan, and Katherine L. Cason. 2004. "Dietary Pattern Change and Acculturation of Chinese Americans in Pennsylvania." *Journal of the American Dietetic Association* 104 (5): 771–78.

Ma, Yingyi. 2020. *Ambitious and Anxious: How Chinese College Students Succeed and Struggle in American Higher Education*. New York: Columbia University Press.

Ma, Yingyi, and Ning Zhan. 2022. "To Mask or Not to Mask amid the COVID-19 Pandemic: How Chinese Students in America Experience and Cope with Stigma." *Chinese Sociological Review* 54 (1): 1–26.

234 Bibliography

Magat, Margaret. 2015. "From Rebounds to Three-Pointers: Linsanity, Racial Insults, and Stereotypes in Flux." *Journal of American Folklore* 128 (510): 438–48.

———. 2019. *Balut: Fertilized Eggs and the Making of Culinary Capital in the Filipino Diaspora.* London: Bloomsbury.

Magliocco, Sabina. 1993. *The Two Madonnas: The Politics of Festival in a Sardinian Community.* New York: Peter Lang.

Mahmood, Saba. 2005. *Politics of Piety: The Islamic Revival and the Feminist Project.* Chicago: University of Chicago Press.

Making Us Visible New Jersey (MUVNJ). 2022. "Thank You So Much for Being Allies on This Important Cause! Let's Do It for Our Kids!" Accessed February 5, 2022. https://us1.campaign-archive.com/?e=[UNIQID]&u=fecb1c466b38c2ff9c570e695&id=603f071899.

Mallett, S. 2004. "Understanding Home: A Critical Review of the Literature." *Sociology Review* 52 (1): 62–89.

Manalansan, Martin F. 2013. "Beyond Authenticity: Rerouting the Filipino Culinary Diaspora." In *Eating Asian America: A Food Studies Reader,* edited by R. Ku, M. Manalansan, and A. Mannur, 288–302. New York: New York University Press.

Marshall, A. W. 2021. "Social Landscape on WeChat: An Ethnographic Study of the Sunshine Dance Club of Central Pennsylvania." *Journal of Ethnic American Literature* 11:92–110.

Martin, Fran. 2022. *Dreams of Flight: The Lives of Chinese Women Students in the West.* Durham, NC: Duke University Press.

May, Tiffany. 2020. "Coronavirus Strands China's Students, in a Dilemma for Beijing." *New York Times,* April 7, 2020. https://cn.nytimes.com/china/20200407/coronavirus-china-students/dual/.

McClain, Charles J. 1994. *In Search of Equality: The Chinese Struggle against Discrimination in Nineteenth-Century America.* Berkeley: University of California Press.

McDonald, David A. 2020. "Critical Folkloristics, Free Speech, and the 'War on Terror.'" *Journal of American Folklore* 133 (530): 392–411.

McKee, Kimberly D. 2022. "8 More Than an Outcome of War: Adoptions from Asia to the United States." *Journal of Asian American Studies* 25 (2): 247–60.

McKinsey & Co. 2021. "Women in the Workplace 2021." Accessed March 23, 2023. https://www.mckinsey.com/featured-insights/diversity-and-inclusion/women-in-the-workplace#/.

McLaren, Margaret A., ed. 2017. *Decolonizing Feminism: Transnational Feminism and Globalization.* London: Rowman and Littlefield International.

McNay, Lois. 2000. *Gender and Agency: Reconfiguring the Subject in Feminist and Social Theory.* Cambridge, UK: Polity.

———. 2003. "Agency, Anticipation, and Indeterminacy in Feminist Theory." *Feminist Theory* 4:139–48.

Mehravari, Nader. 2022. "Persian Comfort Food: A Foodways Exploration." *Digest: A Journal of Foodways and Culture* 9 (2): 7–16.

Meier, Dani I. 1999. "Cultural Identity and Place in Adult Korean-American Intercountry Adoptees." *Adoption Quarterly* 3:15–48.

Micklethwait, John, and Adrian Wooldridge. 2020. *The Wake-Up Call: Why the Pandemic Has Exposed the Weakness of the West, and How to Fix It.* New York: HarperVia.

Mills, Margaret A. 2020. "Introduction: Defining and Creating (A)New Critical Folklore Studies." *Journal of American Folklore* 133 (530): 383–91.

Mills, Margaret A., and William Westerman. 2020. "Critical Folkloristics Today." Special issue, *Journal of American Folklore* 133 (530).

Mirsky, Richard M. 1981. "Perspectives in the Study of Food Habits." *Western Folklore* 40 (1): 125–33.

Mohanty, Chandra Talpade. 2003. *Feminism without Borders: Decolonizing Theory, Practicing Solidarity*. Durham, NC: Duke University Press.

Molnar, Nicholas Trajano. 2017. *American Mestizos, the Philippines, and the Malleability of Race: 1898–1961*. Columbia: University of Missouri Press.

Moraga, Cherríe, and Gloria Anzaldúa, eds. 1981. *This Bridge Called My Back: Writings by Radical Women of Color*. New York: Kitchen Table Press.

Muñoz, José Esteban. 1999. *Disidentifications: Queers of Color and the Performance of Politics*. Minneapolis: University of Minnesota Press.

Murphy, S. 2017. *Zombie University: Thinking Under Control*. London: Repeater Books.

Naples, Nancy A. 1992. "Activist Mothering: Cross-Generational Continuity in the Community Work of Women from Low-Income Urban Neighborhoods." *Gender and Society* 6 (3): 441–63.

N'Diaye, Diana Baird. 2021. "Telling Our Own Stories: Reciprocal Autoethnography at the Intersections of Race, Class, and Gender." *Journal of American Folklore* 134 (533): 252–57.

Ngai, Mae M. 2021. *The Chinese Question: The Gold Rushes and Global Politics*. New York: W. W. Norton.

Nierenberg, Amelia, and Adam Pasick. 2020. "Colleges Are Slashing Budgets: The Pandemic Has Pushed Higher Education Institutions to the Brink." *New York Times*, October 26, 2020. https://www.nytimes.com/2020/10/26/us/colleges-budget-cuts-finance.html?smid=em-share.

Noyes, Dorothy. 2003. *Fire in the Plaça: Catalan Politics after Franco*. Philadelphia: University of Pennsylvania Press.

Numrich, Paul. 1996. *Old Wisdom in the New World: Americanization in Two Immigrant Theravada Buddhist Temples*. Knoxville: University of Tennessee Press.

———. 2000. "How the Swans Came to Lake Michigan: The Social Organization of Buddhist Chicago." *Journal for the Scientific Study of Religion* 39 (2): 189–203.

———. 2003. "Two Buddhisms Further Considered." *Contemporary Buddhism* 4 (1): 55–78.

Obadia, Lionel. 2020. "Buddhist 'Solutions' and Action in the Context of COVID-19, East and West: Complexity, Paradoxes, and Ambivalences." *Contemporary Buddhism* 21 (1–2): 170–89.

OECD (Organisation for Economic Co-operation and Development). n.d. "The Impact of COVID-19 on Employment and Jobs." Accessed March 23, 2023. https://www.oecd.org/employment/covid-19.htm.

Oh, Arissa H. 2015. *To Save the Children of Korea: The Cold War Origins of International Adoption*. Redwood City, CA: Stanford University Press.

Omi, Michael, and Howard Winant. 2015. *Racial Formation in the United States*. 3rd ed. New York: Routledge.

O'Reilly, Andrea. 2021. "'Certainly Not an Equal-Opportunity Pandemic': COVID-19 and Its Impact on Mothers' Carework, Health, and Employment." In *Mothers, Mothering, and COVID-19: Dispatches from the Pandemic*, edited by Andrea O'Reilly and Fiona Joy Green, 41–52. Bradford, ON: Demeter Press.

O'Reilly, Andrea, and Fiona Joy Green, eds. 2021. *Mothers, Mothering, and COVID-19: Dispatches from a Pandemic*. Bradford, ON: Demeter Press.

Otero, Solimar, and Mintzi Auanda Martínez-Rivera, eds. 2021. *Theorizing Folklore from the Margins: Critical and Ethical Approaches*. Bloomington: Indiana University Press.

Papastergiadis, Nikos. 1997. "Tracing Hybridity in Theory." In *Debating Cultural Hybridity: Multicultural Identities and the Politics of Anti-Racism*, ed. Pnina Werbner and Tariq Modood, 257–81. London: ZedBooks.

Parents of Chinese Students. 2020. "An Open Letter from 200 Families of Overseas Students to Ambassador Cui Tiankai of the Consulate General of New York." March 29, 2020. https://mp.weixin.qq.com/s/8SQecxqF4xHJbTk-oHuIbg.

Park, Soyeon. 2012. "Caucasian Parents' Experience with Transnational-Transracial Adoption: A Phenomenological Study." *International Journal of Child, Youth and Family Studies* 3 (4.1): 479–79.

Pellecchia, Umberto. 2017. "Quarantine and Its Malcontents: How Liberians Responded to the Ebola Epidemic Containment Measures." *Anthropology in Action* 24 (2): 15–24.

Pierson, David, Isabelle Qian, Olivia Wang, and Tiffany May. 2022. "China's Abrupt COVID Pivot Leaves Many without Medicines." *New York Times*, December 21, 2022. https://cn.nytimes.com/china/20221221/china-covid-shortages/dual/.

Ponlop, Rinpoche Dzogchen. 2016. *Emotional Rescue: How to Work with Your Emotions to Transform Hurt and Confusion into Energy That Empowers.* New York: TarcherPerigee.

Prahlad, Anand. 2018. "African American Folklore, Folklife, and Race." In *The Oxford Handbook of American Folklore and Folklife Studies*, edited by Simon J. Bronner, 720–40. New York: Oxford University Press.

———. 2021. "Tearing Down Monuments: Missed Opportunities, Silences, and Absences— A Radical Look at Race in American Folklore Studies." *Journal of American Folklore* 134 (533): 258–64.

Prebish, Charles S. 1999. *Luminous Passage: The Practice and Study of Buddhism in America.* Berkeley: University of California Press.

Primiano, Leonard Norman. 1995. "Vernacular Religion and the Search for Method in Religious Folklife." *Western Folklore* 54 (1): 37–56.

PRRI Staff. 2021. "The American Religious Landscape in 2020." 2020 PRRI Census of American Religion: County-Level Data on Religious Identity and Diversity, July 8, 2021. https://www.prri.org/research/2020-census-of-american-religion/#page-section-1.

Puskar-Pasewicz, Margaret, ed. 2010. *Cultural Encyclopedia of Vegetarianism.* Santa Barbara, CA: Greenwood.

Qian, Isabelle, and David Pierson. 2022. "'Tragic Battle': On the Front Lines of China's Covid Crisis." *New York Times*, December 28, 2022. https://cn.nytimes.com/china/20221228/china-covid-hospital-crisis/dual/.

Rattansi, Ari. 2020. *Racism: A Very Short Introduction.* 2nd ed. New York: Oxford University Press.

Reed, Jerry L., III. 2022. "Discomforting Foodways: Reflections on the Challenges Faced by Individuals during the COVID-19 Pandemic." *Digest: A Journal of Foodways and Culture* 9 (2): 1–7.

Rinpoche, Dzongsar Jamyang Khyentse. 2018. *Almost Buddhist.* Beijing: New Star Press.

Rinpoche, Yongey Mingyur. 2019. *In Love with the World: A Monk's Journey Through the Bardos of Living and Dying.* New York: Random House.

Roberts, J. A. G. 2002. *China to Chinatown: Chinese Food in the West.* London: Reaktion Books.

Roberts, John. 2021. "Systemic Racism in American Folkloristics." *Journal of American Folklore* 134 (533): 265–71.

Robyn, Satya. 2019. *Coming Home: Refuge in Pureland Buddhism.* Dorset, England: Woodsmoke Press.

Rocha, Cristina. 2006. *Zen in Brazil: The Quest for Cosmopolitan Modernity.* Honolulu: University of Hawai'i Press.

Rofel, Lisa. 2007. *Desiring China: Experiments in Neoliberalism, Sexuality and Public Culture.* Durham, NC: Duke University Press.

Rogers, Katie, and Cecilia Kang. 2021. "Biden Revokes and Replaces Trump Order That Banned TikTok." *New York Times*, June 10, 2021. https://cn.nytimes.com/usa/20210610/biden-tiktok-ban-trump/dual/.

Roth, LuAnne. 2006. "Beyond Communitas: Cinematic Food Events and the Negotiation of Power, Belonging, and Exclusion." *Western Folklore* 64:163–87.

———. 2014. "Sexing the Turkey: Gender Politics and the Construction of Sexuality at Thanksgiving." In *Unsettling Assumptions: Tradition, Gender, Drag*, edited by Pauline Greenhill and Diane Tye, 148–71. Logan: Utah State University Press.

Ryang, Sonia. 2021. "Afterword: Transnational Asian Studies—Toward More Inclusive Theory and Practice." *Journal of Asian Studies* 80 (4): 1033–44.

Salguero, Pierce. 2020. "How Do Buddhists Handle Coronavirus? The Answer Is Not Just Meditation." *The Conversation*, May 15, 2020. https://theconversation.com/how-do-buddhists-handle-coronavirus-the-answer-is-not-just-meditation-137966.

Seager, Richard Hughes. 2012. *Buddhism in America*. New York: Columbia University Press.

Seymore, Zoe. 2022. "Dance Video: Re-Empowering My Identity." Posted on YouTube, May 4, 2022. https://www.youtube.com/watch?v=nvJHzk2cVow.

———. 2023. "Overlooked Adoptees: The Effects of COVID-19 Racism and Ethnic Identity on the Psychological Well-Being of Chinese Transracial Adoptees in the United States." Independent study thesis, College of Wooster.

Shah, Nayan. 2001. *Contagious Divides: Epidemics and Race in San Francisco's Chinatown*. Berkeley: University of California Press.

Shah, S. 1997. *Dragon Ladies: Asian American Feminists Breathe Fire*. Boston: South End Press.

Shepherd, Nick, ed. 2023. *Rethinking Heritage in Precarious Times: Coloniality, Climate Change, and Covid-19*. London: Routledge.

Shivaram, Deepa. 2021. "Illinois Has Become the First State to Require the Teaching of Asian American History." NPR, July 13, 2021. https://www.npr.org/2021/07/13/1015596570/illinois-has-become-the-first-state-to-require-the-teaching-of-asian-american-hi.

Smith, William A. 2008. "Higher Education: Racial Battle Fatigue." In *Encyclopedia of Race, Ethnicity, and Society*, edited by Richard T. Schaefer, 615–18. Los Angeles: Sage Publications.

Sobti, R. C., and Vipin Sobti, eds. 2023. *Frontline Workers and Women as Warriors in the COVID-19 Pandemic*. Abingdon, UK: Routledge.

Stahl, Sandra Dolby. 1977. "The Personal Narrative as Folklore." *Journal of the Folklore Institute* 14 (1/2): 9–30.

———. 1989. *Literary Folkloristics and the Personal Narrative*. Bloomington: Indiana University Press.

State of New Jersey. 2022. "Governor Murphy Signs Legislation Ensuring AAPI-Inclusive Curriculum Is Taught in New Jersey Schools." January 18, 2022. https://nj.gov/governor/news/news/562022/approved/20220118c.shtml.

Stevenson, Alexandra, and Ben Dooley. 2022. "Major Covid Holdouts in Asia Drop Border Restrictions." *New York Times*, September 26. https://cn.nytimes.com/asia-pacific/20220926/asia-travel-reopening-japan-taiwan-hong-kong/dual/.

Stoddard, Eve, and Grant H. Cornwell. 1999. "Cosmopolitan or Mongrel? Créolité, Hybridity and 'Douglarisation' in Trinidad." *European Journal of Cultural Studies* 2 (3): 331–53.

Stop AAPI Hate (SAH). 2020–22. Reports. Accessed on May 1, 2023. https://stopaapihate.org/reports/.

———. 2021a. *National Report (Through June 2021)*. https://stopaapihate.org/stop-aapi-hate-national-report-2/.

———. 2021b. *National Report (Through September 2021)*. https://stopaapihate.org/national-report-through-september-2021/.

———. 2022. *Two Years and Thousands of Voices: National Report (Through March 31, 2022)*. July 20, 2022. https://stopaapihate.org/2022/07/20/year-2-report/. Accessed on July 15, 2023.

Strega, Susan, and Leslie Brown. 2015. *Research as Resistance: Revisiting Critical, Indigenous, and Anti-Oppressive Approaches*. 2nd ed. Toronto: Canadian Scholars' Press and Women's Press.

Su, Zhaohui, Dean McDonnell, Feng Shi, Bin Liang, Xiaoshan Li, Jun Wen, Yuyang Cai, Yu-Tao Xiang, and Ling Yang. 2021. "Chinese International Students in the United States: The Interplay of Students' Acculturative Stress, Academic Standing, and Quality of Life." *Frontiers in Psychology* 12:1–8. https://doi.org/10.3389/fpsyg.2021.625863.

Sung, Sisi. 2023. *The Economics of Gender in China: Women, Work and the Glass Ceiling*. Abingdon, UK: Routledge.

Takaki, R., 2008. *A Different Mirror: a History of Multicultural America*. New York: Back Bay Books/Little, Brown.

Tambiah, S. 1969. "Animals Are Good to Think and Good to Prohibit." *Ethnology* 8:423–459.

Tan, Chee-Beng. 2018. "Localization and the Chinese Overseas: Acculturation, Assimilation, Hybridization, Creolization, and Identification." *Cultural and Religious Studies* 6 (2): 73–87.

Tate, Claudia, ed. 1983. *Black Women Writers at Work*. New York: Continuum.

Taylor, James. 2015. "Popular Buddhism: Monks, Magic and Amulets." In *Routledge Handbook of Religions in Asia*, edited by Bryan Turner and Oscar Salemink, 219–30. London: Routledge.

Thayer, Millie. 2010. *Making Transnational Feminism: Rural Women, NGO Activists, and Northern Donors in Brazil*. Perspectives on Gender. New York: Routledge.

Thornton Dill, Bonnie, and Ruth Enid Zambrana. 2009. "Critical Thinking about Inequality: An Emerging Lens." In *Emerging Intersections: Race, Class, and Gender in Theory, Policy, and Practice*, edited by Bonnie Thornton Dill and Ruth Enid Zambrana, 1–21. New Brunswick, NJ: Rutgers University Press.

Troisi, Jordan D., and Shira Gabriel. 2011. "Chicken Soup Really Is Good for the Soul: 'Comfort Food' Fulfills the Need to Belong." *Psychological Science* 22:747–53.

Tsing, Anna. 2015. *The Mushroom at the End of the World: On the Possibility of Life in Capitalist Ruins*. Princeton, NJ: Princeton University Press.

Tsomo, Karma Lekshe. 1999. *Buddhist Women across Cultures: Realizations*. Albany: State University of New York Press.

———, ed. 2004. *Buddhist Women and Social Justice: Ideals, Challenges, and Achievements*. Albany: State University of New York Press.

———, ed. 2006. *Out of the Shadows: Socially Engaged Buddhist Women*. Delhi, India: Sri Satguru.

Tung, William L. 1974. *The Chinese in America 1820–1973: A Chronology & Fact Book*. Dobbs Ferry, NY: Oceana.

Turner, Victor. 1967. *Forest of Symbols: Aspects of the Ndembu Ritual*. Ithaca, NY: Cornell University Press.

———. 1969. *The Ritual Process*. New York: Penguin.

Twigg, J. 1979. "Food for Thought: Purity and Vegetarianism." *Religion* 9:13–35.

Tye, Diane. 2010. *Baking as Biography: A Life Story in Recipes*. Montreal: McGill-Queen's University Press.

United Nations Educational, Scientific and Cultural Organization (UNESCO). 2022. "Global Flow of Tertiary-Level Students." Institute for Statistics. Accessed April 8, 2022. http://uis.unesco.org/en/uis-student-flow.

UN News. 2023. "WHO Chief Declares End to COVID-19 as a Global Health Emergency." May 5, 2023. https://news.un.org/en/story/2023/05/1136367.

UN Women. 2020. "Whose Time to Care: Unpaid Care and Domestic Work during COVID-19." Brief, Gender and COVID-19, November 25, 2020. https://data.unwomen.org/publications/whose-time-care-unpaid-care-and-domestic-work-during-covid-19.

US Bureau of Labor Statistics. 2021. "Unemployment Rises in 2020, as the Country Battles the COVID-19 Pandemic." *Monthly Labor Review*, June 2021. https://www.bls.gov/opub/mlr/2021/article/unemployment-rises-in-2020-as-the-country-battles-the-covid-19-pandemic.htm.

Van Gennep, Arnold. 1909. *Les rites de passage*. Paris: Émile Nourry.

Vazquez, Maegan. 2021. "Biden Signs Bill Aimed at Addressing Rise in Anti-Asian Hate Crimes." CNN, May 20, 2021. https://www.cnn.com/2021/05/20/politics/biden-anti-asian-hate-crimes-covid-19-signing/index.html.

Veazey, Leah Williams. 2021. *Migrant Mothers in the Digital Age: Emotion and Belonging in Migrant Maternal Online Communities*. Studies in Migration and Diaspora. Abingdon, UK: Routledge.

Võ, Linda Trinh, and Marian Sciachitano, eds. 2004. *Asian American Women: The Frontiers Reader*. Lincoln: University of Nebraska Press.

Wall, Glenda. 2013. "'Putting Family First': Shifting Discourses of Motherhood and Childhood in Representations of Mothers' Employment and Child Care." *Women's Studies International Forum* 40:162–71.

Wang, Leslie K. 2016. *Outsourced Children: Orphanage Care and Adoption in Globalizing China*. Redwood City, CA: Stanford University Press.

Wang, Vivian. 2022a. "China's 'Zero Covid' Bind: No Easy Way Out Despite the Cost." *New York Times*, September 8, 2022. https://cn.nytimes.com/china/20220908/china-covid-lockdown/dual/.

———. 2022b. "China to Drop Covid Quarantine for Incoming Travelers." *New York Times*, December 27, 2022. https://cn.nytimes.com/china/20221227/china-covid-quarantine-travelers/dual/.

Waterton, Emma, Hayley Saul, and Divya P. Tolia-Kelly. 2023. "Reckoning with Extractivism: Towards an Anti-Colonial Heritage." In *Rethinking Heritage in Precarious Times: Coloniality, Climate Change, and Covid-19*, edited by Nick Shepherd, 143–66. London: Routledge.

Waylen, Georgina. 1997. "Gender, Feminism and Political Economy." *New Political Economy* 2 (2): 205–20.

Wei, Xiaohan. 2021. 一个陌生女人的葬礼 [A Funeral for a Stranger Woman]. April 20, 2021. https://mp.weixin.qq.com/s/YILOaNrfqhrHz979x6im_Q.

Widmayer, Christine J. 2022. "Comfort Food in Activism: Sweet Potato Comfort Pie." *Digest: A Journal of Foodways and Culture* 9 (2): 47–56.

Wilson, Anika. 2013. *Folklore, Gender, and Aids in Malawi: No Secret Under the Sun*. New York: Palgrave Macmillan.

Wing, Hannah M., and Jennie Park-Taylor. 2022. "From Model Minority to Racial Threat: Chinese Transracial Adoptees' Experience Navigating the COVID-19 Pandemic." *Asian American Journal of Psychology* 13 (3): 234–47.

———. 2024. "Female Chinese Transracial Adoptees' Racial Awakening amid Dual Racial Pandemics." *Cultural Diversity & Ethnic Minority Psychology* 30 (2): 395–403.

Winter, Tim. 2023. "Covid-19, Black Lives Matter, and Heritage Futures." In *Rethinking Heritage in Precarious Times: Coloniality, Climate Change, and Covid-19*, edited by Nick Shepherd, 282–96. London: Routledge.

World Economic Forum (WEF). 2022. *Global Gender Gap Report 2022*. Published on July 13, 2022. https://www.weforum.org/reports/global-gender-gap-report-2022/.

World Health Organization (WHO). 2022. *World Mental Health Report: Transforming Mental Health for All*. June 16, 2022. https://www.who.int/publications/i/item/9789240049338.

———. 2023. "WHO Coronavirus (COVID-19) Dashboard." Accessed May 31, 2023. https://covid19.who.int/.

Xinhua News. 2020. "WHO Expert Praises China's COVID-19 Containment Measures." March 6, 2020. http://www.xinhuanet.com/english/2020-03/06/c_138849519.htm.

Yan, Kun, and David C. Berliner. 2011. "An Examination of Individual Level Factors in Stress and Coping Processes: Perspectives of Chinese International Students in the United States." *Journal of College Student Development* 52 (5): 523–42.

Yang, Mayfair Mei-hui. 2020. *Re-Enchanting Modernity: Ritual Economy and Society in Wenzhou, China*. Durham, NC: Duke University Press.

Yano, Christine Reiko. 2020. "Racing the Pandemic: Anti-Asian Racism and COVID-19." In *The Pandemic: Perspectives on Asia*, edited by Vinayak Chaturvedi, 123–36. Ann Arbor, MI: Association for Asian Studies.

———. 2021. "Global Asias: Improvisations on a Theme (a.k.a. Chindon-ya Riffs)." *Journal of Asian Studies* 80 (4): 845–64.

Yavorsky, Jill E., Yue Qian, and Amanda C. Sargent. 2021. "The Gendered Pandemic: The Implications of COVID-19 for Work and Family." *Sociology Compass* 15 (6): e12881. https://doi.org/10.1111/soc4.12881.

Ye, Ruolin. 2020. "Chinese Fear COVID-19 Rebound as Overseas Students Rush Home." *Sixth Tone*, March 20, 2020. https://www.sixthtone.com/news/1005340/chinese-fear-covid-19-rebound-as-overseas-students-rush-home.

Ye, Weili. 2001. *Seeking Modernity in China's Name: Chinese Students in the United States, 1900–1927*. Redwood City: Stanford University Press.

Yeung, Jessie. 2022. "180 Million People Impacted by China's Covid Lockdowns." CNN News, April 28, 2022. https://www.cnn.com/2022/04/28/china/china-covid-lockdown-explainer-intl-hnk/index.html.

Yoder, Don. 1972. "Folk Cookery." In *Folklore and Folklife: An Introduction*, edited by Richard M. Dorson, 325–50. Chicago: University of Chicago Press.

You, Ziying, and Patricia Hardwick, eds. 2020. "Guest Editors' Introduction: Intangible Cultural Heritage (ICH) in Asia: Traditions in Transition." Special issue, *Asian Ethnology* 79 (1). https://asianethnology.org/volume/79-1.

You, Ziying, and Qiaoyun Zhang. 2022. "Graves in One's Heart: Grassroots Memorialization of Dr. Li Wenliang during the COVID-19 Outbreak in China." *Journal of American Folklore* 135 (535): 3–25.

Yü, Chün-fang. 2013. *Passing the Light: The Incense Light Community and Buddhist Nuns in Contemporary Taiwan*. Honolulu: University of Hawai'i Press.

———. 2020. *Chinese Buddhism: A Thematic History*. Honolulu: University of Hawai'i Press.

Yuval-Davis, Nira, Floya Anthias, and Eleonore Kofman. 2005. "Secure Borders and Safe Haven and the Gendered Politics of Belonging: Beyond Social Cohesion." *Ethnic and Racial Studies* 28:513–35.

Z., Alan. 2022. "New Jersey Passes AAPI History Curriculum Bill, Behind 'Making History' Are Their Efforts and Struggles." CAUS.com, January 11, 2022. https://www.caus.com/detail/44084.

Zarafonetis, Nicole. 2017. *Sexuality in a Changing China: Young Women, Sex and Intimate Relations in the Reform Period.* New York: Routledge.

Zhang, Juwen, ed. 2015a. "Introduction: New Perspectives on the Studies of Asian American Folklores." *Journal of American Folklore* 128 (510): 373–94.

———. 2015b. "New Perspectives on the Studies of Asian American Folklores." Special issue, *Journal of American Folklore* 128 (510).

———, ed. 2023a. "Folklore of Epidemics." Special issue, *Journal of Folklore Research* 60 (1).

———. 2023b. "Making Sense of the Pandemic of Racism: From the Asian Exclusion Act in 1924 to the COVID-19 Hate Crimes Act in 2021." In "Pandemics & Politics." Special issue, *Cultural Analysis* Forum Series 1:1–21.

———. 2023c. "Where Were/Are Asian American Folklorists?" *Journal of American Folklore* 136 (540): 199–211.

Zhang, Qiaoyun, and Ziying You. 2022. "'Fear Not the Want of Armor, For Mine Is Also Yours to Wear': Trust and Community Cultivation for Risk Response of a Chinese Immigrant Group in the United States." In *Covid-19 Responses of Local Communities around the World: Exploring Trust in the Context of Risk and Fear,* edited by Khun Eng Kuah, Gilles Guiheux, and Francis Lim, 155–69. London: Routledge.

Zhang-Wu, Qianqian. 2018. "Chinese International Students' Experiences in American Higher Education Institutes: A Critical Review of the Literature." *Journal of International Students* 8 (2): 1173–97.

Zhou, Sasha, Rachel Banawa, and Hans Oh. 2021. "The Mental Health Impact of COVID-19 Racial and Ethnic Discrimination against Asian American and Pacific Islanders." *Front Psychiatry* 12:708426.

Zhou, Xun, and Sander L. Gilman. 2021. *"I Know Who Caused COVID-19": Pandemics and Xenophobia.* London: Reaktion Books.

Zhu, Yujie. 2020. "Memory, Homecoming and the Politics of Diaspora Tourism in China." *Tourism Geographies* 25 (1): 95–112.

Zia, Helen. 2019. *Last Boat Out of Shanghai: The Epic Story of the Chinese Who Fled Mao's Revolution.* New York: Ballantine Books.

INDEX

AAPI Youth Rising (AYR), 189, 190
absence, 12
actions, 23, 26, 55, 56, 62, 64, 66, 81, 82, 100, 101, 102, 105, 109, 141, 151, 152, 155, 171, 184, 186, 189, 196, 207, 210, 211, 213; of AAAPI women, 17, 29, 59; of CCA women, 2, 12, 21, 29, 60, 209, 212; collective, 26, 30, 38, 54; feminist, 18; political, 11, 16
activisms, 63; antiracist, 5; everyday, 39, 60, 63; feminist, 169; political, 17, 33, 34, 36, 39, 54, 56, 59, 63, 64, 129, 142, 143, 210, 211, 214; social, 171; youth, 34, 178, 180, 190
activist mothering, 33, 39, 54, 55, 56, 59, 63
adoptees. *See* Chinese transracial adoptees
adoption, 109–14, 124–25, 128, 129, 136, 138, 141–43, 153–54; international 107–8; transnational, 108–9. *See also* transracial adoption paradox
agencies, 2, 4, 5, 9, 13, 29, 33–34, 209, 211, 212, 213; CCA women's, 30; Chinese adoptees', 106, 109, 120, 124–29, 140, 196–97; Chinese students', 73, 100; feminist, 17, 20, 21, 22, 29, 32; lay Buddhist women's, 145, 148–49, 151–53, 155, 168–69, 172–74, 203–5; mothers', 54, 64, 65
Alliance for Impact, 39
American dream, 25, 84, 194

anti-Asian racisms, 1, 2, 4, 6, 8, 11, 21, 26, 27–29, 34, 38, 101, 103, 106, 141, 179, 210; combat(ing), 149, 167–72, 181, 185–86, 211; course, viii, 9, 34, 131, 134, 141; experiences of, 69–70, 73, 75–78, 86, 94, 107, 114–24, 130, 173; food association with, 192; history, 22–5; impacts of, 109, 131–32, 182, 206; responses to, 12, 30, 31, 32, 39, 54–56, 62–64, 83, 102, 129, 147, 196, 209, 214, 215
antibody, 95, 96, 97
anticapitalist, 19, 20
antidiscrimination, 28
anti-oppressive, 209
antiracist, 2, 4, 5, 10, 18, 19–20, 59, 209, 213, 217; solidarities, 60–1, 104, 129–30, 141, 171
antiwar, 18
Asian, Asian American, and Asian Diaspora Studies, 109
Asian, Asian American, and Pacific Islander (AAAPI), viii, 11, 15, 66, 84, 104, 105, 107, 115, 118–19, 131–33, 136, 144, 150, 186, 187, 193, 194; feminisms, 17–19; festivals, 70, 129, 134–35; histories, 129, 191; individuals and communities, 11, 15–16, 25, 29, 38, 54–60, 69, 75, 82, 103, 116, 118, 122, 129, 142–43, 151, 168–72, 210–11, 215; women, 12, 29, 30, 45, 59–60, 65, 211. *See also* Asian American and Pacific Islander (AAPI)

243

Asian American and Pacific Islander (AAPI), 61–62, 64, 66, 83, 94, 150, 180, 182, 184, 187–90; curriculum bills, viii, 39, 56–59, 61–62, 66, 143, 187–88, 210–11; history, 56–59, 61, 66, 83, 211. *See also* Stop AAPI Hate

Asian American and Pacific Islander Equity Alliance, 27

Asian American Political Alliance, 25

Asian Ethnology, 14

Asian Women United of California (AWUC), 18

Asian Youth Act (AYA), 190

Atlanta spa shootings, viii, 9, 29, 82, 105, 106, 129, 131, 133, 169, 170, 171, 172, 187

authenticity, 176, 178, 190, 194–95, 196, 206

belonging, 5, 22, 30, 31, 32, 37, 42, 60, 61, 62, 63, 72, 92, 98, 104, 108, 109, 125–27, 135, 138, 140, 155, 157, 163, 166, 168, 173, 182, 202, 203, 204, 205, 206; uncertainty and, 75, 101

Black, Indigenous, and people of color (BIPOC), 18, 84, 130, 137, 142

Black Lives Matter (BLM), 82, 106, 131, 136

Buddhism, 34, 62, 145, 147, 148, 152–55, 169, 172–73, 203; coping with the pandemic, 164–67; hybrid communities, 157–64; identifications, 156–57; racisms, 167; Tibetan, 146; in the US, 149–51; vegetarianism, 204–5

Buddhist, 146, 147; in the US, 149–51. *See also* Chinese lay Buddhist women

burnout, 48

California gold rush, 23, 150

Centers for Disease Control and Prevention (CDC), 76, 90, 100

children, 3, 4, 9, 20, 24, 37, 38–41, 42, 46–48, 64–65, 78, 93, 147, 155, 164, 166, 170, 174, 204, 211; adopted, 33, 106, 107–8, 111–12, 142; activist mothering and childrearing, 54–56, 58–59; CCA, 34, 181, 183–88, 190; everyday activisms and childrearing, 60–63; impacts of the pandemic, 49–54

China Eastern Airlines (CEA), 88–89

China's State Council Information Office (CSCIO), 96

Chinese American, 37, 57, 58, 70, 82, 83, 85, 124, 126, 127, 128, 130, 149, 170, 180, 182–83, 184, 185, 189, 192; becoming, 135–41. *See also* Chinese and Chinese American women or CCA women

Chinese and Chinese American women or CCA women, 2, 3, 5, 6, 8, 9, 12, 21, 22, 29, 30, 31, 32, 34, 145, 169, 173, 175, 177, 206, 209–10, 211, 213, 214, 215, 218

Chinese Exclusion Act, 4, 23, 83, 132, 179

Chinese for Affirmative Action, 27

Chinese immigrant mothers, 2, 4, 21, 33, 35, 36, 38–39, 42, 54, 209, 211, 212, 213, 214, 215; activist mothering 55, 59–60

Chinese international students, 69, 70, 73, 86; combat racisms and discrimination, 80–85; discrimination against, 78–79; mental health, 92–94. *See also* Chinese women international students

Chinese lay Buddhist women, 2, 4, 5, 21, 30, 34, 35, 145, 147–49, 172–74, 178, 206, 209, 211, 212, 213, 214, 215, 216; agencies, 151–55; combating racisms, 167–72; coping with the pandemic, 164–67; hybrid communities, 157–64; identifications, 156–57; vegetarianism, 203–5

Chinese School Association in the United States, 39

Chinese Students and Scholars Association (CSSA), 82, 85, 102–3

Chinese transracial adoptees, 4, 5, 21, 30, 33, 34, 35, 104, 106–15, 118–29, 131–32, 134–44, 153–54, 178, 190–96, 205, 209, 211, 212, 213, 214, 215, 221, 222

"Chinese virus," 6, 26, 33, 69, 71, 78, 83, 105, 107, 170

Chinese women international students, 33, 67, 71. *See also* Chinese international students

Civil Aviation Administration of China (CAAC), 86, 95

civil rights, viii, 18, 27, 28, 29, 64, 86, 129, 132, 188, 189

Civil Rights Movement, 6, 25

Cleveland Contemporary Chinese School, 37

coalitions, 16, 18, 19, 29, 30, 33, 59, 62, 64, 80, 82, 84, 86, 101, 135, 136

Cold War, 24

colorblind, 211

comfort foodways, 34, 206; of Chinese women international students, 197–203. *See also* foodways

communities of support, 3, 4, 22, 29, 32, 33, 36, 39, 42, 54, 60, 61, 62, 63, 64, 110, 129, 131, 134, 135, 136, 141, 142, 143, 184, 185, 190, 196; definition, 30, 38. *See also* hybrid communities

244   Index

concentration camps, 24

coronavirus, vii, 1–2, 5, 6, 8, 28, 33, 49, 50, 67, 68, 69, 71, 86, 115, 119, 177

COVID-19, 1–4, 5, 20, 21, 22, 26, 27, 32, 34, 35, 38, 39, 40, 41, 42, 44–45, 48, 54, 58, 63, 64, 65, 67–68, 69, 71, 73, 75, 86, 87, 89, 90, 98, 99, 101, 105, 107, 118, 120, 121, 126, 129, 132, 133, 147, 154, 164, 166, 176, 178, 181, 183, 186, 189, 196, 202, 205, 207, 208, 209, 214–15, 216, 218; co-existence, 159; mental health, 92–94; outbreak, 78, 81, 84, 88, 116, 119, 131, 145, 146, 164, 167, 177, 179; protocols, 79. *See also* COVID-19 tests; lockdown(s)

COVID-19 tests, 67, 71, 90, 94–96, 98, 106, 199–200

Critical Folklore Studies, 11, 13, 14

Critical Latinx Folklore Studies, 16

cross-border, 16

cross-boundary, 18, 19

cross-cultural, 19, 66

cross-generational, 55

cross-racial, 18

cross-spatial, 19

cross-temporal, 19

data (plural), 1, 9, 27–28, 29, 38, 40, 66, 70, 75, 80, 83, 148, 188

death, 1–2, 28, 29, 34, 40, 87, 96, 98, 99, 149, 155, 167, 216, 218; threat, 83

decolonization, 5, 34, 169, 212

decolonize, 151

decolonizing, 2, 5, 10, 11, 17, 19, 151, 159, 169, 173, 209, 212–13

Dharma, 146, 148, 150, 154, 156, 158, 159, 160, 161, 162, 163, 164, 166, 172

discrimination, 5, 16, 18, 23, 24, 25, 26–28, 55, 57, 58, 59, 61, 65, 66, 186, 187, 190, 195, 197, 210, 212; against Chinese adoptees, 104, 109, 114, 116, 118, 119, 121–23, 125, 133, 135, 137, 141; against Chinese international students, 69–70, 71, 72, 73, 74, 77, 78–79, 80; against Chinese lay Buddhist women, 153, 170, 171, 173

empathy, 10, 55, 57, 61, 80, 82, 101, 120, 124, 187, 190, 213

empire-colonizers, 23

ethnicity, 4, 10, 16, 20, 32, 55, 104, 107, 114, 115, 122, 125, 142, 151, 171, 176, 194, 203

Euro-American, 5

everyday lives, 6, 16, 29, 33, 34, 49, 54, 60, 86, 125, 153, 175, 177, 180, 192, 205, 206, 207, 211

Executive Order 9066, 24. *See also* Japanese internment camps

father, 39, 40, 43, 47, 51, 98, 107, 111, 112, 113, 122, 123, 124, 128, 139, 153, 193, 215

Federal Bureau of Investigation (FBI), 168

feminisms, 1, 35, 168, 214; AAAPI feminisms, 17, 19; global Asian feminisms, 17–20, 214; transnational feminisms, 17, 18–19; US Third World feminisms, 18; Women of Color feminisms, 17, 19

Five-One policy, 86, 99

fluid foodways, 34, 177, 178, 190, 206; definition, 175–76; of Chinese adoptees, 190–96; of Chinese lay Buddhist women, 203–5. *See also* foodways.

Food and Religion in China (course title), 9

foodways, 4, 6, 9, 33, 34, 134, 176–78, 179, 206; definition, 175. *See also* comfort foodways and fluid foodways

Four Noble Truths, 148, 156

funeral, 89, 171–72

future-oriented, 11, 16, 143

Garden State Equality (GSE), 62–63

gender, 4, 5, 6, 8, 9, 10, 16, 17, 18, 19, 23, 31, 33, 34, 39, 42, 55, 63, 64, 71, 72, 84, 103, 120, 143, 151, 152, 153, 155, 169, 171, 173, 175, 176, 178, 187, 201, 203, 206, 212, 213, 214. *See also* gendered pandemic.

gendered pandemic, 20–22

geopolitics, vii, 33, 72, 101

Global Asian Folklore Studies (GAFS), 1, 19, 109, 213, 214; definition, 11–14, 15–17

global Asias, 11, 13, 14, 34; definition, 13

Global North, 207

Global South, 207

Greater Cincinnati Chinese School, 37

Han Dynasty, 149, 204

health, 1, 4, 5, 10, 19, 20, 45, 48, 65, 82, 84, 96, 97, 101, 106, 202, 215; code, 95, 96, 98, 100, 145, 164, 175, 177; crisis, 22, 30, 47, 64, 106; experts, professionals, and authorities, 76, 79; inequality, 180; kits, 88; policies, 71; public, 6, 10, 30, 33, 65, 72–73, 87, 90, 92, 99, 100, 101, 177; risks, 42; status, 49; workers, 99, 169. *See also* mental health

hegemony, 6, 18, 210

Historical Record of Chinese Americans, 39

Index   245

home, 33, 36–37, 67, 68, 69, 78, 83, 113, 159, 175, 198, 202, 206; at home, 2, 3, 40, 41, 42, 43, 44, 45, 49–54, 65, 69, 74, 78, 79, 105, 106, 112, 118, 122, 154, 165, 168, 177, 191, 198, 201, 205; culture, 25, 139; definition, 31–2, 148; going home, 79–80, 91, 97, 124, 145, 148, 161, 163, 204; longing for, 91; quarantine, 97; returning, 79, 81, 86, 87–89, 94–96, 106; a sense of, 63, 101, 173; societies and country/countries, 70, 73, 76, 81, 82, 101, 102, 137, 149, 153, 202; a taste of, 200, 201, 206. *See also* homemaking; working from home
homemaking, 22, 30–31
Hong Kong Special Administrative Region, 67
hooks, bell, 30
hope, 1, 3, 8, 34, 82, 132, 141, 171, 177, 178, 206, 212, 215, 216–18
Huagen Chinese School (HCS), vii, 38, 145
Hubei Province, 2, 104
hybrid, 15, 89, 90, 151, 157, 173; definition, 159. *See also* hybrid communities
hybrid communities, 34, 145, 147, 148, 149, 161, 163, 169, 173, 205; definition, 157–58
hybridizations, 163; definition, 159

identifications, 4, 6, 9, 17, 33, 34, 38, 56, 62, 64, 92, 107, 109, 140, 141, 142, 143, 175, 180, 182, 190, 195, 203, 206; disidentifications, 135, 140–41; self-, 149, 151, 156–57
identities, 4, 5, 15, 19, 25, 28, 31, 32, 33, 61, 63, 109, 110, 125, 127, 128, 135, 141, 148, 151, 156, 176, 177, 192, 196–97, 203, 204–5, 206, 212, 214, 217; AAAPI, 70; Chinese/Asian American, 104, 135–40, 178, 180, 181–82, 183, 186; gendered, 20; intersectional, 142; racial, 6
identity crisis, 4, 61, 75, 115, 124, 127, 128
immigrant, 38, 108, 138, 163, 194; anti-, 28, 38; *See also* Chinese immigrant mothers
immigration, 17, 23–25, 125, 150; bans, 179, 194; laws, 92, 132, 149, 179, 204; status, 43, 49, 70, 142, 213; systems, 102
Immigration and Nationality Act of 1965, 24, 149
Institute of International Education (IIE), 70
Intangible Cultural Heritage (ICH), 14
intensive motherhood, 39, 40–42, 63
International Society for the Study of Chinese Overseas, ix
internet, 8, 78, 80, 81, 82, 85, 96, 214
interviews, viii, 4, 8–9, 26, 34, 39, 45, 49, 71, 94, 95–96, 107, 110, 135, 145, 148, 175, 178, 197, 205
invisibility, 7, 12, 17, 118

Japanese internment camps, 83
job loss, 20, 40, 43–45. *See also* unemployment
justice, 63, 170, 212; food, 178; racial, 129, 131, 172, 203, 206. *See also* social justice

Latinx, Latino/a/e, 7, 16, 45, 139, 187
Lesbian, Gay, Bisexual, Transgender, Queer or Questioning (LGBTQ), 62, 187
Lesbian, Gay, Bisexual, Transgender, Queer or Questioning, Intersex, Asexual, and Allies (LGBTQIA+), 28, 62, 63, 142, 214
local character anecdotes, 10
lockdown(s), 2, 33, 40, 42–43, 49, 50, 52, 53, 54, 68, 70, 73, 80, 86, 96, 97, 99, 101, 102, 132, 145, 158, 177, 193, 197, 198; Shanghai, 95; Wuhan, 76
Longquan Monastery, 145, 148, 162
Lunar New Year, 38, 68, 134, 135, 185, 192, 193
lunchbox incident, the, 34, 178, 180–83, 190, 206

Make Us Visible New Jersey (MUVNJ), 39, 56, 57, 58, 59, 62, 188, 190
March for Asian Lives, viii, 9, 82, 106, 129, 131
marginalization, 5, 7, 11, 14, 30, 74, 86, 125
margins, 7, 10, 12, 34, 212
memorates, 10
mental health, 5, 25, 28, 47, 48, 65, 71, 73, 92–94, 102, 103, 120, 132, 133, 142, 143, 188, 197, 202
"merit field," 155, 166
migrant, 23, 30, 38. *See also* immigrant
(im)mobilities, 13, 14, 71, 100
mobility, 31, 72, 86
"model minority," 15, 25, 118, 129, 136, 193
mothers, viii, 30, 38, 40–42. *See also* Chinese immigrant mothers

nation-states, 18, 32
neoliberal, 4, 13, 72, 73, 103; feminism, 42
New England Chinese American Association, 39
New Jersey, viii, 39, 56, 57, 58, 59, 60, 61, 62, 83, 107, 184, 187, 188, 189, 190
nongovernmental organization (NGO), 19

OCCS Parents Group (OPG), 37, 38
Ohio Chinese Culture Link, 37
Ohio Chinese Festival (OCF), 37, 38
Ohio Contemporary Chinese School (OCCS), 37
online learning, 52, 89, 105
"othermothers," 55–56

Parents and Children Education Club (PCE Club), 39, 56, 57, 58, 60, 61, 180, 184, 187
Parents and Children Education Identifications (PCEI), 38–39
personal narratives, 4, 8, 9, 10, 42, 64, 112, 134, 190
personal protection equipment (PPE), 28, 76, 89
policy recommendations, 64–6, 101–3, 142–44, 173–74, 214
political activisms, 17, 33, 34, 36, 39, 54, 56, 59, 63, 64, 129, 142, 143, 210, 211, 214
polymerase chain reaction (PCR), 68, 95, 96, 97, 99
postcolonial, 24, 152
postcolonialism, 212
power, 5, 8, 10, 17, 22, 100, 101, 125, 131, 135, 151, 156, 166, 169, 186, 197, 202, 203, 209, 210, 212, 217; dynamics, 152, 176, 177; hierarchies, 11, 176; inequality, 16; relations, 13; structures, 2, 4, 176, 212
precariousness, 206–7
precarity, 14, 207–8
privilege, 10, 40, 70, 73, 125, 137, 149, 164, 169, 202; White, 119, 151

quarantine, 67, 68, 71, 73, 79–80, 90, 91, 94, 95–97, 98, 99, 177, 199, 207, 216; in critique, 99–101; policies, 33, 86

race, 4, 6–7, 10, 12, 13, 15, 16, 18, 20, 23, 31, 33, 41, 55, 63, 64, 71, 83, 107, 110, 115, 119, 120, 123, 124, 125, 131, 137, 142, 150, 151, 171, 181, 186, 194, 203, 211, 213, 214; definition, 5; mixed, 108
racialization, 6, 25, 33, 71, 129, 181, 192
racisms, viii, 3, 4, 6, 8, 9, 15, 17, 21, 26–27, 28, 29, 33, 34, 210–11, 212, 214; definition, 5. *See also* anti-Asian racisms; systemic racism(s)

Sangha, 148, 156, 164
self-authorship, 21–22
self-expression, 152
self-isolation, 97, 177, 199
sexism, 9, 12, 28, 29, 170, 214
snowball sampling, vii, 8, 145
social justice, viii, 6, 7, 13, 14, 16, 19, 21, 22, 29, 30, 33, 34, 38, 40, 54, 55, 56, 59, 62, 64, 65, 73, 86, 102, 103, 107, 109, 122, 128, 131, 141, 142, 151, 169, 172–73, 187, 190, 196, 212
solidarity/solidarities, 2, 17, 18, 19, 22, 30, 32, 33, 55, 61, 63, 135, 144, 169, 170, 171, 172, 183, 189; antiracist, 60, 104, 129, 141, 171

"stay at home" orders, 20
stereotypes, 15, 25, 26, 55, 56, 66, 71, 74, 78, 80, 81, 82, 104, 118, 129, 136, 139, 173, 180, 181, 190, 196, 211; to change, 84–85, 101
Stop AAPI Hate (SAH), 27–28, 59, 75, 170–71, 210
strategies, 2, 6, 13, 18, 19, 21, 26, 34, 41, 60, 68–69, 73, 90, 140–41, 173, 184, 196, 209; combating racisms and discrimination, 80–86, 101, 109, 206, 211; coping, 9, 33, 54, 63
systemic racism(s), 3, 6, 7, 12, 17, 25, 26, 29, 33, 62, 64, 82, 92, 104, 120, 125, 126, 129, 131, 136, 142, 143, 168, 169, 170, 203; definition, 25–26

Teaching Equitable Asian American Community History (TEAACH) Act, 56–57
Tibetan Buddhist Center or Tibetan Buddhist meditation and practice center (TBC), 146, 148, 158, 160, 161, 162, 163,
Three Treasures, 155, 156; take refuge in, 155, 156
Transcontinental Railroad, 23
transnational, 4, 13, 15, 16, 30, 31, 32, 63, 67, 72, 86–87, 153, 155, 157, 158, 172, 173, 201; adoptee, 132; adoptions, 108, 109; feminisms, 17–19
transracial adoptees, 2, 4, 5, 21, 106, 108–9, 126, 132, 134, 209, 212, 213; definition, 107. *See also* Chinese transracial adoptees
transracial adoption, 143
transracial adoption paradox, 108, 126
trauma, 4, 10, 28, 32, 64, 114, 141, 154, 172
truth, 11, 83, 85, 129, 148, 156, 157, 165

unemployment, 42, 43–45, 80, 120, 178, 193
United Nations (UN) Women, 40
US Third World feminisms, 18

vegetarianism, 178, 203–5, 206
vernacular, 10, 30, 33, 197, 210; culture, 178, 190, 196, 206; definition, 195–96
"vernacular turn," 10, 195
violence, viii, 6, 7, 9, 14, 25, 29, 114, 135, 142, 143, 180, 189, 207, 211; anti-Asian, 56, 59, 116, 150, 167, 189; domestic, 153; gun, 38, 70; physical, 27; racist, 130, 131, 202, 210
"virtual Chinatown," 39
"virtual ethnic town hall," 39
virtual ethnography, 4, 34, 39, 145, 148, 175, 205; definition, 8–9

Index   247

well-being, vii, 2, 20, 47, 56, 60, 61, 65, 84, 92,
100, 142, 143, 164, 166, 198, 202, 206, 213;
community, 21; mental, 48, 215; personal, 34,
175; psychological, 134, 215; public, 73, 103;
spiritual, 166, 179
White, 2, 4, 6, 17, 18, 22, 23, 25–26, 34, 41–42, 58,
64, 77, 104, 107, 109, 110, 112–13, 114–15, 116,
118, 119–20, 121–24, 127, 128, 131, 132, 136, 139,
140, 146, 148, 153, 160, 190, 191–92, 193, 205;
dominance, 8, 135; logic(s), 195, 196, 209, 210;
lunchbox incident, 180–81, 183; matrix, 2,
209; racist logics, 142; supremacy, 122, 125,
129, 150–51, 194, 203
Whiteness, 5, 151
Women of Color (cross-racial feminist
coalitional meaning), 18; definition, 18;
feminisms, 17, 19

women of color (US-based classification), 29,
48; definition, 18
Wooster Adoptee Student Union
(WASU), 134
working from home, 42, 45–49, 65, 131
World Health Organization (WHO), 1–2,
40, 92
World War II, 24, 83, 108, 150
Wuhan, China, 2, 27, 58, 67, 84, 119, 216;
hot dry noodles, 197; lockdowns, 76
"Wuhan flu," 83
"Wuhan virus," 26, 105

yellow perils, 4, 5, 22,
129, 136

"zero-COVID," 80, 96, 99

ZIYING YOU is Associate Professor of Comparative Literature and Intercultural Studies at the University of Georgia. She is author of *Folk Literati, Contested Tradition, and Heritage in Contemporary China: Incense Is Kept Burning* (IUP, 2020) and editor (with Lijun Zhang) of *Chinese Folklore Studies Today: Discourse and Practice* (IUP, 2019).

FOR INDIANA UNIVERSITY PRESS

Sabrina Black, *Editorial Assistant*

Tony Brewer, *Artist and Book Designer*

Allison Chaplin, *Acquisitions Editor*

Anna Garnai, *Production Coordinator*

Sophia Hebert, *Assistant Acquisitions Editor*

Samantha Heffner, *Marketing and Publicity Manager*

Katie Huggins, *Production Manager*

Gigi Lamm, *Director of Sales and Marketing*

Nancy Lightfoot, *Project Manager/Editor*

Annie L. Martin, *Editorial Director*

Dan Pyle, *Online Publishing Manager*

Michael Regoli, *Director of Publishing Operations*

Leyla Salamova, *Senior Artist and Book Designer*

Stephen Williams, *Assistant Director of Marketing*